Land evaluation

S. G. McRAE
C. P. BURNHAM

Lecturer and Senior Lecturer
in Land Resources Science,
Wye College (University of London)

CLARENDON PRESS · OXFORD
1981

Oxford University Press, Walton Street, Oxford OX2 6DP

LONDON GLASGOW NEW YORK TORONTO
DELHI BOMBAY CALCUTTA MADRAS KARACHI
KUALA LUMPUR SINGAPORE HONG KONG TOKYO
NAIROBI DAR ES SALAAM CAPE TOWN
MELBOURNE WELLINGTON
and associate companies in
BEIRUT BERLIN IBADAN MEXICO CITY

Published in the United States
by Oxford University Press, New York

British Library Cataloguing in Publication Data

McRae, S. G.
    Land evaluation.—(Monographs on soil survey)
    1. Land use
    I.   Title II. Burnham, C. P. III. Series
    333.73   HD111

ISBN 0 19 854518 5

13923230

$S19 \underline{Q48} \atop D$

Typeset by Oxford Verbatim Limited.
Printed and bound in Great Britain
by Billing and Sons Limited
Guildford, London, Oxford, Worcester

Acknowledgements

We are grateful to the following authors, publishers, and institutions who have permitted the reproduction of their diagrams and tables, often little modified: the American Society of Agronomy; the American Water Works Association; Mr M. A. B. Boddington; the British Grassland Society; the Building Research Establishment; Dr H. M. Churchward; the Department of Agronomy, Cornell University; the Division of Agricultural Sciences, University of California; Dr J. Doornkamp; the Elsevier Scientific Publishing Co.; the Food and Agriculture Organization of the United Nations; the Forestry Commission; the Macmillan Publishing Co. Inc.; the Ministry of Agriculture, Fisheries and Food; Dr H. C. Moss; New Mexico State University Agricultural Experiment Station; the New Zealand Soil Bureau; Oregon State University Press; Prentice-Hall Inc.; Dr R. Protz; Mr I. G. Reid; M. J. Riquier; the Royal Geographical Society; the Saskatchewan Institute of Pedology; the Science Research Council of Jamaica; the Soil Conservation Service of the United States Department of Agriculture; the Soil Conservation Society of America; the Soil Science Society of America; the Soil Survey of England and Wales; Springer-Verlag; Dr D. Teaci; the United States Bureau of Reclamation; the United States Department of Defence; the University of California Cooperative Extension Service; Professor A. P. A. Vink; Professor A. Young. Copyright remains vested in the original holders.

Thanks are due to the librarians at Wye College (University of London), Rothamsted Experimental Station, and at many other libraries in and around London where source material, often of very obscure origin was obtained.

Our typing team consisted of Mrs S. Briant, Mrs T. Dimsdale, Mrs J. Harber, Miss P. Hull, Mrs S. Kingsnorth, Mrs J. Rigby, Miss C. Tettmar, and Mrs B. Underdown, and to them is owed a special debt of gratitude. Secretarial facilities were provided by Wye College and by Rural Planning Services Ltd.

The contribution of our indefatigable editor Dr P. H. T. Beckett cannot be overestimated. Many other friends too numerous to mention have contributed ideas and information, and given us opportunities of practising the art of land evaluation.

Wye College   SGM
April 1981   CPB

Contents

1. Introduction

Land evaluation

Almost every activity of man uses land and, as human numbers and activities have multiplied, land has become a scarce resource. Decisions to change the use of land may lead to great benefits or great losses, sometimes in economic terms, sometimes in less tangible environmental changes. So decision-making about land use is a political activity, often raising strong emotions and much influenced by the social and economic situation. Land varies greatly, in topography, climate, geology, soil, and vegetation cover. A clear understanding of the opportunities and limitations presented by these relatively permanent factors of the environment is an essential part of the rational discussion of changes in land use.

Land evaluation concerns these opportunities and limitations and attempts to translate the plentiful information now being accumulated about land into a form usable by practical men, such as farmers and engineers, asking questions such as 'Can I grow carrots in this field?' or 'Will this route for a buried steel pipeline involve difficulties in installation or maintenance?' It is to be hoped that planners and politicians too will ask objective questions before building a road, offering an agricultural subsidy, or planting a large area with groundnuts.

The definition of land

A tract of *land* is defined geographically as a specific area of the earth's surface: its characteristics embrace all reasonably stable, or predictably cyclic, attributes of the biosphere vertically above and below this area, including those of the atmosphere, the soil and underlying geology, the hydrology, the plant and animal populations, and the results of past and present human activity to the extent that these attributes exert a significant influence on present and future uses of land by man (Brinkman and Smyth 1973).

Thus land is not the same as soil. Other groups of physical properties also influence the nature and usefulness of land. Also land has area, and the suitability of a parcel of land for use also involves its size, shape, and location. Maps will usually be needed in land evaluation.

Direct and indirect methods of land evaluation

Land may be evaluated *directly*, by trial, that is by growing the crop or building a length of the pipeline, to see what happens. Strictly speaking, the results are applicable only to the specific trial sites and for that particular use. In practice they are often extrapolated to apply to the whole of a natural environmental unit such as Chalk Downland or more specifically to a soil-map unit.

Direct evaluation is of limited value unless the evaluator has the resources to collect a large amount of data. Existing information is usually inadequate, or biased and open to challenge. Even apparently firm evaluations such as those implicit in sale prices or agreed rents will have been affected by many irrational factors and may not be closely related to inherent productivity. Such values may provide compelling precedents in a quasi-legal context, e.g. in determining compensation payments, but they provide a unreliable basis for rational land planning.

Thus most land evaluation systems are *indirect*. They assume that certain soil and site properties influence the success of a particular land use in a reasonably predictable manner, and that the quality of land can be deduced from observations of those properties.

Stages in indirect land evaluation

The process of indirect land evaluation can be divided into six steps, representing successive interpretative stages (Fig. 1.1). The first interpretative stage must be to ascertain which land properties are likely to be relevant and can be measured or assessed without excessive effort, and then to measure or assess them. Such properties have been called *land characteristics* (FAO 1976). In practice, data concerning these are often collected in the course of a soil survey, including topographical, meteorological, and ecological information.

The effect of land characteristics on systems of land use is seldom direct and uncomplicated. For example a plant is not directly affected by rainfall or by soil texture, but it is affected by the availability of water and of chemical nutrients and by the incidence of poor aeration due to waterlogging. In the FAO terminology the latter properties are *land qualities*, i.e. 'complex attributes, relevant to use, which are determined by a set of interacting single land characteristics' (FAO 1976).

The usefulness of land may be assessed in three ways: suitability, capability, and value. *Suitability* refers to one tightly defined use or practice, e.g. suitability for carrot growing, for golf courses, or for septic-tank drainage schemes. Land *capability* refers to a range of uses, e.g. for agricultural, or forestry, or recreational development. Land capability is more difficult to assess than suitability since priorities must be established between uses, e.g. is mediocre arable land better than high-yielding grassland unsuitable for cultivation, or is land capable of growing only one sort of crop (but that very

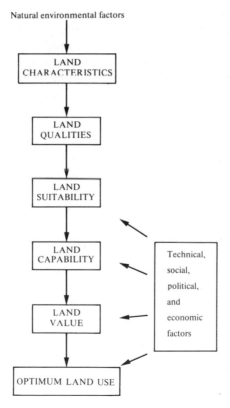

Fig. 1.1. The stages in indirect land evaluation.

successfully) better or worse than versatile land which will grow a number of crops but none quite so successfully? This distinction between suitability and capability is commonly made. The Canada Land Inventory (p. 196) employs classifications of capability for agriculture, forestry, recreation, and wildlife and of suitability for common field-crops, perennial forage, and organized camping. The USDA Land Capability Classification (Chapter 5) has been applied to a wide range of rural land uses including agriculture, grazing, and forestry. Capability assessments usually involve a bundle of suitability judgements, e.g. 'this land is unsuitable for arable crops or improved grassland, but is suitable for rough grazing or for forestry'. However, FAO does not use the term capability and Vink (1975) considers that there is no essential difference between land suitability and land capability.

The concept of *value* involves a monetary or similar basis, whether as an annual sum, e.g. a rental value, or as a capital payment. In many cases the value is notional, e.g. assessments for taxation purposes. Boddington (1978) argues forcefully that planners too need to translate capability classes into economic terms in order to compute the gains and losses involved in a proposed change of land use. The end product of land evaluation is a decision on *optimum land use*, whether private ('Shall I plant an orchard in this field?') or public ('On which site shall we build this new airport?').

In the development of suitability and capability classifications, technical data is used, e.g. from agronomy, forestry, and engineering. Socio-economic factors also have a significance, and usually become dominant in determining the value and optimum use of land.

Socio-economic factors range from easily quantifiable geographical circumstances, such as position in relation to settlement, transportation, and other human activities, to political and administrative decisions like eligibility for planning permission or for subsidies, and such unquantifiable factors as the availability of managerial skill or the existence of religious constraints such as the unclean pig or the sacred cow. This book concentrates on the limitations imposed on land by the natural environment, not because social, economic, and political factors are unimportant, but because discussion of such factors is facilitated by a prior, objective assessment of natural limitations.

The development and implementation of systems

The *development* of an indirect land-evaluation system involves the identification of the important soil and site properties which affect the success of an enterprise. The system is then constructed so that values of these properties either define categories *(Categoric Systems)* or may be combined mathematically to give an index on a sliding scale *(Parametric Systems)*.

In practice, few land evaluators wish to develop an entirely new system. Generally they will choose an existing system depending on the purpose of the evaluation, and modify it to suit local conditions and the availability of data.

This book presents a wide range of systems from which the evaluator can choose the most suitable for his purpose.

The evaluator then has to *implement* the chosen system by assigning particular parcels of land (artificially or naturally bounded) to their appropriate category or index. If he is to evaluate only a single or relatively small number of specified sites, he will probably combine the results of direct on-site investigations (point-source data) with information extracted from other sources. If he is to evaluate substantial areas he will need to extrapolate point-source data to a wider area.

Both procedures lead to inaccuracies and once the data have been incorporated within the evaluation process, their doubtful accuracy and/or value is often obscured. The legends of land evaluation maps, parametric indices, and particularly computer print-outs often imply a precision that the ground-truth does not justify. It is important that the evaluator should appraise his own data and procedures and take care that the form of his evaluation gives a fair indication of their precision. In particular whatever method of evaluation is chosen, it should have been tested against actual performance of the land both in its initial development and after local modifications have been made.

The most direct method of land evaluation for agricultural purposes is the collection and processing of crop-yield data, dealt with in Chapter 2. Chapter 3 deals with the collection of the data needed for indirect land evaluation and with the general strategy of data use, particularly procedures for using soil-survey information. Thereafter the arrangement of chapters is by purpose. Chapters 4 to 7 deal with land evaluation for agriculture, including the assessment of land suitability for crops and agricultural practices (Chapter 4), land capability for general agriculture using either categoric systems (Chapter 5) or parametric systems (Chapter 6), and the evaluation of land for irrigation (Chapter 7). Forestry is concerned with a crop whose growth or yield may readily be measured non-destructively before harvest; so the literature is distinctive (Chapter 8). Chapter 9 discusses the suitability of land for other purposes such as building, waste disposal, or recreation. Finally Chapter 10 discusses natural resource surveys and the use of land evaluations in land use planning.

2. Measuring agricultural productivity

Introduction

To an agriculturalist good land means productive land. Productivity may be measured by collecting yield data for commonly grown crops (pp. 7–15) or, better still, by calculating the profit from farming the land (p. 16). Crop yields from a few sites can be used to derive mathematical models (pp. 18–19) which relate yields to environmental factors. Yield data normally relate to small areas (plots, fields, or farms) and require extrapolation if they are to be used in evaluating large areas (pp. 19–20).

Collection of yield data

The main sources of yield information are:
- (i) trial plots (pp. 7–9);
- (ii) pot tests (p. 9);
- (iii) crop sampling (pp. 9–13);
- (iv) farm records (p. 13);
- (v) other agricultural statistics (pp. 13–14);
- (vi) informed opinion (p. 14).

Trial plots

There are many field trials in progress, and some have continued for a very long time. They have usually been set up to study some particular management problem, e.g. fertilizer application, liming, comparison of varieties, etc. and typically comprise a large number of replicated treatments on a relatively small number of sites. Such trials should be examined critically before using their results, for many are unsatisfactory in their siting or management. If time and resources permit, a programme of new trials should be set up, observing the following principles:

(i) The trial sites should be on single soil series and, as far as possible, should be representative of the whole of the mapping unit dominated by a single series.

(ii) Inextensive mapping units should be avoided.

(iii) The sites should be comparable in terms of important environmental factors such as slope position, particularly where soil erosion is a problem (e.g. Simonson and Englehorn 1938; Shrader, Schaller, Pesek, Slusher, and Rieckers 1960; Spratt and McIver 1972; Malo and Worcester 1975), aspect (e.g. Rennie and Clayton 1966), and likely meteorological conditions (e.g. Simonson and Englehorn 1943; Shrader, Riecken, and Englehorn 1957; Shrader *et al.* 1960; McKenzie 1970; Odell and Oschwald 1970; Gardiner 1972a, b; Wilkinson 1974). If these cannot be standardized, at least their local values should be recorded.

(iv) Where the soil map unit being investigated has a wide geographic and hence climatic range, then relevant climatic data need to be collected for each trial site (e.g. Shrader *et al.* 1957, 1960; Gardiner 1972a, b; Fenton 1975).

(v) The trials should continue for a period long enough to include effective samples of climatic variation. A minimum of five years is required (e.g. Rust and Odell 1957; Schrader *et al.* 1960; Odell and Oschwald 1970; Fenton, Duncan, Schrader, and Dumenil 1971). Ten years is preferable even in regions with a humid climate, and, where rainfall is low and erratic, 20 years is recommended.

(vi) Management regime must be standardized to represent either typical or good farming practice in the area. However, farm yields, even at a high level of management are typically only 75–95 per cent of field-plot yields (Odell 1958; Schrader *et al.* 1960). There should be standardization of fertilizer inputs, sowing or planting dates, crop varieties, etc.

(vii) Comprehensive records of the yields, management factors, and any other relevant information, collected and preserved in an orderly fashion, are essential. Piecemeal data and reliance on memory are to be avoided at all costs. (See Soil Survey Staff (1951) for suggested record sheets).

(viii) The actual siting of the plots within a field should take into account the convenience to the experimenter (e.g. access, proximity to irrigation if this is to be employed) and the farmer. Farmers are inconvenienced by plots in the middle of their fields, but experimenters should beware of sites offered near field edges or corners which may have atypical soils, past treatments or micrometeorological conditions, as well as being liable to wildlife damage or interference by vandals.

(ix) There should be sufficient replication to allow valid statistical analysis of the results. A statistician should be consulted before work begins, for field work is wasted if poor sampling techniques have invalidated subsequent statistical analysis.

Ideal trial plots are usually called *benchmark* plots, data from which can be applied to the appropriate map unit as a whole, and also, perhaps with minor adjustment, to similar map-units not in themselves represented by trial plots (e.g. Kellogg 1961, 1962; Wilkinson 1974; Fenton 1975). It is on these benchmark plots that most attention should be lavished to secure the most comprehensive results possible. Steele (1967) noted 'It is better to have full field and laboratory studies including field experiments, on a few key kinds of soil than scattered data from many kinds'. On the other hand, with limited resources it is probably better to increase the number of soils studied rather than the number of different treatments at each site (Loveday and MacIntyre 1966). So long as a consistent set of treatments is established at each site this advice is not in conflict with Steele's. What is to be avoided is a large number of sites providing incomplete or incompatible data. Hauser (1970) and Pearce (1976) give practical advice on how to establish and analyse field-trials.

Pot experiments

Pot trials are simpler to manage since all the pots are in one locality, and climatic variations between sites can be eliminated. The great disadvantage is the artificiality of the situation (de Vries 1980). It is probably for this reason that pot trials are not used as practical tools for yield prediction. Pot experiments would be more useful if they dealt with entire profile monoliths rather than disturbed samples of topsoil, but this would negate the advantage of convenience. Other cumbersome attempts to combine the advantages of pot trials in a glasshouse with more realistic field conditions involve re-constituting soil profiles from a wide area at one trial site or taking boxes of standard soils to sites varying climatically (e.g. Hunter and Grant 1971).

Crop sampling

Yield data may be obtained relatively easily by taking small samples from fields, orchards etc. where the crop is being grown under normal farm conditions. These yields are truly representative of conventional farming. On the other hand there must be much replication to overcome variations due to differing management techniques. This variation can be reduced by stratifying the data according to the level of management. The USDA (Soil Survey Staff 1951) suggests three management levels for which data might be sought:

> Level 1 — The most *common* combinations of management practices followed by the majority of successful farmers using the soil being dealt with.
> Level 2 — The *superior* combinations of management practices followed by the leading farmers using the soil, perhaps 1 per cent or perhaps over 10 per cent.

Level 3 — The *optimum* combinations of management practices developed on pilot-research farms, if any, or on other farms that represent
the best (or 'ceiling') that can be achieved in the present state of the
agricultural arts.

A fourth category, a *low* or *poor* level of farming can also be
recognized, but 'few who go to the trouble to read and use the soil
survey, or to seek advice based upon it, are interested in estimates
at the low level'. However the guidelines for the recognition of even
two different management levels are cumbersome (e.g. Shrader *et
al.* 1960; Odell and Oschwald 1970).

A low level of management may be the norm in some developing
countries and Young (1973*b*) suggested that three levels might be
specified:

Level 1 — *Ordinary management* — The most common existing farming
practices.
Level 2 — *Improved management* — The methods adopted by the more
progressive farmers at the present day; including standard 'better farming' practices, as locally recommended, but excluding methods requiring
a high capital input, or sophisticated skills.
Level 3 — *Optimim management* — As used on experiment stations;
including all known methods of obtaining sustained high yields.

Young suggested that yield estimates based on Level 2 are most
appropriate to development schemes, but that comparable data for
Level 1 would indicate the magnitude of the benefits likely to be
attained. Young and Goldsmith (1977) found that there was a
substantial group of farmers in Malawi who had partly adopted
better farming methods, a *low–improved* management between
Levels 1 and 2. Adequate data from optimally managed land (Level
3) was rarely available. Fivefold differences in yield due to differences in management were found (Table 2.1). Differences due to
soil type were no more than ± 33 per cent.

Ideally evaluation of yields should take account of all common
combinations of crop, environmental factors, and level of management as shown in Fig. 2.1.

Some investigators have restricted their studies only to the *best
holdings* growing the crops in question (e.g. Van Liere 1948; Lee
and Ryan 1966; Sturdy and Eldridge 1976). Even crop samples
taken apparently at random may be biased towards best holdings,
since a greater proportion of the better farmers are likely to prove
co-operative.

The choice of sample sites will also be influenced by the existence of other data such as farm records (e.g. Odell 1950 *a*, *b*), and the range of crops or varieties to be studied. Crops vary so much in their requirements (p. 44) that soils which might give higher yields of one crop might give lower yields of another.

Many workers have sought to choose fields in which more than one soil series was represented so that differences in management were eliminated, allowing direct comparison of yields (e.g. Murray, Englehorn, and Griffin 1939; de Leenheer and Simon 1950; Sturdy and Eldridge 1976). This resembles the *poor patch* approach used particularly to investigate horticultural crops (e.g. de Bakker 1950; Baeyens, Sweldens, and Deckers 1964) where differences in soil and site conditions were studied between normally growing crops and those with visibly poorer growth. As Edelman (1953) and Riecken (1963) have pointed out the management of the field or orchard is probably governed by the best soil present and is inappropriate for the poorer soil or patch, which might give better yields with the technology appropriate to its particular problems. Another disadvantage of working across a soil boundary is that the soils may be unrepresentative intergrades. For these reasons there is an argument for restricting investigations to fields occupied by a single soil series (e.g. Lee and Spillane 1970). Selection of fields with only one or with two or more soil series implies that a soil map already exists. Even so the experimenter should verify that plots really are modal examples of the soil unit.

TABLE 2.1
Estimated mean crop yields (kg/ha) for different management levels in Malawi

Management level	Maize	Groundnuts	Tobacco	Irish potatoes	Field beans
Traditional (1)	740	440	480	2000	350
Low-improved (1–2)	2900	810	920	7800	850
Improved (2)	5700	1000	1150	11 600	1000

Source: Young and Goldsmith (1977), by permission.

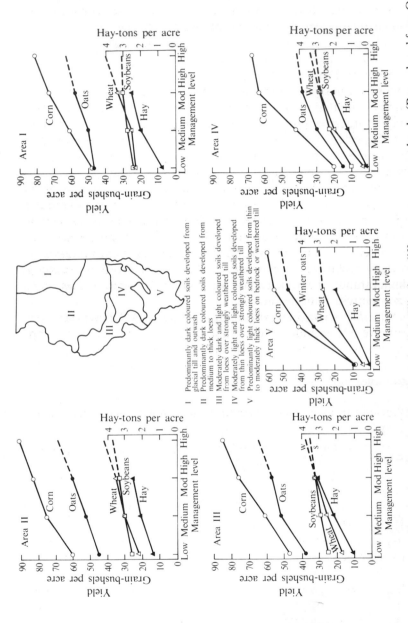

Fig. 2.1. The productivity of some broad groups of soils in Illinois at different management levels. (Reproduced from Odell (1958). *Soil Science Society of America Proceedings*, Volume 22, by permission of the Soil Science Society of America.)

The general considerations listed for the choice of trial plots (p. 7) also apply to crop sampling, particularly the need for statistical advice before the sampling programme begins.

Farm records

Many farmers keep records of the yields obtained on their various fields and these can be useful, particularly if they cover several years. A major problem is that fields often contain more than one soil type. Thus an early study in Illinois by Smith and Smith (1939) was limited to records which had been kept for at least 7 years, fields with only one soil series present, and specified management levels. Odell and Smith (1941) included data for fields with up to 10 per cent of a second soil series, provided this did not differ greatly in productivity from the dominant soil. Fields mapped as associations of two soil types had to contain 40–60 per cent of each soil and were rejected if a third soil was present. The long-term average farm yields for various crops on each soil type were found to have only a small standard deviation, and therefore gave a valid estimate of the productivity of each soil.

The USDA (Soil Survey Staff 1951, pp. 374–82) gives advice on how to extract data from actual farm record-books, with sample field record-sheets and questionnaires.

Other agricultural statistics

Agricultural statistics collected by government and other agencies may be used as the basis for yield predictions, e.g.:

(i) Wheat yields from the Saskatchewan Wheat Pool and Line Elevator Companies (Moss 1962).

(ii) Cereal yields from the Alberta Hail and Crop Insurance Corporation (Peters 1977).

(iii) Sugar-beet yields from the Irish Sugar Company (Lee and Ryan 1966).

(iv) Tobacco yields from marketing board records in Malawi (Young and Goldsmith 1977).

The main problem is that each yield refers to a large area, not limited to one soil type or management level. Often only information on the effects of climate can be derived from them (e.g. Williams, Joynt, and McCormick 1975; Peters 1977).

Informed opinion and existing land use

Yield estimates may be based on informed local opinion, described euphemistically as 'comparison of crop requirements (known or assumed) with soil properties', 'verbal sources', 'farm interviews', or 'the crystallized expression of the experiences of the people who use the land' although the term 'guesstimate' is more apt. This is not to say that such methods are to be shunned. If they are made by experienced workers they can be quite accurate.

Many of the yield estimates presented in USDA soil survey reports are subjective assessments (Ableiter 1937, 1940) made thus:

> Approximate estimates are made of the yields of several crops for 5 to 15 of the key soils of the area and several management levels by one or two soil surveyors or agricultural advisers with local experience, these are checked by as many other colleagues as possible, the original estimators then prepare a fuller set of results and add those for the other soils of the region. This set of predictions is finally checked by their colleagues before publication.

Land-agents often estimate the general productivity of an agricultural holding from the quality of its equipment, including buildings, roads, and machinery, since this is assumed to reflect the past profitability of farming. More systematically, the Cornell system used in New York State (Conklin 1959) involves estimation of farm incomes by observations of buildings, fields, crops and livestock, and other visible characteristics of the farms, coupled with the results of farm-management surveyors, and climatic and soil data. Three classes of farms are recognized:

(i) those which appear capable of supporting viable farm businesses for the forseeable future;

(ii) those near enough the economic margin to make their future somewhat uncertain; and

(iii) those judged obsolete for full-time farming use under modern farming conditions.

Many regional studies of agricultural geography, such as those of Veatch (1941) in Michigan and Stamp (1962) in Britain, have assumed that the locations of different land uses in an old and stable landscape reflected variations in productivity. Stamp defined some categories of his classification (Table 5.4) on existing land use. However, existing land use may not be optimal. O'Connor (1962), for example, has shown that horticulture in England has often spread from a nucleus of suitable land on to adjacent poorer land because farmers wish to enlarge their enterprises or to copy the success of their neighbours, while horticulture does not occur at all in other more distant areas where suitable land exists. In such cases excessive attention to existing land use is a most damaging form of circular reasoning.

The presentation of the results of yield surveys

The productivity capacities of the soils of a region may be presented as predicted yields in kg/ha, etc.; such figures are easily understood, but soon become outdated. Productivity tends to rise with time (e.g. Shrader *et al.* 1960; Odell and Oschwald 1970) due to changes in technology particularly crop varieties and optimal use of fertilizers, but the effect of the changes can vary on different soils.

Alternatively the results can be expressed as a percentage of the standard yield for that crop. In the United States the *Crop Productivity Index* was originally based on a 'standard yield obtained without amendments on the best soil of the region in which the crop is principally grown' (Ableiter 1937). Inextensive soil types which were especially well adapted to a particular crop could receive Indices above 100. These *Inherent Productivity Indices* were accompanied, and soon replaced, by indices reflecting the *Potential Productivity* when farmers applied a reasonably high management input. Thus the *Productivity Index* became the 'predicted yield of an individual adapted crop under alternative physically defined systems of management' (Ableiter and Barnes 1950). At high management levels the Indices commonly exceed 100 (e.g. Odell and Oschwald 1970). A general productivity rating can be calculated for each soil and all adapted crops with roughly similar requirements by weighting Productivity Indices for individual crops in accord with their relative areal extent (e.g. Odell and Oschwald 1970). The weighting should be not only by relative areal extent but also by some arbitrary amount to allow for the relative management inputs. Kellogg (1961) has pointed out that it is difficult to produce a general rating for crops which vary widely in their requirements. Productivity Indices have been extensively used to assess rural land for taxation purposes (e.g. Aandahl 1953; Mausal, Runge, and Carmer 1975; Odell and Oschwald 1970). USDA (1978*b*) has suggested ranking soils by a generalized *Soil Potential Index,* taking into account not only the relative yield of a crop, but also indices relating to the costs of corrective measures or the costs due to continuing limitations.

Economic evaluation of agricultural productivity

Crops must be sold or used to advantage and production costs defrayed. It is the balance which determines profit or loss, as shown in Fig. 2.2. Variable costs are directly attributable to an enterprise, i.e. they are incurred by growing a crop rather than leaving the field idle. Other costs are attributable to the farm as a whole, and even though they do vary with the type and size of the enterprise they are called *fixed costs*. The most convenient basis for budgeting a single field is the *gross margin*, which is the value of production less the variable costs. Fixed costs can be allocated to individual enterprises or fields, but with more difficulty than variable costs, to allow calculation of the *net income*. The calculations in Table 2.2 from Norfolk, England and similar calculations made in the United States (e.g. Kinney 1966) show that net income varies with crop and soil. Crops like potatoes have high variable and field costs compared with cereals, so that high yields and/or a high price for the produce are necessary to ensure a positive return. It is essential to choose a crop adapted to the particular soil so as to minimize the

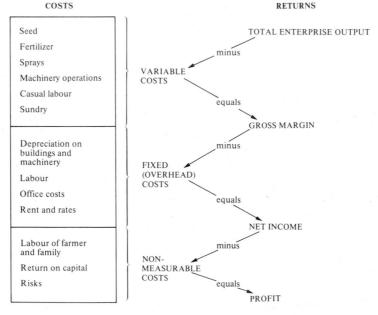

Fig. 2.2. The distribution of costs and returns in farming.

risks of failure. Soil variations affect gross margins not only through yield differences but also through their variable fertilizer requirements or the effect of soil textures and drainage on the amount of labour and machinery needed to service a given area (e.g. Richey, Griffith, and Parsons 1977; Shelton, von Bargen, and Al-Jiburi 1979).

Economic calculations can produce a single index figure which is claimed to represent the relative quality of land, for example the 'Soil Aptitude' Index (S_A) of Vink (1960), defined as:

$$S_A - [(R \times Y) \times E_1] - [R \times (F + C) \times F_2],$$

summed over all the crops in a given rotation, where R = percentage of land in a given rotation which is growing the particular crop; Y = yield of crop (kg/ha); F = cost of fertilizers; C = all other farming costs; and E_1 and E_2 = economic parameters valid for a certain technical and economic situation (F, C, E_1, and E_2 are in arbitrary monetary units/ha).

TABLE 2.2
*Economic analysis of two arable rotations
in Norfolk, England*

Crop	Proportion of area (%)	Yield (tonnes/ ha)	Gross margin (£/ha)	Net income (£/ha)
Adventurers series (thick peat requiring pump drainage, Land Use Capability Class 1)				
Winter wheat	40	4.4	144	37
French beans	20	10.0	154	44
Sugar beet	20	50.6	196	122
Potatoes	20	38.0	268	158
			762	362
St. Albans series (well drained stony sand, Land Use Capability Subclass 4s)				
Spring barley	80	1.9	72	− 140
Sugar beet	20	23.8	64	− 12
			134	− 152

Notes: 1. See Chapter 5, especially Table 5.1 for the description of Land Use Capability Classification.
2. Calculations based on estimated 1980 prices (Nix 1979).

Table 2.3 shows the calculated Soil Aptitude Indices for a number of Dutch soil types corrected for the different levels of management.

TABLE 2.3
'Soil Aptitude Indices' calculated for Dutch soils in arbitrary monetary units per hectare

Soil type	Soil Aptitude Index (S_A)
Humus podzol, sandy, excessively drained	24
Deep humose soil, loamy sand, somewhat excessively drained	153
Brown podzolic soil, loamy sand, excessively drained	276
Gray brown podzolic soil, sandy loam, excessively drained	387
Alluvial soil, sandy loam, well drained	1036
Alluvial soil, loam, well drained	1122

Source: Vink (1960), by permission.

Crop yield models

Yield estimates are only fully applicable to sites for which records have been made, and preferably over a number of years (p. 8). Satisfactory models relating yield to environmental factors would provide a secure basis for the extrapolation of the estimates to any site for which the environmental information could be obtained, whether or not the crop had ever been grown there. This procedure has been described by Nelson and McCracken (1962) as the Inductive Method, by Butler (1964) as the Soil Property Approach, by Nix (1968) as the Site Factor Method, and by Allgood and Gray (1978) as the Soil Properties Model. The usual form of the model is a yield prediction equation based on simple or multiple regression analysis. Unfortunately, published relationships often depend on relatively small data sets and/or have not been tested on data not used to derive them. This is true of the forestry examples on p. 156. Simple examples for arable crops include:

(i) Percentage relative yield (Y) of cotton in the Sudan Gezira (Finck and Ochtman 1961):

$$Y = 2.57x - 49.3,$$

where x is the percentage of clay in the 0–40 cm layer.

(ii) Yield of spring wheat (Y) in kg/ha in the Southern Urals (Taichinov 1971):

$$Y = 8.25x + 945,$$

where x is the thickness of the humus horizon (cm).

A much more complicated equation taking account of eight variables has been used by Rust and Odell (1957) to explain variation in maize yields in Illinois, and several other examples are given by Butler (1964), and Nix (1968).

However, studies involving only a limited number of soil and site attributes are likely to be of only local significance. Avery (1962) and Butler (1964) have pointed out that there can be no general relationship between any one soil or site attribute and crop performance since very many properties influence yield and they do not act independently. Progress can best be made by conducting field experiments which take all likely relevant factors into consideration. Collis-George and Davey (1960) suggested that the number of conventional field-trials should be restricted and replaced with fewer but much more comprehensively instrumented experiments. Barley (1964) replied that it would never be possible to study a complete system, and that economic or technical reasons oblige researchers to select certain parts of a system for study. Nevertheless, the more information that can collected about a given system the better the mathematical model of crop yields is likely to be. Ferrari (1966), Nix (1968), de Jager (1971), and Scotney and de Jager (1971) discuss comprehensive models of crop yields. They have not yet been applied to practical land evaluation, although they are obviously related to parametric systems (Chapter 6), which also attempt to predict agricultural productivity from environmental variables. However, existing parametric systems have been developed on a pragmatic basis; the attempts of Riquier (1972) to use a form of mathematical modelling are still inconclusive.

Using soil maps to predict yields

The usual method of extrapolating crop-yield predictions is to record yields from an adequate sample of sites typical of a soil mapping unit (or analogous landscape division) and to assume that similar yields will be obtained throughout the extent of the mapping unit. Butler (1964) described this as the Soil Type Concept, and Nix (1968) used the term Analogue Method. Butler points out that few such studies have been statistically satisfactory, and fewer still have shown significant correlations between soil types and production levels. This is probably because most areas contain several wide-spread soil series that do not differ much in agronomically relevant properties. If large enough samples of yield measurements on contrasting soils were available, doubtless differences would be shown.

In the United States virtually all soil-survey reports present yield predictions for the crops commonly grown on each map unit, and there is often considerable variation between map units.

3. Soil and site information for land evaluation

Introduction

Information about soil and site properties is the raw material for indirect land evaluation. These are often land characteristics (p. 2) which can be directly observed or assessed. Land qualities (p. 3) would be more useful, but are much more difficult to measure and usually have to be derived from measurable land characteristics or are assessed subjectively. Indirect land evaluations normally use a combination of characteristics and qualities. What data are required depends on the systems (Table 3.1).

The first task of the land evaluator is to choose the system most appropriate to his needs and determine what *kind* of data he needs in order to implement it. His next task is to investigate possible *sources* of data. Suitable data may:

(i) be derived from remote sensing, e.g. airphotos or satellite imagery;

(ii) exist as maps, especially soil maps and topographic maps;

(iii) exist as spatially located data, not in map form, e.g. climatic data;

(iv) have to be directly acquired by field observations and measurements, interviews with farmers, etc.

At this stage, he may find that the system he has chosen may have to be modified or even rejected because he would be unable to implement it with the resources at his disposal.

Finally he has to process and use the data. Sometimes the processing is simply conversion of data on land characteristics to information on land qualities. Examples of this are given later in this chapter. The *overall strategy* of data use is more fundamental and is concerned both with the reliability of the data and ways of extrapolating point-source or other spatially dependent data (p. 34).

The kind of data required

There are many lists of useful soil and site attributes (e.g. Northcote 1964; Butler 1964; Mulcahy and Humphries 1967; Riquier,

TABLE 3.1
Data required by different land evaluation systems

Data	California Parametric Storie Index Rating (1)	Britain Land Use Capability Classification (2)	Ghana Land Capability Classification (3)	Tropics Suitability for sugarcane (4)	United States Suitability for effluent disposal (5)
Texture	X	X	X	X	
Organic matter	X				X
Stoniness		X			
Soil structure		(X)			
Soil depth	X	X	X	X	X
Genetic profile	X			X	
Soil pattern		X			
Parent material	X			X	
Salinity/alkalinity	X			X	
Nutrients/fertility	X	(X)	X	X	
pH/base status	X			X	X
CEC/clay mineralogy				X	X
Soil temperature regime				X	
AWC/soil moisture regime		(X)	(X)	X	X
Permeability/infiltration		(X)	X	X	X
Drainage/wetness/watertable	X	X	X	X	X
Flooding	X	X		X	
Microrelief	X	X			
Erosion	X	X	X	X	X
Slope/relief		X	X		
Elevation		X		X	
Rainfall/evapo-transpiration		X			
Temperature/growing season		X			
Wind				X	

( ) Indicates data which may be taken into account.
(1) — Storie (1978); (2) — Bibby and Mackney (1969); (3) — Obeng (1963); (4) — Arens (1978); (5) — Hall *et al* (1976).

Bramao, and Cornet 1970; Beek 1977; Bartelli 1979; Miller and Nichols 1979; and Tables 3.2, 3.3, 3.4, and 3.6). Those useful for indirect land evaluation can be grouped under the following headings:

   (i)   soils (pp. 23–5);
   (ii) climate (pp. 25–6);
   (iii) topography (pp. 27–9);
   (iv) composite environmental data (pp. 29–32);
   (v) socio-economic data (pp. 32–3).

Soil information

Soil maps

Many of the soil properties which are important in land evaluation (Table 3.2) are normally collected during routine soil surveys, and indeed serve to distinguish the different kinds of soils encountered. However, if the soil map and the other information collected by the soil surveyor are intended to provide a basis for land evaluation, the soil surveyor should discuss his aims and methods with the evaluator before he begins the survey. For example, the soil surveyor may find a convenient and mappable division by separating two otherwise similar soils on a total soil depth greater or less than 40 cm, while it may be crucial to the land evaluator to know the distribution of soils with depths of less than 25 cm, 25 to 50 cm, 50 to 75 cm, and greater than 75 cm.

On the other hand soil mapping is expensive, so a soil map should normally be planned to remain useful for several decades. However in a new context, such as suburban or recreational development, an agricultural soil survey may have to be used to answer new questions (Bartelli, Klingebiel, Baird, and Heddleson 1966), for which rather different characteristics or qualities have to be assessed. Thus, as noted by Kellogg (1951, 1955, 1961), it is more efficient in the long run to make a general soil survey from which various interpretations can be made.

Other sources of soil information

Few soil characteristics can be reliably observed by remote sensing. Visible boulders and rock outcrops and, sometimes, the colour and moisture content of surface soils can be assessed. Other

TABLE 3.2

Soil characteristics and related land qualities used in land evaluation

Soil characteristic	Main methods of assessment	Related land qualities
SOIL CHARACTERISTICS COMMONLY USED		
Soil texture and stoniness	M	Ease of cultivation; moisture
	DL	availability; drainage and aeration;
	DF	fertility; water erosion hazard;
		wind erosion hazard, soil permea-
		bility; irrigability; rootability
Visible boulders/rock outcrops	R	Ease of cultivation; moisture
	M	availability
	DF	
Soil depth	M	Moisture availability, ease of
	DF	cultivation, rootability
SOIL CHARACTERISTICS SOMETIMES USED		
Soil structure, including pans, crusting, compaction	R	wind erosion hazard, water erosion
	M	hazard; rootability; moisture
	DF	availability
	DL	
Organic matter and root distribution	M	Moisture availability; wind erosion
	DF	hazard; water erosion hazard; ease
	DL	of cultivation
pH (reaction)/CaCO$_3$/gypsum	M	Soil fertility; soil alkalinity
	DF	
	DL	
Clay mineralogy	M	Water erosion hazard; ease of
	DL	cultivation
Chemical analysis, e.g. extractable NPK, toxic constituents	DL	Fertility (i.e. nutrient availability); toxicities
Soil permeability	M	Drainage and aeration; moisture
	DF	availability; irrigability
	DL	
Available water capacity	DL	Moisture availability
Infiltration/run off	DF	Water erosion hazard
	S	
Soil salinity	DL	
Soil colour and mottling	M	Drainage and aeration
	DF	
	R	
Soil parent material	M	Fertility (i.e. nutrient availability
	DF	including deficiencies and toxicities)

R — remote sensing; M — maps; S — spacially located data; DF — direct observation in the field; DL — direct measurement in the laboratory.

characteristics can be studied only on the spot, usually after digging or augering. Soil survey manuals (e.g. Soil Survey Staff 1951; Hodgson 1974, 1978) explain how to make field assessments of depth, texture, colour, stoniness, structure, root distribution, and consistence. There are field methods for measuring pH, electrical conductivity, bulk density, permeability and infiltration capacity, and the approximate content of calcium carbonate, calcium sulphate, and certain other soil constituents (Avery and Bascomb 1974). As it is usually not possible to make more than a limited number of such observations it is important to understand the nature of their natural variability (e.g. Beckett and Webster 1971). These considerations apply even more strongly to observations that can be made only in the laboratory, such as most chemical estimations (e.g. organic matter or the conductivity of soil extracts or mineralogy and micromorphology).

It may be realistic not to include assessments of chemical fertility, other than salinity and/or alkalinity, in land evaluation. Fertility is difficult to categorize, is changeable, and depends much on management. It is perhaps only in the developing tropical areas, with nutrient-poor soils and no history of fertilizer use that the inherent fertility of soils is worth considering in land evaluation.

Climatic information

Climatic data (Table 3.3) are usually obtained from meteorological agencies within the country involved; maps and/or records of temperature, precipitation, and wind speed and direction are fairly readily available. More specialist information, such as net radiation, may be restricted. For some purposes, the land evaluator may have to collect information himself or to make simple meterological observations, especially of meso- or microclimates, e.g. windiness on sites which might have an exposure problem (Lines and Howell 1963) or the frequency of frosts where sensitive crops are to be grown (Smith 1953; Hogg 1964). Some climatic information can be derived from satellite imagery, e.g. cloud cover, snow cover, date of snow melt, date of the 'greening' of vegetation that indicates the commencement of the growing season, etc. (Barrett and Curtis 1976).

The relevant temperature regime of an area can be expressed in different ways, e.g. the temperature of a period representative of

TABLE 3.3

*Climatic characteristics and related land qualities
used in land evaluation*

Climatic characteristic	Main methods of assessment	Related land qualities
Temperature	M S DF	Frost risk; temperature regime, (length of growing season, etc.); moisture availability; evapotranspiration
Precipitation, including distribution and intensity	M S DF	Water erosion hazard; flood risk; moisture availability
Wind speed and direction	S DF	Evapotranspiration; exposure; climatic hazard (storms)
Net radiation	S DF	Evapotranspiration
Hail/snow	S DF	Climatic hazard
Evaporation	S DF	Evapotranspiration

M — maps; S — spatially located data; DF — direct observation in the field; DL — direct measurement in the laboratory.

the growing season, the length of frost-free period, or the length of the growing season which is usually taken as the period above a limiting temperature, e.g. 5.6°C (42°F), or 'accumulated temperature', the product of days and degrees above the limiting temperature. Thus 'The Climates of Canada for Agriculture' suggests that 2000 degree days above 42°F are needed for wheat growing (Chapman & Brown 1966). Birse and Dry (1970) have prepared a map of Scotland showing accumulated air temperatures above 5.6°C. Robertson (1968) used a more sophisticated equation combining day and night temperatures with photoperiod to calculate a 'biometeorological time scale' for cereal crops.

Calculated soil moisture deficits, i.e. the difference between precipitation and potential evapotranspiration, are more useful than rainfall data alone. The British system of Land Use Capability Classification (Table 5.1), for example, relates class limits to the potential moisture deficit in the period April–September (approximately the growing season), though local modifications have sometimes been necessary (Bendelow and Hartnup 1977).

Topographic information

Altitude, slope angle and length, and position in the landscape are easily measured or assessed, and are relevant in land evaluation (Curtis, Doornkamp, and Gregory 1965; Speight 1968; Higginson 1975; Wright 1982; and Table 3.4). Topographic factors may act through their effect on soil qualities such as erosion hazard (e.g. Hudson 1971), or ease of cultivation or mechanized farm operations (e.g. Finkenzeller 1957; Ruhmann 1957; Spoor and Muckle 1974). They are most commonly incorporated in land evaluation systems, however, by reference to critical values of slope angle or altitude (Table 3.5). The mean slope angle θ (degrees) between two points on adjacent contours of a topographic map is

$$\theta = \mathrm{Cot}^{-1} \frac{SH}{100V},$$

where S is the denominator of the map scale, H the contour separation in mm, and V the vertical contour interval in m. Limiting distances between contours for the various categories can usefully be marked on the edge of a strip of paper. This method gives a

TABLE 3.4

Topographic characteristics and related land qualities used in land evaluation

Topographic characteristic	Main methods of assessment	Related land qualities
Slope angle and length	R	Ease of cultivation; local access; water erosion hazard; civil engineering factors; irrigability
Altitude	R M DF	Climatic predictions (temperature, length of growing season, rainfall, exposure)
Landscape position including aspect	R M DF	Related to soil-mapping unit; climatic factors (temperature regime, exposure, frost risk); ease of cultivation; water erosion hazard; wind erosion hazard; salinity/nutrient availability; drainage; civil engineering factors; flood risk

R — remote sensing; M — maps; DF — direct observation in the field; DL — direct measurement in the laboratory.

TABLE 3.5
Critical slope angles

Steepness (%)	Critical for
1	International airport runways
2	Main-line passenger and freight rail transport
	Maximum for loaded commercial vehicles without speed restriction
	Local airport runways
	Unrestricted ploughing and cultivation
	Below 2 per cent — flooding and drainage problems in site development
4	Major roads
5	Agricultural machinery for weeding, seeding
	Soil erosion begins to become a problem
	Land development (constructional) difficult above 5 per cent
	Housing, roads
	Excessive slope for general development
	Intensive camp and picnic areas
9	Absolute maximum for railways
10	Heavy agricultural machinery
	Large-scale industrial site development
15	Site development
	Standard wheeled tractor
20	Two-way ploughing
	Combine harvesting
	Housing-site development
25	Continuous arable cropping
	Loading trailers
	Recreational paths and trails

Source: Cooke and Doornkamp (1974), by permission.

reasonable estimate of the mean angle of a long slope but may underestimate short slopes (Young 1972).

On air photographs, the slope θ (degrees) between any two points is

$$\theta = \text{Tan}^{-1} \frac{fp}{cw},$$

where f is the focal length of the camera lens, p is the parallax difference between the two points measured with a stereometer (see Wright 1982), c is the horizontal distance between the two points, as measured on the photographs, and w is the mean distance between the principal point and the transferred principal point, all in mm (Young 1972).

Slope angles can be expressed as percentage grade (e.g. in the United States), or in degrees (as in Britain). This book uses percentage grades. These can be converted to degrees (θ) by the expression

$$\theta = \text{Tan}^{-1} \frac{G}{100},$$

where G is the percentage grade (Young 1972).

Composite environmental data

Information about soil and site wetness (Table 3.6)

General indications of site wetness can be inferred from topographic maps. Remote sensors may recognize wet land as dark tones in the visible and infrared range (Barrett and Curtis 1976), but this may require observations throughout the year, which are most easily achieved by satellite imagery. Satellite imagery is also useful for assessing the extent of flooding (e.g. Andrawis, Moore, and Doka 1980).

During a soil survey, internal soil drainage is usually assessed from profile morphology (Fig. 3.1) and is often one of the differentiating criteria between soil-mapping units. Thus information on soil drainage can often be derived from a soil map. However, profile morphology may be a relict feature unrelated to present drainage conditions, so that the associated water regime can only be

TABLE 3.6

Soil and site wetness characteristics and related land qualities used in land evaluation

Soil and site wetness characteristics	Main methods of assessment	Related land qualities
Depth to water-table	M DF	Moisture availability; drainage and aeration; civil engineering factors
Presence of springs	R DF M	Ease of cultivation; civil engineering factors
Frequency of flooding	DF	Flood risk; civil engineering factors

R — remote sensing; M — maps; DF — direct observations in the field.

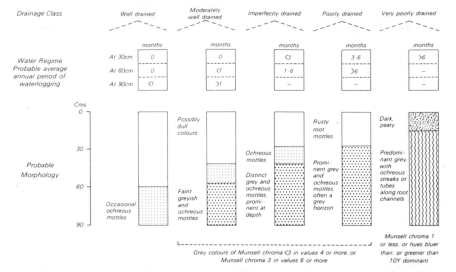

Fig. 3.1. Drainage Class (see Table 3.7), water regime, and probable soil morphology as recognized by Soil Survey of England and Wales. (By permission.)

Well drained (*excessive*). Coarse textured soils with small available water capacity and only saturated during and just after heavy rain. Surplus water is removed very rapidly. Any water table is well below the solum.

Well drained. Soil is rarely saturated in any horizon within 90 cm. Mottling is usually absent throughout the profile.

Moderately well drained. Some part of the soil in the upper 90 cm is saturated for short periods in winter or after heavy rain but no horizon within 50 cm remains saturated for more than one month in the year.

Colours typical of well drained soils on similar materials are usually dominant but may be slightly lower in chroma, especially on ped faces and faint to distinct ochreous or grey mottling may occur below 50 cm.

Imperfectly drained. Some part of the soil in the upper 50 cm is saturated for several months but not for most of the year.

Subsurface horizon colours are commonly lower in chroma and/or yellower in hue than those of well drained soils on similar materials. Greyish or ochreous mottling is usually distinct by 50 cm and may be prominent below this depth. There is rarely any gleying in the upper 25 cm.

Poorly drained. The soil is saturated for at least half the year in the upper 50 cm but the upper 25 cm is unsaturated during most of the growing season.

The profiles normally show strong gleying. A horizons are usually darker and/or greyer than those of well drained soils on similar materials and contain rusty mottles. Grey colours are prominent on ped faces in fissured clayey soils or in the matrix of weakly structured soils.

Very poorly drained. Some part of the soil is saturated at less than 25 cm for at least half the year. Some part of the soil within the upper 60 cm is permanently saturated.

The profiles usually have peaty or humose surface horizons and the subsurface horizon colours have low (near neutral) chroma and yellowish to bluish hues.

roughly inferred. Where possible it is better to base the evaluation on more precisely defined Wetness Classes (Table 3.7) to which soils can be allocated on the basis of quantitative data from dip wells, tensiometers, etc. on at least a few representative sites. However, this requires measurements over a period of years (e.g. van Heesen 1970), so direct observations are rarely used except where they are of major importance as in irrigation studies, or where observation is relatively easy, as of springs and floods.

Assessment of the overall moisture regime of a soil also needs information about the available water capacity of its profile. Salter and Williams (1967) and Ghosh (1980) have proposed schemes for deducing the available water capacity of a soil profile from its texture and depth. Dryness categories have been defined (Table 3.8) and used as subclass divisions of drainage classes (Table 3.7) to give a fuller description of the soil moisture regime as IIa, IIIc, etc.

Farquharson, Mackney, Newson, and Thomasson (1978) have

TABLE 3.7

Categories of soil wetness (Wetness Classes) used by the Soil Survey of England and Wales and corresponding Drainage Classes based on profile morphology (see Fig. 3.1)

Wetness Class	Duration of wet states	Drainage Class‡
I	The soil profile is not wet within 70 cm depth for more than 30 days* in most years†	Well drained
II	The soil profile is wet within 70 cm depth for 30–90 days in most years	Moderately well drained
III	The soil profile is wet within 70 cm depth for 90–180 days in most years	Imperfectly drained
IV	The soil profile is wet within 70 cm depth for more than 180 days, but not wet within 40 cm depth for more than 180 days in most years.	Poorly drained
V	The soil profile is wet within 40 cm depth for more than 180 days and usually wet within 70 cm for more than 335 days in most years	Very poorly drained
VI	The soil profile is wet within 40 cm depth for more than 335 days in most years	Very poorly drained

*The number of days specified is not necessarily a continuous period.
†'In most years' is defined as more than 10 out of 20 years.
‡The Drainage Classes (see Fig. 3.1) only correspond approximately to Wetness Classes. See Table 3.8 for Dryness Subclasses.
Source: Jarvis and Mackney (1973), by permission.

TABLE 3.8

*Categories of soil dryness (Dryness Subclasses) used by the
Soil Survey of England and Wales*

Available water capacity of soil profile (mm)	Average potential maximum soil moisture deficit (mm)			
	0–50	50–100	100–150	> 150
<100	b	c	d	d
100–150	a	b	c	d
150–200	a	a	b	c
>200	a	a	a	b

See Table 3.7 for Wetness Classes.
Source: Hodgson (1974), by permission.

combined wetness classes, soil depth, soil permeability, and slope
to give a measure of Winter Rain Acceptance Potential (Fig. 3.2),
useful in the evaluation of water catchment areas. Chiang (1971)
has devised ratings for the run-off potential of soils in the United
States for the same purpose.

Soil erosion

The likelihood of soil erosion is usually assessed subjectively from
the evidence of past erosion (by ground inspection or remote sensing) and features of climate and topography. The universal soil-loss
equation is an elegant example of the use of land characteristics to
determine a land quality. It predicts liability to soil erosion by water
from variables related to rainfall, soil characteristics, length and
angle of slope, land use, and application of conservation practices
(FAO 1965; Hudson 1971; Soil Conservation Society of America
1977a). Woodruff and Siddoway (1965) have given a similar equation for wind erosion (see also FAO 1960).

Socio-economic data

There are three main problems in using socio-economic data in land
evaluation:

(i) The evaluator may not be well acquainted with economic
nomenclature and concepts.

(ii) The available economic data are usually based on a different
spatial framework from his other information. Economic data such

as crop yields, fertilizer costs, gross margins, etc. are usually available for fields, whole farms, parishes, or other socio-economic divisions which do not match classifications on soil, climate, topography, etc.

(iii) Economic factors are constantly changing.

For these reasons, most land evaluation systems deliberately avoid consideration of socio-economic factors. Conversely those which do take such factors into account (e.g. the Cornell system, p. 33) do not pay much attention to the factors of the natural environment which affect crop growth. The economic appraisal which usually precedes an expensive development project is usually undertaken by a trained economist, and the natural scientist is a member of a multidisciplinary team. A good example is the Irrigation Suitability Classification of the United States Bureau of Reclamation (p. 127). Tabor, Bell, Buntley, Fribourg, and Springer (1974) do point out, however, that the agronomic potential of an area can be greatly overestimated if restrictions such as soil pattern, field size, field shape, and necessary conservation practices are ignored.

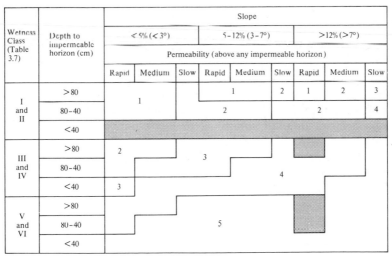

Wetness Class (Table 3.7)	Depth to impermeable horizon (cm)	Slope								
		< 5% (< 3°)			5–12% (3–7°)			>12% (>7°)		
		Permeability (above any impermeable horizon)								
		Rapid	Medium	Slow	Rapid	Medium	Slow	Rapid	Medium	Slow
I and II	>80		1			1	2	1	2	3
	80–40					2			2	4
	<40	░	░	░	░	░	░	░	░	░
III and IV	>80	2				3			░	░
	80–40				3			4		
	<40	3								
V and VI	>80					5			░	░
	80–40								░	░
	<40									

Classes of winter rain acceptance 1-Very high; 2-High; 3-Moderate; 4-Low; 5-Very low

Fig. 3.2. Identification of Winter Rainfall Acceptance Potential (WRAP) Class in England and Wales from soil and site properties. (From Farquharson *et al.* (1978), by permission.)

General strategy of data use

Logically, the evaluator could start by dividing the whole area into apparently uniform divisions, e.g. by *remote sensing*, and then use site-specific properties of typical sites in each to evaluate the major divisions. Alternatively he might start with *direct observations* from a limited number of specific sites and try to extrapolate from these well-understood situations to a regional framework. In practice he usually follows the first procedure. He looks for existing *maps* as a general basis for the work and adds whatever information is already to hand. Then he seeks new information to clarify or check his assessment of the map units, guided by relevance and cost. A soil map, or an analysis of the landscape by remote sensing, often provides a convenient framework for the selection of representative sites for further examination, and also for rational extrapolation of any other information, which relates to just a few *spatially located* sites, e.g. meteorological stations or experimental plots.

Remote sensing is a general term meaning the use of optical cameras or other sensing devices (such as radar) mounted in any airborne vehicle, typically an aircraft or satellite. All forms of remote sensing provide a relatively rapid overview of territory regardless of the problems of traversing it on the ground, but in most cases reliable interpretation requires some ground check.

There have been numerous attempts to use satellite imagery for resource assessment. Satellites have some advantages. Large areas can be overflown virtually at one time, whereas an air photograph cover takes longer to complete so that seasonal changes may affect interpretation. The location, orientation, and matching of large numbers of air photographs is time-consuming. Furthermore, a satellite may overfly an area many times throughout the year giving an opportunity of following changes and approximately dating them. Also the small scale imagery can be cheaply reproduced.

Satellite imagery also has a number of disadvantages. The scale is very small, e.g. 35 000 km^2 per frame, and the resolution poor, e.g. 80 m in early LANDSAT imagery. There are political objections against improving resolution, e.g. to 30 m in the proposed LAND-SAT D. Most of the earlier cover was of countries within 50° latitude of the equator, and some persistently cloudy areas still lack adequate cover. Worst of all, ground check has shown that some interpretations of detail, e.g. recognition of crops, are difficult, and the results unreliable. So satellite imagery is most likely to be chosen for rapid surveys at scales of 1:250 000 and smaller (e.g. Brink, Partridge, and Williams 1981) but more detailed maps will usually have to be based on photographs taken from aircraft.

Barrett and Curtis (1976), White (1977), and Stoner and Baumgardner (1979) have provided good reviews. Early accounts of the use of satellite imagery tended to be over-optimistic (e.g. Short, Lowman, and Freden 1976) but a more critical attitude prevails now (e.g. Allan 1980). Methods of air photograph interpretation for soil and related surveys are well established (Soil Survey Staff 1966; Brenchley 1974; Carroll, Evans, and Bendelow 1977).

The advantages of *direct acquisition* of data on the ground is that the evaluator will obtain exactly the information he requires, and can assure himself of its reliability. However, specially commissioned observations are often expensive. Some kinds of point data can easily be extrapolated over broad areas, e.g. macroclimatic features such as average rainfall, and easily visible properties such as land slope, existing vegetation, etc. Some data, including practically all soil-based properties, are much more variable over short distances and/or more difficult to observe. The length of time needed to make reliable estimates of flood hazard, level of water-table, etc. can be another complicating factor. For many kinds of data a close network of observations is impracticable. The evaluator will then have to search for the best compromise between exact values for a limited number of sites and personal judgement to supply the missing data.

The major cost in a land evaluation exercise for a broad area is field work. So it makes economic sense to make this as efficient as possible. This might seem to indicate that observation not directly relevant to the evaluation in hand should not be made, e.g. why bother to make observations of surface soil structure when the intention is to plant a deep-rooted tree crop? However, evaluation for another use may be required in the future, and observations which may seem irrelevant now may later become crucial. If they are not recorded an expensive re-survey will be necessary. Thus, most workers recommend comprehensive data collection, although observations requiring excessive time and/or elaborate equipment should be avoided unless an immediate need is proven. Usually it will be more effective to reduce the number of observation points rather than reduce the amount of information collected at each point (Robertson 1970). The work of Beckett and co-workers on the quality and usefulness of soil maps (e.g. Webster and Beckett 1968; Burrough and Beckett 1971) should also be considered, the aim being low within-unit variability. Scale is one of the most important decisions (Vink 1975) in planning any evaluation programe involving the production of maps, because it is closely linked to the density of observations needed and hence to cost (Table 3.9). If the aim is regional planning, uses may be allocated to parcels of 10 km² or more, e.g. for new towns, plantations, irrigation schemes, etc. If the use is planning within the farm, 1 ha may be the smallest parcel for which a different management would be considered. If the initial soil map on which a land evaluation is to be based makes excessively small separations, then the effort in producing such a detailed map may be wasted. Conversely, a broad land evaluation, such as the Agricultural Land Classification of the British Ministry of Agriculture (p. 38) where the general limit of precision allows no separation of units smaller than 80 ha is of little practical value at the field level. The amount of data to be collected depends on the size of the project area. For a small area or single site, a thorough investigation will usually be worthwhile; the costs being only a fraction of the project costs. The preliminary investigation of the use potential of a wide area, however, will demand inexpensive methods which can be applied to a large number of sites .

If the soil map is sufficiently detailed most of the soil boundaries will also separate areas of different land suitability or capability. If so it may suffice to calibrate the units of the soil map in terms of their suitability or capability. The three procedures described below are in order of their decreasing dependence on the information produced by soil survey (cf. p. 151):

(i) The land evaluator extracts data from the soil survey memoir and from other maps of climate, topography, etc. He assumes that the whole extent of a soil map unit or simple divisions of a map unit behave similarly, and proceeds by saying, for example, 'the soil and site factors used by the soil surveyor to define or describe map unit Y indicate that it would be suitable for growing celery. Therefore (unless there is information to the contrary) all areas of map unit Y are suitable for celery production. This also assumes that every map-unit definition encapsulates all the factors which may be relevant to the evaluations. This is frequently not the case (e.g. McArthur, Wheeler, and Goodall 1966; McDonald 1975; Western 1978).

TABLE 3.9

Soil and Land Capability maps : factors related to scale

Type of map	Scale	Typical soil mapping units	Typical Land Capability mapping units	Smallest area conveniently shown (Planning Unit)	Typical purpose of map
Very detailed	1 : 10 000 or larger	Types, variants, and phases of soil series	Capability Unit	0.2 ha (Plot)	Detailed planning within project area, e.g. for civil engineering
Detailed	1 : 25 000	Soil series and phases	Capability Unit	1.2 ha (Field)	Planning within farm or project; land re-apportionment; land taxation
Semi-detailed	1 : 50 000	Soil series and complexes	Capability Subclass	5 ha (Farm)	Maps of extensive projects; detailed regional planning; guide to advisory officers
Reconnaisance	1 : 200 000	Associations of series	Dominant Capability Class or Subclass	80 ha (Village or Large Farm)	Broad regional planning (e.g. location of projects)
National	1 : 1 000 000	Associations of major groups	Associations of Capability Classes or Subclasses	20 km² (Region)	National land planning; education

(ii) The evaluator uses an existing soil map (or an equivalent terrain analysis) as a sampling framework for his own observations or assessments of land capability or suitability, and uses the map units to extrapolate his findings. The thought process is: 'I need information about soil infiltration characteristics over the area of a proposed irrigation scheme. I will measure infiltration at a number of sites on each map unit and assume that their results are applicable to all other occurrences of those map units'. The success of this approach still depends on the predictive value of the soil map but, unlike procedure (i), this value can be tested statistically (Bie and Beckett 1971).

Soil series, divided if necessary into phases on the basis of slope and/or climate, usually provide as suitable 'pigeonholes' for collating soil information as any other. A wide range of land properties should be recorded for the most extensive soil series. They then become *benchmarks* from which the values of these attributes in other less extensive series can be estimated on the basis of general knowledge as 'a little lower', 'about the same', or 'a little higher' than the most similar benchmark series (cf. p. 8).

If a new soil survey is to be commissioned for a land evaluation exercise, probably the soil surveyor should also make the evaluation. He may be the only trained observer who actually traverses the area systematically, and can thus easily gather any ancillary information required.

(iii) The evaluator uses soil maps just as one source of information among others and draws boundaries on any basis that seems to make sense, so that a rainfull isohyet, a contour, or a land use change is as likely to be chosen as a soil boundary. This procedure is particularly appropriate when there is no complete cover of soil maps and/or where a uniform legend has not been used in soil mapping. This is the case in the Agricultural Land Classification of England and Wales used by the Ministry of Agriculture Fisheries and Food (MAFF 1966), a categoric system (Table 5.1) which grades agricultural land in England and Wales into five ranked categories according to the degree to which certain physical characteristics impose long-term limitations on agricultural use.

The procedure followed was:

Firstly, all available information was assembled; soil-survey maps, drift geological maps, books and monographs on soils, meteorology and farming relating to the area in question, aerial photographs, the 1:625 000 map of average rainfall, the reports accompanying the Stamp Land Utilization Survey maps, and any other relevant material. Soil survey maps can be particularly helpful but their cover over England and Wales is limited.

Assignment to Grade 5 was then made where it was clear that adverse physical characteristics, individually or collectively, impose very severe limitations on, or even preclude, agriculture. High altitude, high rainfall, heavy dissection, and a short growing season could be assessed as a desk exercise by reference to relevant reports and maps. Tentative boundaries were drawn. Analysis of aerial photographs (where they existed) greatly assisted the identification of Grade 5 land particularly in the hills and uplands. Boundaries were confirmed, as necessary, in the field.

Less severe limitations were analysed in the mapping of Grade 4 and greater attention paid to soil and drainage limitations. The main limitations, however, are still those of high altitude and moderately dissected topography. At this stage there were closer consultations with advisory officers, discussions with farmers and further field inspection. Grade 4 and 5 sites also exist in the lowlands but their locations were mapped during the intensified sampling procedure used on higher quality land.

Moderate limitations characterize Grade 3 and the physical factors required more detailed examination and became more selective. The climatic and relief requirements for the Grade must be satisfied: geological and soil changes become critical. Where soil maps were available they were used. Solid and drift geology maps were examined in detail and soil associations were projected by relating geology to known associations elsewhere. Advisory officers and local farmers were increasingly consulted and the opinions expressed were noted and used not only in the boundary mapping of Grade 3 but also in the mapping of Grades 1 and 2.

Within Grade 3, restrictions in soil capability and likely response were important grade determinates. Mainly these were — slight drainage impedence; high water-table; shallowness; lightness of texture which can cause instability under certain conditions; and lack of water-retentive capacity. These could occur individually or in a combination. Aerial photographs were used, textural and tonal differences were noted and related to other information. Boundaries for the Grade were subsequently fixed during fieldwork.

The residual areas with minor or apparently no physical limitations were examined in detail in the field with particularly close attention to soil profile characteristics. The appropriate characteristics for Grades 1 and 2 were discussed with the Regional Soil Scientists and the Grades assigned accordingly. Any exceptions to these high gradings were thus mapped over smaller areas than with the lower grades.

In addition to the frequent consultations with advisory officers during fieldwork the gradings adopted were formally agreed at a final panel meeting of those who had participated in the assessment (excluding farmers). These consultations were done with particular care at the boundaries of maps being surveyed by different research officers (MAFF 1974).

Land evaluations based on detailed soil surveys are usually more satisfactory. Indeed, a soil surveyor often makes the best land evaluator, for he is often the only person who systematically traverses a given area. Soil-survey reports should be prepared with the needs of future land evaluations in mind. For each mapping unit the properties likely to be relevant should be clearly set out (as in Mackney and Burnham 1966, or in most USDA soil reports, for example). Single factor maps are particularly useful (e.g. Barnes 1949; Kellogg 1951, 1961; Vink 1963*a*, 1963*b*; Coulter 1964; Mackney and Burnham 1966; Steele 1967; Stobbs 1970; Young 1973*b*; Knox 1977).

A farmer, horticulturalist, forester, or other user can then identify an area on the soil map, note the kinds of soils present, and then hope to look for information about their properties and predictions of their behaviour in the soil survey report. As Aandahl (1958) noted 'Soil survey interpretation comprises the organisation and presentation of knowledge about characteristics, qualities and behaviour of soils as they are classified and outlined on maps. . . . The purpose is to provide people with the best possible information about every acre of soil on a farm that is directly useful.'

4. Land suitability for individual crops and agricultural practices

Introduction

Suitability and *capability* have often been confused or even regarded as synonymous. This book (p. 3) draws a distinction between *suitability* for a single clearly defined, reasonably homogenous purpose or practice, e.g. carrot production or mole drainage, and *capability* for a broader use such as agriculture or urban development. Thus *suitability* assessment has a sharp focus, looking for sites possessing the positive features associated with successful production or use, whereas *capability* must be vaguer, and is often defined in terms of negative limitations, which hinder or prevent some or all of the individual activities being considered.

A detailed soil map can be interpreted to give a suitability appraisal for a comprehensive list of crops, and specific guidance can be given on appropriate management practices. This has great advantages over a general capability assessment, where a low rating might conceal high suitability for a single crop with relatively unusual requirements, e.g. padi rice, blueberries, asparagus, or coconuts. Such an emphasis on positive opportunities is well suited to development projects and it is not surprising that the FAO system of land classification is of this kind. Land not inherently well suited for agriculture can be improved, e.g. by drainage or terracing, and many soil-survey reports give evaluations of the map units for these improvements. The major improvement of irrigation is dealt with separately in Chapter 7.

Thus land suitability assessments fall into five groups:

(i)   choosing suitable land for a specific crop (pp. 42–3);

(ii)   interpreting a soil map in terms of the suitability for various crops and management practices (pp. 43–7);

(iii) using the FAO 'Framework' in development projects (pp. 48–56);

(iv)   assessing the feasibility of land improvements (p. 57);

(v)   assessing land grazed by livestock (pp. 57–66).

Choosing suitable land for a specific crop

Suitability is largely a matter of producing high yields with relatively low inputs (Vink 1960). There are two stages in finding land that is suited to a specific crop. Firstly the requirements of the crop need to be known, or alternatively what soil and site attributes adversely influence the crop. This requires studies similar to those discussed in Chapter 2. The second stage is to identify and to delineate land with the desirable attributes but without the undesirable ones. A soil map makes both steps easier. Observations of crop performance can be related to particular kinds of soil and the results extrapolated to all areas of the same soil. This assumes that the criteria used to distinguish the various soil types have an agronomic significance. In several soil surveys of fruit-growing areas in Britain (e.g. Wallace, Spinks, and Ball 1931; Bane and Jones 1934; Osmond, Swarbrick, Thompson, and Wallace 1949; Bagenal and Furneaux 1949) such an assumption was valid, since the soil surveyor and the assessor of crop suitability were the same person.

In studies such as these it is often found that only a few soil and site factors, e.g. drainage, soil texture, or susceptibility to frost, are important. Thus, some workers have chosen simply to subdivide their study area on the basis of these few features rather than to make a full scale soil survey in which other factors would have to be considered e.g. Sweet 1935; Walsh and Clarke 1943; Rigg and Chittenden 1951; Edelman 1953; Pijils 1956; Brzesovsky 1963). The danger in this *single-factor mapping* is that if subsequent research shows some other feature or features to be important the area has to be re-surveyed. Also, as Gibbons (1961) noted, different factors may be important for different crops so that a single-factor map for one crop would not necessarily help in assessing land suitability for another crop with different requirements.

Soil data banks (p. 197) are particularly relevant to this approach (e.g. Kloosterman and Lavkulitch 1973). Information is stored on every soil-mapping unit and it only requires appropriate specifications to select all map units with, say, freely drained soils and sandy texture.

The most difficult step in choosing land for a specific crop is to define the requirements of the crop in terms of the soil properties about which information can be obtained. The requirements of some crops have been specified in some detail, e.g. bananas (Arens

1978), cocoa (Smyth 1966), oil palm (Wong 1966; Ama 1970), padi rice (Brinkman 1978), rubber (Sys 1975a), and sugarcane (Arens 1978; Yates 1978; Thompson 1978) and there also exist more generalized statements on the requirements of temperate region crops such as arable crops (Haans and Westerveld 1970; Vink 1975; Sys 1975b; Dyke 1976), vegetables (Page 1976; Lees 1976), fruit (Clements 1976), grassland (Vink and Van Zuilen 1974; Morrison and Idle 1972; Lee and Diamond 1972; Mudd 1976; Forbes 1976), and vines (Blacquière and Meriaux 1969). Godin and Spensley (1971), Kay (1973), Vink (1975), Young (1976), and Protz (1977) have discussed the requirements of a number of tropical crops (Tables 4.1 and 4.2). Young (1975, 1976) stresses that the optimal conditions for a crop (which are the same for many crops) may be less important than its tolerance to adverse factors, since many decisions relate to sub-optimal conditions. Choice of crop is also dictated by socio-economic factors.

Interpretation of soil maps in terms of crop suitability and management practices

A soil surveyor usually notes information about the land use of his soil-mapping units. If this reveals that particular crops are restricted to, or at least concentrated upon, certain soil types, it can be fairly safely assumed that all areas of these soils are suitable, so long as there are no changes in other factors limiting to crop growth. Sometimes he can estimate the degree of suitability from observations of how well the crops grow on the soils. The surveyor's records can be presented as a simple list of the crops suitable for each map unit or by ranking soil types according to their degree of suitability for each crop. Soil reports may include information on the management practices appropriate to different combinations of soil and crop, and these are often linked to a generalized capability classification (Chapter 5). In the soil-survey report for the Ventura Area of California, for example, Edwards, Rabey, and Kover (1970) describe the growing of one typical crop, celery, as follows:

> Celery is climatically suited to the Oxnard Plain. Celery transplants are set out during a period that extends from August through March. Planting is scheduled so that harvesting is continuous and uniform. Harvesting is done by hand, from early in November, through the middle of July.

TABLE 4.1
Soil requirements of different crops

Crop	Requirement for					Tolerance of				
	Water	Clayey texture	Good structure	Calcium	Acid conditions	Water-logging	Drought	Clayey texture	Acid conditions	Salinity
Rice	H	M	L	L	L	H	L	H	H	L/M
Maize	L/M	L	M	L	L	L	M/H	L	L	L/M
Tapioca	M	M	M	M	L	L	M	M	M	L
Sisal	M	M	L*	M	L	M*	M	H*	M	M
Rubber	H	H	L	L	M	H	L	H	M	L
Coffee	M	L	H	M	L	L	M	L	L	L
Cocoa	M	M	H	M	L	M	M	L	L	L
Tea	H	L	H	L	H	M	L	L	H	L
Tobacco	M	L	H	M	L	L	M	L	L	L
Date palm	M	L	H	H	L	L	M	L	?	H
Citrus	M	M	H	H	L	L	M	L	M	L/M*
Wheat	L/M	H	H	H	L	L	M	M*	M	M
Barley	L/M	L	L	L	L	L	M/H	M/H	L	H
Oats	M	L	L	L	L	H	L	M	H	L
Rye	L	L	L	L	H	H	L/M	H	H	M
Potatoes	M/H	L	H	L	H	M/H	L	H	H	M
Mangolds	H	L	M	L	L	H	L	L	H	M
Sugar beet	H	M	H	M	L	M	L	H	M	M/H
Peas	M	M	H*	M	L	L	M	M	M	L*
Beans	M	M*	M*	M*	L	L/M*	L*	M/H	L	L*
Flax	M	M	H	M	L	L	L	L	L	L
Cherry	M/L	L	M	L	L	L	M	L/M	M	L
Apple	M/H	M	H	M	L	L	L/M	L	L	L
Pear	H	L/M	H	M	L	M	L	M	L	L

L — low; M — medium; H — high. *Depending on variety.
Source: adapted from Vink (1975), by permission.

TABLE 4.2

Major criteria used in assessing soil suitability for crops in Malaysia

Crop	Max. slope (%)	Soil depth (cm)	Texture	Drainage	Water release (months)	Maximum salinity (mmho/cm)	to depth (cm)	pH	Minimum depth to acid sulphate (cm)	Maximum thickness of drained peat (cm)	Work-ability
Rubber	36	125	Not LS or coarser	Not P	12	2	150	4.0–6.0	150	50	NI
Oil palm	29	125	Not SL or coarser	Some F	12	2	150	4.0–6.5	100	100	NI
Sago palm	3.5	100	Not SL or coarser	VP–P only	—	2	150	4.0–6.0	125	50	NI
Tapioca	10.5	50	Not C	Not P	12	2	100	4.3–7.3	50	NR	NWR
Sweet potato	10.5	50	Not C	Not P	12	2	100	4.3–6.0	50	NR	NWR
Soyabean	10.5	25	Not C	W–I	GS	4	50	5.5–6.5	50	25	NWR
Vegetables	10.5	25	Not C	W–I	GS	4	50	4.5–6.5	50	NR	NWR
Tea	35	100	Not S or C	W–I	12	2	150	4.0–6.0	25	0	NI
Grass (cut)	21	25	Not LS or coarser	W–P	12	4	50	4.3–7.0	50	NR	NWR
Citrus	35	125	Not S or C	W–I	12	2	150	5.0–7.0	150	50	NS
Pineapple	10.5	25	All	W–I	12	2	100	4.5–5.5	50	NR	NS
Guava	21	50	Not LS or coarser	W–I	12	2	100	4.5–6.5	100	100	NS
Banana	21	125	Not LS or coarser	W–I	12	2	100	4.0–7.0	125	25	NS
Cashew	36	100	Not C	W–I	9	2	150	4.0–7.3	150	100	NI
Cocoa	21	150	Not SL or coarser	W–I	12	2	150	5.0–7.5	150	50	NI
Coffee	21	125	Not S	W–I	12	2	150	4.5–6.5	150	125	NI
Coconut	10.5	100	Not LS or coarser	W–I	12	2	150	4.5–7.5	100	100	NI
Maize	10.5	50	Not S or C	W–I	GS	2	50	>5.0	125	NR	NWR
Sorghum	10.5	50	Not S	W–I	GS	4	50	>5.0	125	NR	NWR
Groundnut	10.5	25	Not S or C	W–MW	GS	4	50	5.5–7.0	50	0	NWR
Padi Rice	0.4	25	SCL or finer	Controlled	Dry at harvest	4	25	>4.0	25	0	NWR

LS — Loamy sand; SL — Sandy loam; C — CLay; S — Sand; SCL — Sandy clay loam; W — Well drained: MW — Moderately well drained: I — Imperfectly drained; P — Poorly drained; VP — Very poorly drained; GS — Growing season; NR — No restrictions; NI — Not important; NS — No stones; NWR — No workability restrictions allowed.

Source : adapted from Protz (1977), by permission.

Cultural practices include applying manure, plowing, disking, rolling, land planing, spring-tooth harrowing, furrowing, and shaping seedbeds. About 450 kg nitrogen, 100 kg of phosphorus, and 90 kg of potassium are applied per hectare. Manure is commonly applied before the transplants are set out, at the rate of 2.5 tonnes per hectare. Diseases are controlled by treating the seeds and by using fungicides, and worms by applying insecticides. Weeds are controlled by applying selective herbicides after the transplants are set out and by cultivating and hand hoeing.

The gross irrigation requirement for celery is about 6,000 litres of water per hectare. Furrows are used for irrigating.

Specific factors important in management for groups of soils, by Capability Units (p. 87) follow:

Group 1 — Soils of capability units I-1 and IIs-5 are in this group. Irrigation water is applied 10 times during the growing season. Runs are shortest on the sandy loams and longest on the clays.

Group 2 — Soils of capability units IIe-1, IIe-3, and IIe-5 are in this group. Irrigation water is applied 10 times during the growing season. All tillage is done across the slope.

Group 3 — Soils of capability units IIs-4, IIIs-4, and IIs-0 are in this group. Irrigation water is applied 10 to 12 times during the growing season. On Corrolitas and Metz series soils on 2—9% slopes, furrows are laid out across the slope or on the contour.

Group 4 — Soils of capability units IIw-2 and IIw-6 are in this group. Tile drains or open ditches are used to keep the water table below the root zone. In areas affected by excess salts, the gross irrigation requirement is about 7,500 litres of water per hectare. The additional water is needed to leach salts from the soil. Irrigation runs are shortest on the sandy loams and longest on the clays..

In Britain, soil maps have been interpreted to assess land suitability for specific management practices, such as direct drilling, a technique of seeding directly into soils without preliminary cultivation (Cannell, Davies, Mackney, and Pidgeon 1979), acceptance of animal wastes in the form of slurries (Lea 1979; and p. 179), and cultivation techniques (Jones 1979; and Table 4.3).

Suitability classifications can be devised for particular land uses, often with divisions very similar to those of the Land Capability Classification (p. 68). Thus the suitability of land for cropping (Table 4.4) or for pastoral use in New Zealand is expressed in two six-class systems based on soil limitations. Chun (1971) illustrates this type of approach for padi rice, upland crops, orchards, woodland, and grass in Korea.

TABLE 4.3

Suitability Groups according to ease of cultivation (as used in the interpretation of the 1:250 000 soil map of Kent, England)

Group	Ease of ploughing, preparation of seedbeds	Requirements	Remarks
1	Easy	Autumn ploughing not essential, traditional machinery adequate, timeliness essential	Can be ploughed during drier periods in winter and spring with little risk of structural damage
2	Moderate	Autumn ploughing desirable, traditional machinery adequate, timeliness essential	Easily damaged by ill-timed ploughing if the organic content is small. Winter ploughing is not precluded if undertaken after rain-free periods, but timeliness is important.
3	Moderately difficult	Autumn ploughing essential, traditional machinery adequate, timeliness essential.	Soils are easily damaged by farm machinery when wet and dry out slowly so that timely cultivations are essential particularly in Spring. Autumn drilling is desirable to avoid Spring cultivations
4	Difficult	Autumn ploughing essential, crawler tractor and/or offset machinery advantageous, timeliness critical	Soils should be ploughed in autumn when conditions are favourable, cage wheels or other aids may be required to avoid or minimize structural damage. Frost weathering is essential for the formation of a good seedbed: timely spring cultivations are critical and the number of passes should be kept to a minimum.
5	—	—	Not normally ploughed, or impossible because of steep slopes, permanently high groundwater-table, strong microrelief, extreme droughtiness or infertility.

Source: Fordham and Green (1980), by permission.

TABLE 4.4

Soil limitation classes for potential cropping use in
New Zealand

Class	Subclass	Definition
C1		Soils of flat and easy rolling land with minimal to slight soil limitations for crop production
	1A	Soils most suitable for cropping with only minimal limitations or limitations that can be easily overcome
	1B	Soils with medium to high nutrient requirements, including some shallow and poorly drained soils
	1C	Soils which require drainage before they can be successfully cropped
C2		Soils of flat and rolling land with moderate soil limitations for crop production
	2A	Soils with insufficient moisture
	2B	Soils with impeded drainage and with heavy textured subsoils
C3		Soils of flat and rolling land with severe soil limitations for crop production
	3A	Soils with limitations of coarse texture, stoniness, and frequent flooding
	3B	Soils of medium to high elevations
C4		Soils of the hilly and steep land unsuitable for crop production
C5		Soils on moderately steep and moderately steep to steep land with severe soil limitations to crop production
C6		Soils on steep land where slope precludes cultivation for crop production

Source : Information from Cutler (1968), Campbell (1977), and Rijkse (1977).

The FAO Framework

The FAO Framework for Land Evaluation (1976) was preceded by a background document (FAO 1972), a draft (FAO 1973), and the Proceedings of two meetings of international expert consultants (Brinkman and Smyth 1973; FAO 1975). Smyth (1970b, 1971, 1974), Higgins (1975, 1978), Purnell (1978, 1979), and reports on various pilot studies, e.g. in Malawi (Young and Goldsmith 1977); Sri Lanka (Desaunettes, Somapala, Hettiga, and Amarasinghe 1974); Mauritius (Arlidge and Wong 1975); the Sudan (Van der Kevie 1976); the Cameroons (Muller and Gavaud 1976); and Brazil, Surinam, and Kenya (FAO 1976) illustrate the development of the Framework towards its final form. The Framework was designed mainly for use in developing countries, but may also have future applications in more advanced countries (Sys 1978).

There are six basic principles (Young 1978):

(i) Land suitability is assessed for specified kinds of use.

(ii) Evaluation requires a comparison of benefit obtained with inputs needed.

(iii) A multidisciplinary approach is required.

(iv) Evaluation is made in terms relevant to local or national conditions.

(v) Suitability is for use on a sustained basis, i.e. the use must not bring about severe or progressive degradation.

(vi) Evaluation involves a comparison of two or more kinds of use, which are not exclusively agricultural.

The structure of the Framework is shown in Table 4.5. There are four levels of decreasing generalization:

(i) Land Suitability Orders which reflect kinds of suitability.

(ii) Land Suitability Classes which reflect degrees of suitability within Orders.

(iii) Land Suitability Subclasses which reflect kinds of limitation, or the main kinds of improvements required, within Classes.

(iv) Land Suitability Units which reflect minor differences within Subclasses in the management required.

TABLE 4.5

The FAO Framework for Land Evaluation

Order		Class	Subclass	Unit
S	Suitable	S1 S2 S3 etc.	S2m S2e S2me etc.	S2e–1 S2e–2 etc.
Sc	Conditionally Suitable (This is a phase of the Order Suitable: see text)	Sc2	Sc2m	–
N	Not suitable	N1 N2	N1m N1e etc.	

Source : FAO (1976), by permission.

In its basic structure the Framework resembles the USDA Land Capability Classification (p. 69). The S1, S2, etc. and N1, N2, etc. Classes of the Framework parallel Classes I—VIII in the Land Capability Classification. In both systems Subclasses are represented by a letter notation after the Class number which denotes the main kind of limitation (or improvements required), and Units are represented by a numerical notation of the form -1, -2, etc. Like the Land Capability Classification the Framework can be employed at any level of generalization.

Land Suitability Orders denote whether the land is suitable (S) or not suitable (N) for the particular use under consideration. Order S is defined as 'Land on which sustained use of the kind under consideration is expected to yield benefits which justify the inputs, without unacceptable risk of damage to land resources'; and Order N as 'Land which has qualities that appear to preclude sustained use of the kind under consideration'.

The designation Conditionally Suitable (Sc) is a phase of the Order Suitable, and caters for small areas of land which are unsuitable or poorly suited for the use being considered under the management specified, but which would be suitable provided certain conditions were fulfilled, e.g. different management techniques to cope with localized poor drainage or cropping restrictions to cope with local microclimates. This phase should be avoided whenever possible, and it may only be employed where a number of detailed stipulations are met (see FAO 1976, p. 21). It is not to be used to indicate an uncertain interpretation.

Within each Order, *Land Suitability Classes* are numbered according to decreasing degrees of suitability. Although there is no limit to the number of Classes within the Order Suitable, five is the recommended maximum and three the norm as below:

Class S1 Highly Suitable Land having no significant limitation to sustained application of a given use, or only minor limitations that will not significantly reduce productivity or benefits and will not raise inputs above an acceptable level. (This Class may not always occur.)

Class S2 Moderately Suitable Land having limitations which in aggregate are moderately severe for sustained application of a given use; the limitations will reduce productivity or benefits and increase required inputs to the extent that the overall advantage to be gained from the use, although still attractive, will be appreciably inferior to that expected on Class S1 land.

Class S3 Marginally Suitable Land having limitations which in aggregate are severe for sustained application of a given use and will so reduce productivity or benefits, or increase required inputs, that this expenditure will be only marginally justified.

Variation in the number of Classes may cause confusion in indexing, e.g. the marginally suitable category could be S3 in some cases, S4 or S5 in others depending on the total number of Classes recognized. An alternative which gives a constant numbering to the lowest Suitability Class by subdividing Classes, e.g. S2.1, S2.2 etc., is permitted, but not recommended.

There are normally two Classes within the Order Not Suitable:

Class N1 Currently Not Suitable Land having limitations which may be surmountable in time but which cannot be corrected with existing knowledge at currently acceptable cost; the limitations are so severe as to preclude successful sustained use of the land in the given manner.

Class N2 Permanently Not Suitable Land having limitations which appear so severe as to preclude any possibilities of successful sustained use of land in the given manner .

The boundary between N1 (Currently Not Suitable) and the lowest category of the Order Suitable (Marginally Suitable) may vary with economic and social conditions, but the boundary between Currently and Permanently Not Suitable is essentially fixed.

All Classes except S1 can be subdivided into *Land Suitability Subclasses* according to the nature of the major limitation or limitations; Classes in the Order Not Suitable need not be divided. The required Subclasses will be established on an *ad hoc* basis as each situation demands; there is no formal list of Subclasses.

The number of Subclasses should be kept to a minimum, and the symbol for any Subclass should list as few limitations as possible. Usually one letter should suffice and two should be used only when their limitations are equally severe.

Land Suitability Units, like Land Capability Units (p. 87), are of most use at the farm planning level, since they differ from each other on 'production characteristics or in minor aspects of their management requirements'. Land Suitability Units can be created in the numbers deemed necessary.

It should be stressed that 'The Framework does not by itself constitute an evaluation system. . . . The Framework is a set of principles and concepts on the basis of which local, national or regional evaluation systems can be constructed' (FAO 1976, p. 7). There are four major kinds of evaluation system according to whether they are qualitative or quantitative, and refer to current or potential suitability (FAO 1976, p. 22).

Qualitative classifications are general appraisals normally based on the physical properties of the land with only ancillary economic information. Quantitative suitability classifications also include a considerable input of economic, social, and environmental information. For land evaluation in the developing countries where the FAO Framework is most likely to be employed it is very useful to differentiate between Current suitability and Potential suitability (FAO 1976, p. 22):

> A classification of *Current Suitability* refers to the suitability for a defined use of land in its present condition, without major improvements. A current suitability classification may refer to the present use of the land, either with existing or improved management practices, or to a different use.
>
> A classification of *Potential Suitability* refers to the suitability, for a defined use, of land units in their condition at some future date, after specified major improvements have been completed where necessary. It is necessary to specify the economic factors included in the estimated costs of these improvements, e.g. amortization of capital costs.

Land improvements (as distinct from changes in land use) are major or minor activities which cause beneficial changes in the qualities of land itself. The main distinction between major and minor improvements is on the capacity of individual farmers to carry them out. Thus terracing or field drainage might be minor improvements in some social contexts, major improvements in others.

Because a suitability classification sets different Class limits for each use, it is quite likely that a particular map unit may be regarded as highly suitable (S1) for one use such as forest but only marginally suitable (S3) for another use such as arable farming (e.g. Fig. 4.1).

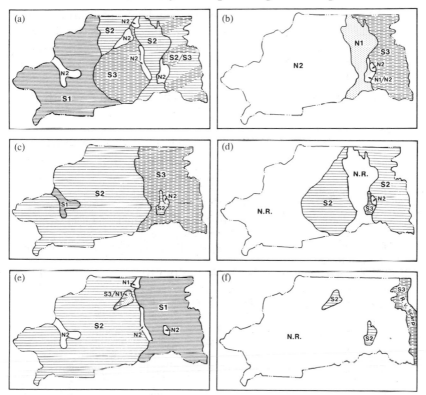

Fig. 4.1. Qualitative Current Suitability Classes (FAO Framework) for major kinds of land use in Malawi. (a) arable farming: annual crops, (b) arable farming: perennial crops; (c) livestock production: (d) forestry: natural woodland; (e) forestry: plantations; (f) tourism and conservation. S1 — Highly suitable; S2 — Moderately suitable; S3 — Marginally suitable; N1 — Currently not suitable; N2 — Permanently not suitable; NR — Not relevant. (From Young and Goldsmith (1977), by permission.)

This does not automatically mean that the best use of the land is for forestry. The actual choice between alternative uses depends on other socio-economic or political factors. The aim of the suitability classification is to provide an input to the overall planning discussion.

At the core of the Framework is the concept of a *Land Utilization Type* (LUT), discussed at length by Beek (1974, 1975*a*, 1975*b*). This is defined as 'a specific subdivision of a major kind of land use serving as the subject of land evaluation and defined as precisely as is practical in terms of produce, level of management, farm size, etc. It is a technical organizational unit in a specific socio-economic and institutional setting' (Beek 1975*b*). The identification of LUTs is an essential first step in implementing a suitability classification, and is an important aid in the pooling, co-ordination, and processing of relevant land-use data.

LUTs may either be defined fully at the beginning of a land evaluation exercise or may be broadly defined at the start and modified as the evaluation proceeds. The specification of LUTs may involve a variety of *key attributes* or *distinguishing factors* (FAO) 1976) such as:

(i) Produce, including goods (e.g. crops, livestock, timber), services (e.g. recreational facilities) or other benefits (e.g. wildlife conservation).
(ii) Market orientation, including whether towards subsistence or commercial production.
(iii) Capital intensity.
(iv) Labour intensity.
(v) Power sources (e.g. human labour, draught animals, machinery using fuels).
(vi) Technical knowledge and attitudes of land users.
(vii) Technology employed (e.g. implements and machinery, fertilizers, livestock breeds, farm transport, methods of timber felling).
(viii) Infrastructure required (e.g. sawmills, tea factories, agricultural advisory services).
(ix) Size and configuration of land holdings, including whether consolidated or fragmented.
(x) Land tenure, the legal or customary manner in which rights to land are held, by individuals or groups.
(xi) Income levels, expressed *per capita*, per unit of production (e.g. farm) or per unit area.

Management practices need not be identical in all parts of one LUT. For example, if the LUT is 'mixed farming', part of the land may be under arable use and part allocated to grazing. Such differences may arise from variation in the land, from the requirements of the management system, or both.

Some examples of LUTs are:

(i) Rainfed annual cropping based on groundnuts with subsistence maize, by smallholders with low capital resources, using cattle-drawn farm implements, with high labour intensity, on freehold farms of 5–10 ha.

(ii) Farming similar to (i) in respect of production, capital, labour, power, and technology, but on farms of 200–500 ha operated on a communal basis.

(iii) Commercial wheat production on large freehold farms, with high capital and low labour intensity, and a high level of mechanization and inputs.

(iv) Extensive cattle ranching, with medium levels of capital and labour intensity, with land held and central services operated by a government agency.

(v) Softwood plantations operated by a government Department of Forestry, with high capital intensity, low labour intensity, and advanced technology.

(vi) A national park for recreation and tourism.

Thus both agricultural and non-agricultural uses, and uses at different levels of management are considered (e.g. Fig. 4.1). Multiple and compound land utilization types may also be recognized. *Multiple land use* is the situation where more than one kind of land use is undertaken simultaneously on the same area of land, e.g. timber plantations and recreation. A *Compound land use* contains several uses within a single evaluation unit, e.g. mixed farming with arable and grass grown in rotation.

The limitations on which the FAO Suitability Classes and Sub-classes are distinguished are 'land qualities, or their expression by means of diagnostic criteria, which adversely affect a kind of land use'. A diagnostic criterion is 'a variable which has an understood influence upon the output from, or the required inputs to, a specified use, and which serves as a basis for assessing the suitability of a given area of land for that use. This variable may be a land quality (p. 3), a land characteristic (p. 2), or a function of several land characteristics.' For every diagnostic criterion there will be a critical value or a set of critical values to define the limits of Suitability Classes (e.g. Table 4.6).

The main objective of FAO and other development agencies e.g. the Land Resources Division of the Ministry of Overseas Development in Britain (Baulkwill 1972; Lang 1975; Murdoch, Lang, and Smyth 1976) is to help developing countries to make rational choices between land use alternatives. As techniques have developed, investigation projects have become more specific and of more direct application. Many now require a multidisciplinary approach to which the input from agronomists and soil scientists is only a part.

TABLE 4.6
The degrees of limitation for use of agricultural implements in Brazil

Land Utilization Type No.	1	2	3	4	5	6
Level of technology	Modern	Intermediate	Primitive (draught animals)	Very primitive (hand labour)	Modern	Primitive (hand labour)
Crops	Mainly annual	Mainly annual	Mainly annual	Mainly annual	Tree crops	Tree crops
Suitability Class						
S1 (Good)	None	Slight	Slight	Moderate	Slight	Moderate
S2 (Fair)	Slight	Moderate	Moderate	Moderate to Strong	Moderate	Strong
S3 (Poor)	Moderate	Moderate	Moderate	Strong	Strong	Strong
N (Not)			Limitations stronger than in Class S3			

The degrees of limitation define the boundaries of the suitability Class, e.g. a Strong limitation would rate the land S2 for LUT6, S3 for LUTs 4 and 5, and N for LUTs 1, 2, and 3
Source : FAO (1976), by permission.

Assessing the feasibility of land improvements

Land can be assessed not only for the nature and degree of the factors which limit crop growth but also for the feasibility of improvement measures which can remove or reduce these limitations. A simple interpretation of soil-map units will often suffice, for example, the advice on drainage schemes given in British soil survey memoirs and records (e.g. Thomasson 1975; and Table 4.7), or the need for deep ploughing to improve topsoil quality in the Netherlands (Haans and Westerveld 1970).

Sometimes suitability classifications are based on the recommended treatments to overcome the limitations of the land, e.g. Table 4.8. A soil capability classification used in Quebec (Mailloux, Dubé, and Tardif 1964) defines Classes according to the seriousness of their limitations but the Subclasses are based on the nature and scale of the improvement measurements which are thought necessary, e.g. Subclass c is for land requiring expensive stone removal work and Subclass f for land requiring major erosion control measures. The USDA Land Capability Classification (p. 68) began as such a classification, to help plan soil conservation measures (see Figs. 5.2 and 5.3). The parametric system of Riquier et al. (1970; and p. 112) can be applied both to the existing circumstances and to the predicted situation when land improvements have been implemented.

Productivity of grassland and livestock grazing potential

Improved grassland

Grass grown in enclosed fields is an important crop particularly in temperate regions. Where it is harvested for direct feeding or conservation, e.g. as hay, silage, or dried grass, productivity can be assessed by field trials, harvesting sample plots, or from farm records as for arable crops (t'Mannetje, Jones, and Stobbs 1976; t'Mannetje 1978).

A grazing regime, however, is different, and the weight of the herbage removed by grazing is not readily assessed. Direct measures of livestock production (e.g. Corbett 1978) may be too coarse to reveal the influence of the environment. Grazing from a particular field often makes up only part of the diet of an animal and indeed one field may be grazed at intervals by several kinds of stock,

TABLE 4.7
Guidelines for the drainage of land for arable use in Berkshire, England

Soil series	Subsoil permeability	Type of system	Pipe interval (m)	Depth to pipe invert (cm)
Bursledon	Moderate	Pipe drains with no permeable fill over drains	Random drains in depressions or gulleys	75
Berkhamsted	Moderate		Random drains in plateaux depressions	75
Swinley†	Moderate		20	75
Holidays Hill†	Moderate–slow			
Rapley†	Moderate		20–30	75–90
Curdridge	Moderate–slow			
Swanwick†	Moderate		20	>90
Hurst†	Moderate–slow			
Park Gate‡	Moderate			
Hook	Moderate–rapid		40	90
Wickham	Slow	Pipe drains with permeable fill over drains up to 40 cm from surface and mole drains at 55–65 cm spaced at maximum of 2.5 m	20	75–90
Ferrel	Slow			
Windsor	Very slow		40–60	75
Netley	Moderate–rapid	Pipe drains but with filter over or with filter-wrapped pipe	Deep interceptor; random drains	>120

*Arable land includes long ley grass rotations; acceptance of these guidelines will not render land suitable for all types of arable farming. Intensification may be necessary werĕ root crops are to be harvested in late autumn. The guidelines are not recommendations; each site will need thorough investigation by the drainage designer to take account of all circumstances. The design may need to be varied to take account of outfall conditions, surface slopes and contours, soil structure weaknesses, and existing underdrainage treatment.

†Subsoiling will be advantageous where profile examination shows this to be necessary and when soil is sufficiently dry.

‡If underlain directly by clay, place pipes above the clay layer.

Source: Jarvis *et al.* (1979), by permission.

TABLE 4.8

A treatment oriented land classification for use in hilly tropical regions

Soil depth (cm)	Slopes					
	Gently sloping <12% (<7°)	Moderately sloping 12–27% (7–15°)	Strongly sloping 27–36% (15–20°)	Very strongly sloping 36–47% (20–25°)	Steep 47–58% (25–30°)	Very steep >58% (>30°)
>90	C_1	C_2	C_3	C_4	FT	F
50–90	C_1	C_2	C_3	C_4/P	FT/F	F
20–50	C_1	C_2/P	C_3/P	P	F	F
<20	C_1/P	P	P	P	F	F

Notes: 1. Symbols for most intensive tillage or uses:

C_1 : Cultivable land requiring no or few intensive conservation measures, e.g. contour cultivation, strip cropping, vegetative barriers, rock barriers and in larger farms, broadbase terraces.

C_2 : Cultivable land with moderately deep soils, needing more intensive conservation, e.g. bench-terracing, hexagons, mini-convertible terracing for the convenience of four wheel tractor farming. The conservation treatments can be done by medium-sized machines.

C_3 : Cultivable land needing bench-terracing, hexagons and mini-convertible terracing on deep soil and hillside ditching, individual basins on less deep soil. Mechanization is limited to small tractor or walking tractor because of the steepness of the slope. Terracing can be done by a smaller machine.

C_4 : Cultivable land, all the necessary treatments are likely to be done by manual labour. Cultivation is to be practised by walking tractor and hand labour.

P : Pasture, improved and managed. Where the slope is approaching 47% (25°) and when the land is too wet, zero grazing should be practised. Rotational grazing is recommended for all kinds of slopes.

FT : Food trees or fruit trees. Orchard terracing is the main treatment supplemented with contour planting, diversion ditching and mulching. Because of steepness of the slopes, interspaces should be kept in permanent grass cover.

F: Forest land, where the soil is too shallow for any of the soil conservation treatments.

2. Any land which is too wet, occasionally flooded or too stony which prevents tillage treatment should be classified as follows:

(a) Below 47% (25°): Pasture
(b) Above 47% (25°): Forest

3. Gully dissected lands which prevent normal tillage activities: Forest.

Source: Sheng (1972), by permission.

or may be both grazed and cut in the same year. It is thus exceedingly difficult to demonstrate the actual productivity of a particular field.

Grassland productivity is greatly affected by the level of management, and particularly fertilizers which may outweigh any differences due to land quality (Holmes 1968; Hughes 1970; Lee and Diamond 1971). Sward deterioration caused by reversion to non-sown species of lower grazing value also affects grassland productivity and, where climatic conditions are marginal, this is much affected by soil conditions (Davies 1968).

Damage to the grass sward by treading (poaching) under wet conditions severely restricts the grazing season, and is the most important limitation to grassland utilization in Britain (Patto, Clement, and Forbes 1978). Livestock farmers can also be hit by occasional climatic extremes such as severe droughts or winter snows or floods that are concealed in longterm averages.

Faced with all these problems, the soil surveyor attempting to interpret his soil map for the benefit of livestock farmers has three options:

(i) He can simply provide basic information on the suitability of the land for the various management operations involved.

(ii) He can attempt some prediction of grass yield, or the carrying capacity of the land for livestock as in Ireland (Lee and Diamond 1972).

(iii) He can use a classification of suitability for grassland.

For the first option he should record:

(i) Liability to soil erosion by wind and/or water.

(ii) Drainage (including flood risk) particularly as it affects the length of the grazing season; the feasibility of artificial drainage (if required) and the likely benefits which might follow.

(iii) The resistance to drought in terms of soil moisture holding capacity and soil depth, together with a consideration of the feasibility and benefits of irrigation.

(iv) The structural stability of the soil to poaching by stock and/or rutting by machinery; this is particularly affected by drainage and by soil texture and organic matter content (including peatiness).

(v) Soil salinity and the availability and quality of irrigation water.

(vi) Slopes and surface irregularities and their effect on the operation of agricultural machinery.

(vii) The ease of cultivation, as influenced by slope, soil texture, soil depth, stoniness, presence of boulders and rock outcrops which affect the suitability of the land for mechanized reseeding.

(viii) The pH and chemical fertility, with any information on previous responses to applications of lime and fertilizer.
(ix) Variability of soil conditions over any particular field.
(x) Climatic limitations, e.g. rainfall, temperature, length of growing season, accumulated degree days, exposure, etc. Rainfall may often be the most important factor of all even when the range of rainfall is not extreme, as in Britain (Kilkenny, Holmes, Baker, Walsh, and Shaw 1977; Harrod 1979).

The prediction of the carrying capacity of land needs to take account of the differing requirements of the different categories of stock appropriate to the region and the period over which the land can usefully be grazed. In Britain the Grazing Livestock Unit (Nix 1979) rates dairy cows 1.0, beef cattle 0.8, calves under one year 0.4, lowland sheep 0.2, and hill sheep 0.1 GLU. The specified number of GLU/ha does not necessarily represent the number of stock that will be carried by the land since other factors (e.g. lack of capital) play a part. Cowlishaw (1969) has shown how to determine carrying capacity experimentally as the stocking rate giving the highest mean liveweight gain (Fig. 4.2). Alternatively, Chisholm (1965) measured the stocking rate giving the highest profit. Carrying capacity may be determined either for the grazing season or for the whole year, the latter often determined by the carrying capacity of

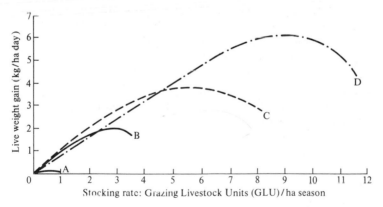

Fig. 4.2. Graphical determination of the optimum stock carrying capacity of grazing land. A — Rangeland in Georgia, United States (0.6 GLU/ha season); B — Unirrigated pasture in Texas (3.0 GLU/ha season); C — Irrigated pasture in Britain (5.7 GLU/ha season); D — Irrigated pasture in California (9.1 GLU/ha season). (Adapted from Cowlishaw (1969), by permission.)

the land when little or no grazing is available (e.g. in the winter or the dry season). For individual fields GLU–grazing days per year is usually the more suitable measure of carrying capacity.

Classifications of the suitability of land for grassland have been proposed in New Zealand (Gibbs 1963), the Netherlands (Vink and van Zuilen 1974) and Britain (Morrison and Idle 1972; Harrod 1979; Harrod and Thomasson 1980). Harrod's classification is of special interest. He ranks land in England and Wales for grassland suitability according to its potential production and the trafficability of the land. This affects the utilization of the grass and maintenance of a good sward. These in turn (Fig. 4.3) depend on the climate and soil moisture properties (dryness, wetness, retained water capacity, and depth to impermeable layer).

Grassland yield categories (Table 4.9) are based on soil Dryness Subclasses (Table 3.6) and three general climatic divisions (i) dry lowlands, (ii) moist areas, and (iii) areas with short growing seasons (less than 240 days) due to higher altitude and/or latitude. The boundary between dry and moist climates follows the 100 mm isopleth of average potential cumulative soil water deficit (Hodgson 1974; Avery, Findlay, and Mackney 1975; Hall, Reeve, Thomasson, and Wright 1977), but includes with the moist areas those parts of the lowlands which experience an autumn flush of grass growth (the Cheshire plain with adjacent areas and south-west England).

Trafficability is categorized in Table 4.10, which uses the Wetness Classes of Table 3.5. The scheme was originally devised to evaluate poaching risk, i.e. damage by the hooves of grazing animals, but has been extended to cover the use of wheeled machinery since the significant soil properties are similar.

Yield and trafficability categories then define the Grassland Suitability Classes (Table 4.11).

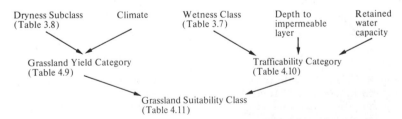

Fig. 4.3. The derivation of Grassland Suitability Classes in England and Wales. (See Table 4.11.)

TABLE 4.9
Grassland Yield Categories in England and
Wales

Dryness Subclass (Table 3.8)	Yield Category		
	Dry lowlands*	Moist lowlands*	Short growing season*
a	*a*	*a*	*b*
b	*b*	*a*	*c*
c	*c*	*b*	*d*
d	*d*	*c*	*d*

*See text for definitions.
Source: Harrod (1979), by permission.

Harrod (1979) describes the Grassland Suitability Classes:

Class A: soils well suited to pasture   Potential yields are high with ample growth throughout the season. The land is readily trafficked, poaching risk is low, and the high stock densities associated with intensive grassland use can be sustained with ease. Re-seeding presents no problems on these soils.

Class B: soils suited to pasture, with only minor limitations   Suitability is slightly restricted owing to small imbalances of yield and trafficability, but satisfactory extensive use is commonly possible. Difficulties with re-seeding are unlikely. The minor limitation of this class can result from:
1. impeded drainage;
2. shallow, stony, or sandy soils with low total available water inducing slight droughtiness;
3. unfavourable particle-size class interacting with other soil properties to give moderate poaching and trafficability problems;
4. risk of freshwater flooding which occasionally interferes with use or management and encourages deterioration of the pasture;
5. short growing season (less than 240 days).

Class C: soils suited to seasonal pasture   Soils have serious limitations to potential yield and/or trafficability and the balance between these cannot be sustained throughout the summer. Therefore they are unsuited for use as intensive pasture.
    Limitations can be attributed to the effects of:
1. wetness, including frequent freshwater flood risk;
2. droughtiness;
3. moderately steep or steep slopes of 19–47 per cent (11–25°);

TABLE 4.10
The classification of grassland trafficability in England and Wales

Wetness Class (Table 3.7)	Depth to impermeable layer (cm)	Dry climate* Volumetric retained water capacity of mineral A horizon			Moist climate* Volumetric retained water capacity of mineral A horizon		
		45%	35–45%	35%	45%	35–45%	35%
I	>80	1	1	1	1	2	2
and							
II	80–40	1	1	2	2	2	3
III	>80	1	2	2	3	3	3
and	80–40	2	2	3	3	3	4
IV	<40	3	3	4	4	4	5
V	>80	4	4	5	5	5	5
and	80–40	5	5	5	5	5	5
VI	<40	5	5	5	5	5	5

Trafficability and poaching risk categories are as follows:

Trafficability		Poaching risk	
1.	Very high	1.	Very low
2.	Very high	2.	Low
3.	Moderate	3.	Moderate
4.	Low	4.	High
5.	Very low	5.	Very high

*See text for definitions.
Source: Harrod (1979), by permission.

4. boulders or rock outcrops (rocky or very rocky land with up to 50 per cent of outcrops);

5. short growing season (less than 240 days).

Within these specifications several kinds of soils differently suited for seasonal grass can be recognised, (using the nomenclature of Harrod and Thomasson (1980) for the major limitations):

Cp — soils with high potential yields but poor trafficability and high poaching risk;

Cy — soils with low potential yields but good trafficability;

Cyp — soils with low potential yields and poor trafficability;

Cv — upland soils with restricted growing season and surface wetness;

Cg — moderate steep and steep slopes of 19–47 per cent (11–25°).

Class D: soils ill-suited to pasture Very low yield potential with extremely difficult going conditions severely restrict the value of this land for pasture.

Limitations arise from one or more of the following:

1. very wet, economically undrainable soils;

2. very wet peaty topped soils very difficult to improve (for example, cultivating to mix a clayey subsoil with peaty material will not be beneficial);

3. extremely stony or raw soils;

4. extremely rocky (>50 per cent rock outcrops) or boulderstrewn land;

5. short growing season (<240 days);

6. very steep slopes >47 per cent (>25°);

7. frequent salt water flooding.

A map at 1 : 1 000 000 showing the distribution of these Classes in England and Wales has been published (Harrod and Thomasson 1980).

TABLE 4.11

Classification of grassland suitability in England and Wales

Yield Category (Table 4.9)	Trafficability Category (Table 4.10)				
	1	2	3	4	5
a	A	A	B	Cp	Cy
b	A	B	B	Cp	Cy/D
c	B	B	Cyp	Cyp	Cyp or Cu/D
d	Cy	Cy	Cyp	Cyp	Cyp or Cu/D

For description of Grassland Suitability Classes A, B, C, and D see text.

y — yield; p — poaching; u — upland.

Source: Harrod (1979) and Harrod and Thomasson (1980), by permission.

Rangeland

The soil surveyor himself is unlikely to have all the necessary skills to evaluate extensively grazed rangeland. The productivity and livestock carrying capacity of rangeland is determined by its botanical composition, and how this changes in response to managment inputs and grazing (USDA 1970). Under heavy grazing the most palatable plants tend to decrease in number and vigour, less desirable plants increase and there may be invasion by hardy and undesirable plants which were not originally present (Steele 1967). In the end only 'the barbed-wire plants and the stinkers' survive (Bellamy 1976). Good management techniques favour the desirable species by controlled grazing, the use of chemicals or machines to control weeds and brushwood, or, more rarely, deliberate reseeding or fertilizing.

Grazing experiments are expensive (t'Mannetje *et al.* 1976) and need careful planning if their value is fully to be realized (cf. Fig. 4.2). However Condon (1968) has described a procedure for evaluating several tracts once the grazing capacity of one tract has been fairly accurately determined by such experiments or from its behaviour in actual productive use. The USDA has grouped soils that produce similar kinds and amount of forage into *range sites* on their soil and site characteristics (Bartelli 1978), using terms such as 'loamy prairie', 'shallow savannah' or 'saline subirrigated range site'. For each soil mapping unit the characteristic vegetation and potential production (dry weight/area/a) for favourable, normal, and unfavourable years are often given.

Rangeland has a capacity for multiple uses besides grazing (Box and Dwyer 1979) so evaluation and management for visual resources, wildlife recreation, and historic and archaeological resources may also be appropriate (Elsner, MacGill, Schwarz, and Thor 1979).

5. Agricultural land capability: category systems

Introduction

Evaluation of agricultural land *capability* refers to broad agricultural systems and not specific crops or practices (p. 3; cf. Chapter 4). Land with the highest capability is expected to be versatile and allow intensive use for a reasonably large range of enterprises (Fig. 5.1).

Category systems group land into small number of discrete ranked categories, usually no more than ten, according to the limiting

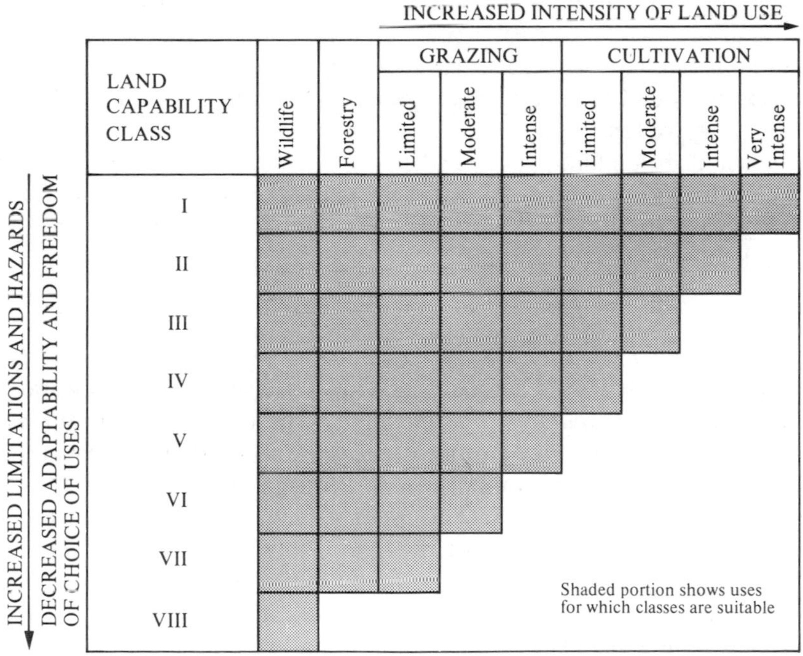

Fig. 5.1. The relationship between USDA Land Capability Classification Classes and the intensity with which each Class can be used safely. (Adapted from Hockensmith and Steele (1949) by Brady (1974). Copyright (1974) Macmillan Publishing Co., Inc. Reproduced by permission.)

values of a number of soil and site properties. These properties are believed to be those which impose permanent limitations on the range and success of suitable land uses (Chapter 3).

Categoric systems are implemented by testing the values of the appropriate soil and site properties against the criteria set for each category, by a sieving process. The values are tested first against the criteria for the best Class of land, and unless all criteria are met, the land automatically falls to the next lower Class. The values are then tested against the less stringent criteria for that Class and so on until a Class is found at which all the criteria are met. Commonly land meets many of the criteria for a superior Class easily and is downgraded to a lower Class because of failure to meet only one criterion. Categoric systems cannot easily deal with those situations where no single factor is limiting but where a number of properties show relatively low values simultaneously, yet none sufficiently severely in themselves to require downgrading of the land.

Parametric systems (Chapter 6) deal better with these interactions but have other disadvantages (pp. 96 and 114), and particularly the need for exact values for each soil or site property. For category systems one only needs to know if the value is above or below a certain limit.

Categoric systems are also widely used in assessing land for irrigation (p. 127), forestry (p. 147), and a wide range of non-agricultural uses (Chapter 9).

Land capability classification

The most widely used categoric systems for evaluating agricultural land are *land capability classifications*. These divide land into a small number of ranked categories according to the number and extent of its physical limitations to crop growth (Fig. 5.1). The highest level is the *Class*. This is, in effect, an expansion of the layman's classification of land into 'good, bad, or indifferent'. In the *Subclass* the main limitation or limitations affecting the land are recognized, while the lowest level of classification or *Capability Unit* is a grouping of soils which respond similarly to particular management systems.

Land capability classifications of this kind were developed in the United States Department of Agriculture (USDA) during the 1930s as part of the programme to control soil erosion. Classes of land were to be distinguished so as to 'indicate the most intensive tillage that can be practised safely with permanent maintenance of the soil or, in regions where cultivation is not practiced, the most intensive utilization for range or forestry that is consistent with preservation of the soil and its plant cover' (Norton 1939).

Initially the USDA Land Capability Classification had nine Classes, but it became established with eight (Norton 1940; Hockensmith and Steele 1943). By convention, Roman numerals are used to designate Classes, with Class I the best land, and Class VIII the poorest. During the 1940s increasing attention was given to problems other than soil erosion and the new more general *Class* descriptions emphasized the *degree of limitations* to the use of the land. *Land Capability Subclasses* indicating the *kind of limitation* and a lowest level of *Land Capability Units*, each consisting of land which was nearly uniform in *use possibilities* and *management needs* were also introduced.

The next stage was the rationalization and clarification of the Subclass (e.g. Hedge and Klingebiel 1957; Klingebiel 1958). A suffix notation was introduced for the four major kinds of limitation recognized at the Subclass level:

    e   erosion hazard
    w   excess water
    s   soil limitations within the rooting zone
    c   climatic limitation

Subclasses were denoted by the appropriate suffix or suffixes (with a maximum of two) placed after the class number, e.g. IIe, IIIws. Class I had no Subclasses.

Klingebiel and Montgomery (1961) presented the following definitive descriptions of the Classes of the USDA Land Capability Classification:

Class I   soils in Class I have few limitations that restrict their use.

These soils are suited to a wide range of plants and may be used safely for cultivated crops, pasture, range, woodland, and wildlife. They are nearly level or only gently sloping and the erosion hazard from wind or water is low. The soils are deep, generally well drained, and easily worked. They hold water well and are either fairly well supplied with plant nutrients or highly responsive to inputs of fertilizer.

The soils in Class I are not subject to damaging overflow. They are productive and suited to intensive cropping. The local climate must be favourable for growing many of the common field-crops.

In irrigated areas, soils may be placed in Class I if the limitation of the arid climate has been removed by relatively permanent irrigation works. Such irrigated soils (or soils potentially useful under irrigation) are nearly level, have deep rooting zones, favourable permeability and water-holding capacity, and are easily maintained in good tilth. Some of the soils may require initial conditioning, including levelling to the desired grade, leaching of a slight accumulation of soluble salts, or lowering of the seasonal water-table. Where limitations due to salts, water-table, overflow, or erosion are likely to recur, the soils are regarded as subject to permanent natural limitations and are not included in Class I.

Soils that are wet, and have slowly permeable subsoils, are not placed in Class I, although some Class I soils may be drained as an improvement measure for increased production and ease of operation.

Soils in Class I that are used for crops need ordinary management practices to maintain productivity — both soil fertility and soil structure. Such practices may include the use of fertilizers and lime, cover and green-manure crops, conservation of crop residues and animal manures, and sequences of adapted crops.

Class II soils in Class II have some limitations that reduce the choice of plants or require moderate conservation practices.

These soils require careful soil management, including conservation practices, to prevent deterioration or to improve air and water relations when the soils are cultivated. The limitations are few and the practices are easy to apply. The soils may be used for cultivated crops, pasture, range, woodland, or wildlife food and cover.

Limitations of soils in this Class may include (singly or in combination) the effects of gentle slopes, moderate susceptibility to wind or water erosion or moderate adverse effects of past erosion, less than ideal soil depth, somewhat unfavourable soil structure and workability, slight to moderate salinity or sodium easily corrected but likely to recur, occasional damaging overflow, wetness correctable by drainage but existing permanently as a moderate limitation, and slight climatic limitations on soil use and management.

These soils provide the farm operators less latitude in the choice of either crops or management practices than those in Class I. They may also require special soil-conserving cropping systems, soil conservation practices, water-control devices, or tillage methods when used for cultivated crops. For example, deep soils of this class with gentle slopes subject to moderate erosion when cultivated may need terracing, stripcropping, contour tillage, crop rotations that include grasses and legumes, vegetated water-disposal areas, cover or green-manure crops, stubble mulching, fertilizers, manure, and lime. The exact combinations of practices vary from place to place, depending on the characteristics of the soil, the local climate, and the farming systems.

Class III   soils in Class III have severe limitations that reduce the choice of plants or require special conservation practices, or both.

Soils in Class III have more restrictions than those in Class II and when used for cultivated crops the conservation practices are usually more difficult to apply and to maintain. They may be used for cultivated crops, pasture, woodland, range, or wildlife food and cover.

Limitations of these soils restrict the amount of clean cultivation; the timing of planting, tillage and harvesting, and the choice of crops; or some combination of these limitations. The limitation may result from the effects of one or more of the following: moderately steep slopes; high susceptibility to water or wind erosion or severe adverse effects of past erosion; frequent overflow accompanied by some crop damage; very slow permeability of the subsoil; wetness or some continuing waterlogging after drainage; shallow depths to bedrock, hardpan, fragipan, or claypan that limits the rooting zone and the water storage; low moisture-holding capacity; low fertility not easily corrected; moderate salinity or sodium; or moderate climatic limitations.

When cultivated, many of the wet, slowly permeable, but nearly level soils in this class require drainage and a cropping system that maintains or improves the structure and tilth of the soil. To prevent puddling and to improve permeability, it is commonly necessary to supply organic material to such soils and to avoid working them when they are wet. In some irrigated areas, part of these soils have limited use because of a water-table, slow permeability, and the hazard of salt or sodic accumulation. Each distinctive kind of soil in Class III has one or more alternative combinations of use and practices required for safe use, but the number of practical alternatives for average farmers is less than that for soils in Class II.

Class IV   soils in Class IV have very severe limitations that restrict the choice of plants, require very careful managment, or both.

The restrictions in use for soils in Class IV are greater than for those in Class III and the choice of plants is more limited. When these soils are cultivated, more careful management is required and conservation practices are more difficult to apply and maintain. Soils in Class IV may be used for crops, pasture, woodland, range, or wildlife food and cover.

Soils in this Class may be well suited to only two or three of the common crops, the harvest produced may be low in relation to inputs over a long period of time. Use for cultivated crops is limited as a result of the effects of one or more permanent features such as: steep slopes, severe susceptibility to water or wind erosion, severe effects of past erosion, shallow soils, low moisture-holding capacity, frequent overflows accompanied by severe crop damage, excessive wetness with continuing hazard of waterlogging after drainage, severe salinity or sodium, or moderately adverse climate.

Many sloping Class IV soils in humid areas are suited to occasional but not regular cultivation. Some of the poorly drained, nearly level soils put in Class IV are not subject to erosion but are poorly suited to intertillable crops because a long time is required for drying out in the spring and productivity for cultivated crops is low. Some of these soils are well suited to one or more special crops, such as fruits and ornamental trees and shrubs, but this suitability itself is not sufficient to place a soil in Class IV.

In subhumid and semiarid areas, soils in Class IV may produce good yields of adapted cultivated crops during years of above-average rainfall; low yields during years of average rainfall; and failure during years of below-average rainfall. During the low-rainfall years the soil must be protected, even though there can be little or no expectancy of a marketable crop. Special treatments and practices to prevent soil blowing, conserve moisture, and maintain soil productivity are required. Sometimes crops must be planted or emergency tillage used for the primary purpose of maintaining the soil during years of low rainfall. These treatments must be applied more frequently or more intensively than on soils in Class III.

Class V   soils in Class V have little or no erosion hazards but have other limitations, impractical to remove, that limit their use largely to pasture, range, woodland, or wildlife food and cover.

Class V soils have limitations that restrict the kind of plants that can be grown and that prevent normal tillage of cultivated crops. Though nearly level, some are wet, are frequently overflowed by streams, are stony, have climatic limitations or some combination of these limitations. Examples of Class V soils are: those on bottom lands subject to frequent overflow that prevents the normal production of cultivated crops; nearly level soils with a growing season that prevents the normal production of cultivated crops; level or nearly level, stony or rocky soils; and ponded areas where drainage for cultivated crops is not feasible but where soils are suitable for grasses or trees. Because of those limitations, cultivation of the common crops is not feasible, but pastures can be improved and benefits from proper management can be expected.

Class VI   soils in Class VI have severe limitations that make them generally unsuited to cultivation and limit their use largely to pasture or range, woodland, or wildlife food and cover.

Physical conditions of soils placed in this Class may require application of range or pasture improvements such as seeding, liming, fertilizing, and water control with contour furrows, drainage ditches, diversions, or water spreaders. They may have continuing limitations that cannot be corrected, such as steep slope, severe erosion hazard, effects of past erosion, stoniness, shallow rooting zone, excessive wetness or overflow, low moisture capacity, salinity or sodium, or severe climate. One or more of these limitations may render soils generally unsuitable for cultivated crops. But they may be used for pasture, range, woodland, or wildlife cover, or some combination of these.

Some soils in Class VI can be safely used for the common crops, provided intensive management is used. Some are also adapted to special crops such as sodded orchards, blueberries, or the like, requiring soil conditions unlike those demanded by the common crops. Depending on soil features and local climate, they may be well or poorly suited to woodlands.

Class VII   Soils in Class VII have very severe limitations that make them unsuited to cultivation and that restrict their use largely to grazing, woodland or wildlife.

The physical conditions of Class VII soils make it impractical to apply such pasture or range improvements as seeding, liming, fertilizing, and water control with contour furrows, ditches, diversions or water spreaders. Soil restrictions are more severe than those in Class VI because of one or more continuing limitations that cannot be corrected, such as very steep slope, erosion, shallow soil, stones, wet soil, salts or sodium, unfavourable climate or other limitations that make them unsuited to common cultivated crops. They can be used safely for grazing, woodland, wildlife food and cover, or for a combination of these under proper management.

Depending upon the soil characteristics and local climate, soils in this Class may be well or poorly suited to woodland. They are not suited to any of the common cultivated crops; in rare instances, some of these soils may be used for special crops under unusual management practices. Some areas of Class VII may need seeding or planting to protect the soil and to prevent damage to adjoining areas.

Class VIII   soils and landforms in Class VIII have limitations that preclude their use for commercial plant production and restrict their use to recreation, wildlife, water supply, or to aesthetic purposes.

Soils and landforms in Class VIII cannot be expected to return significant on-site benefits from management for crops, grasses, or trees, although benefits from wildlife use, watershed protection, or recreation may be possible.

Limitations that cannot be corrected may result from the effects of erosion or erosion hazard, severe climate, wet soil, stones, low moisture capacity, and salinity or sodium.

Badlands, rock outcrop, sandy beaches, river wash, mine tailings, and other nearly barren lands are included in Class VIII. It may be necessary to give protection and management for plant growth to soils and landforms in this class in order to protect other more valuable soils, to control water, or for wildlife or aesthetic reasons.

Classifying land capability in this way makes the following assumptions (summarized from Klingebiel and Montgomery 1961):

(i) Land Capability Classification is an interpretative classification based on permanent qualities and characteristics of the land. Existing vegetation (including shrubs, trees, or stumps) is not considered a permanent characteristic.

(ii) Land within a Class is similar in the severity of its limitations, but not necessarily in the kind of limitation or in the management practices required, so that, for example, there may be quite different soils in the same Class.

(iii) Land Capability Classification is not a productivity rating for specific crops, though the ratio of input to output may help determine the Class.

(iv) A moderately high level of management is assumed.

(v) The system does not, in itself, indicate the most profitable use that could be made of the land.

(vi) Where removal of limiting factors is feasible or has been carried out (e.g. drainage, irrigation, stone removal) the land is assessed according to the limitations remaining after the improvements have been made. The costs of such improvements do not influence the assessment. (See, however, the more recent concept of the Soil Potential Index, USDA 1978*b* and p. 15);

(vii) The Land Capability assessment of an area may be changed by major reclamation projects that permanently change the nature and/or extent of the limitations, e.g. large scale drainage, irrigation, or flood prevention schemes.

(viii) Capability groupings are subject to change as new information about the behaviour and responses of the soils becomes available.

(ix) Distance to market, kinds of roads, size and shape of the soil area, locations within fields, skill or resource of individual operators, and other characteristics of land ownership patterns are not criteria for Capability groupings.

The limitations recognized at the Subclass level are:

Subclass e (erosion) is made up of soils for which the susceptibility to erosion is the dominant limitation or hazard. Erosion susceptibility and past erosion damage are the major soil factors that place land in this Subclass.

Subclass w (excess water) is made up of soils where excess water is the dominant hazard or limitation. Poor soil drainage, wetness, high water-table, and overflow are the criteria for placing land in this Subclass.

Subclass s (soil limitations within the rooting zone) includes, as the name implies, soils that have such limitations as shallowness of rooting zones, stones, low moisture-holding capacity, low fertility difficult to correct, and salinity or high sodium content.

Subclass c (climatic limitations) is made up of land for which climate (temperature or lack of moisture) is the only major hazard or limitation.

Modifications for use outside the United States

The modifications which have been made to adapt the USDA Land Capability Classification for use outside the United States can be grouped into:

(i)   changes in the number of Classes (pp. 75–7);

(ii)   different limiting factors (pp. 77–8);

(iii) subdivisions of Classes other than on the basis of the major limitation or limitations (pp. 78–9);

(iv) quantifying the limiting factors (pp. 79–82);

(v) modifications consequent upon non-acceptance of some of the basic assumptions (pp. 82–3).

Changes in the number of Classes

India (Murthy, Jain, and Naga 1968), Pakistan (McVean and Robertson 1969), Queensland (Murtha 1975), Venezuela (Comerma and Arias 1971), and Southern Africa (Thomas 1962; Thomas and Vincent 1962; Loxton 1962; PTB 1962; Mann 1963; Davis 1976) have retained all eight Classes without modification. Class V (which was specifically for wet soils in level sites, poorly adapted for arable crops) is sometimes redefined to give an additional class for 'normal' non-cultivable land (e.g. Barrera 1961; Prickett 1966; Obeng 1968). Sometimes Class V is simply omitted and Classes I to IV and VI to VIII retained (e.g. Gowaiker and Barde 1964), usually renumbered to give seven consecutively numbered Classes, for example the Soil Capability Classification for Agriculture (Canada Land Inventory 1965*b*,) and the Land Use Capability Classification used in British soil surveys (Bibby and Mackney 1969; and Table 5.1).

Some modifications group the various non-cultivable categories (V, VI, VII, and VIII) into a single Class V (e.g. MAFF 1966, 1968; and Table 5.1; Islam 1966; Tahir and Robinson 1969). In some cases two consecutively numbered Classes are considered necessary for non-cultivable land (e.g. Digar and Sen 1960; Azevedo and Cardoso 1962; Mailloux *et al.* 1964; Gardiner 1974). Non-cultivable land may be ignored altogether (Oyama 1965).

These modifications usually leave Classes I to IV for cultivable agricultural land of decreasing quality, so that these Classes are broadly comparable between systems. Confusingly, however, some modifications have reduced the number of Classes for cultivable land so that only the first two (e.g. Cutler 1962; Ryan 1962) or three apply (e.g. Grange 1944; Azevedo and Cardoso 1962; Short 1973; Carroll 1974). In Malaysia Class I is reserved for land with a potential for mining (p. 187), with agricultural land in Classes II and III. In contrast, two systems increase the total number of classes, to nine in the Philippines (Barrera 1961) or ten in Romania (Carstea 1964; and p. 82).

TABLE 5.1
*The definition of Classes in the Land Use
Capability Classification and corresponding Grades of
the Agricultural Land Classification in England and
Wales*

Class or Grade	Land Use Capability Classification definition	Agricultural Land Classification definition
1	Land with very minor or no physical limitations to use	Land with very minor or no physical limitations to agricultural use
2	Land with minor limitations that reduce the choice of crops and interfere with cultivations	Land with some minor limitations which exclude it from Grade 1
3	Land with moderate limitations that restrict the choice of crops and/or demand careful management	Land with moderate limitations due to the soil, relief or climate or some combination of these factors which restrict the choice of crops, timing of cultivation, or level of yield
4	Land with moderately severe limitations that restrict the choice of crops and/or require very careful management practices	Land with severe limitations due to adverse soil, relief or climate or a combination of these
5	Land with severe limitations that restrict its use to pasture forestry and recreation	*Grade 5* Land of little agricultural value with very severe limitations due to adverse soil, relief, or climate or a combination of these
6	Land with very severe limitations that restrict use to rough grazing, forestry, and recreation	
7	Land with extremely severe limitations that cannot be rectified	
	Subclasses (for Classes other than Class 1) are based on the kinds of limitation affecting land use w—wetness s—soil limitations g—gradient and soil pattern limitations e—liability to erosion c—climatic limitations	Subgrades of Grade 3 (only) are in ranked order 3a, 3b, and 3c.

Source: information from Bibby and Mackney (1966) and MAFF (1966, 1976), by permission.

The net result of these adjustments to class numbering is that usually Classes I, II, III, and IV can be taken fairly safely as similar in concept to the corresponding classes of the USDA Land Capability Classification, but that the significance of Classes V, VI, and VII should be checked, since these have very variable significance. The risk of confusion is greatest when the class symbols are Roman numerals, as in the original system, and is reduced where revisions in the concepts of the various classes are labelled by Arabic numerals (e.g. Bibby and Mackney 1969; and Table 5.1; Canada Land Inventory 1965*b*), by a letter notation (e.g. Azevedo and Cardoso 1962; Gardiner 1974), or by calling the categories Grades rather than Classes (MAFF 1966, 1968, 1976; and Table 5.1).

Different limiting factors

In a broad survey of the resources of an area a simple division of land into a small number of ranked categories without specifying the nature of the limitations may be all that is required. This may be accompanied by a few fairly bland statements that factors such as climate, gradient, erosion risk, nature of the soil, drainage characteristics, etc., were considered in assessing any particular piece of land. However, the user of such a map is given no guidance as to why a particular tract of land is placed in its Class. For example in the Agricultural Land Classification (Table 5.1) 'land may be assigned to a Grade for widely different reasons. It may be placed in Grade 4 because it is a poorly drained clay in an area of high rainfall, or, in the alternative, because it is an excessively drained sandy soil in an area of low rainfall' (MAFF 1968).

Two trends are recognizable in the development of Subclasses defined on the major limiting factors. Firstly, in regions with tropical and mediterranean climates climatic limitations are sometimes thought unimportant, and Subclass (c) is dropped, e.g. India (Murthy *et al.* 1968), Ghana (Obeng 1968), Nigeria (Carroll 1974), Philippines (Barrera 1961), and Portugal (Azevedo and Cardoso 1962).

More commonly, however, the number of Subclasses is increased. A Subclass for land with adverse topography is often included as in the Subclasses T or t (for topography) in the Canada Land Inventory (1977), Venezuela (Comerma and Arias 1971), and Sarawak (Andriesse 1966); g (for gradient and soil pattern limitations) in the Land Use Capability Classification of the British soil surveys (Bibby and Mackney 1969; and Table 5.1); r (for relief) in Pakistan (Islam 1966; Brammer and Brinkman 1967); and s (for slope) in Japan (Oyama 1965). The USDA system assumes that land with a marked slope will always have an erosion hazard (e). Some modifications allow more specific treatment of the main limiting factors, especially soil factors. For Alberta the Canada Land Inventory (1977) introduced D — soil structure or permeability; F — fertility; M — moisture holding capacity; N — salinity; P — stoniness; and R — shallowness, all of which would be covered by the Subclass S (soil limitations) in the original national Soil Capability Classification for Agriculture. The general wetness limitation has been similarly subdivided, in Venezuela where three Subclasses are recognized n — internal drainage; a — external drainage; and i — flood, and in Pakistan into w — excess water; z — rapid floods, and x — for the associated problem of fresh young alluvium.

The number of Subclass limiting factors can become unacceptably large, e.g. for 14 factors used in Alberta (Canada Land Inventory 1977) or Japan (Oyama 1965). In Venezuela Comerma and Arias (1971) make a useful compromise in recognizing four major Subclasses labelled with the upper-case letter T (Topography), E (Erosion), S (Soil), and D (Drainage), and using lower-case letters, when required to denote the nature of the limitation more specifically.

Unfortunately the letters for Subclass notation are not used consistently, particularly 's' which indicates a general soil limitation in the original USDA system and most derivatives, but salinity in Venezuela (Comerma and Arias 1971) and Pakistan (Islam 1966; Brammer and Brinkman 1967), and slope in Japan (Oyama 1965).

Subdivisions of Classes other than on limitations

Most derivatives of the USDA Land Capability Classification which include Subclasses base them on the nature of the main limiting factor or factors, but occasionally Classes have been subdivided in other ways. Thus in England and Wales Grade 3 of the Agricultural Land Classification (Table 5.1) is subdivided into three ranked categories 3a, 3b, and 3c (MAFF 1976) on the basis of the increasing severity of the limitations so that 3c means land having 'some physical characteristics which give a poorer production than that of other land in the grade' and not land specifically with a climatic limitation.

There are pragmatic subdivisions in the systems proposed for New Zealand (Cutler 1962) and Pakistan (McVean and Robertson 1969). In the latter, for example, some (but not all) classes are subdivided into Subclasses a, b, or c depending on either their main limitations, the conservation measures necessary, or their potential use. Such systems may have great practical value in their areas, but their close similarity to conventional land capability classifications maybe misleading. This is particularly so for a system proposed for Papua New Guinea (Haantjens 1965, 1969), which looks like the USDA Land Capability Classification but is, in effect, an additive parametric system (p. 102).

Category systems which superficially look like land capability classifications, i.e. based on the nature and degree of limitations, but which are really suitability classifications are described on pp. 46 and 57.

Quantifying the limiting factors

Implementation of the USDA Land Capability is very largely subjective since the criteria for Class limits are not generally specified. It is, in effect, a formal representation of the best available experience and judgement. Bartelli (1978) states the limits at which some factors become sufficiently adverse to require the downgrading of land from one Class to another (Table 5.2). Even when the criteria are not specified, the final assessment is usually quite acceptable so long as the assessor is experienced and has taken sufficient local advice.

Normally the sponsor of a land capability classification will have established some of the criteria on which land is to be assigned to particular Capability Classes. These may be published as guidelines whereby other workers, often inexperienced, can apply the classification. Formal publication of such rules gives them a certain degree of authority, but it must not be forgotten that they may still be subjective judgements. The benefit is simply that subsequent judgements are made consistently.

Obviously the limits of a particular Class will differ in different areas, depending on local conditions, as shown in Table 5.3 which gives some limiting values for percentage slope. Many of these slope limits are related to erosion risk. In this case quite gentle slopes downgrade land into lower Classes. Erosion is less of a problem in

TABLE 5.2
Suggested criteria for allocating land to USDA Land
Capability Classification Classes in Texas and Oklahoma*

Class	I	II	III	IV	V	VI	VII
Soil moisture and temperature regime*	Udic soil moisture regime and mesic or warmer soil temperature regimes	Udic intergrades of Ustic	Typic Ustic	Torric intergrades of Ustic	—	Ustic intergrades of Torric	Torric
Soil wetness: conductivity after drainage (cm/h)	>2.0	>2.0	0.125–2.0	<0.125	—	—	—
Salt content effect on crops	—	slight	moderate	serious on cultivated land	—	serious on cultivated land	satisfactory growth virtually impossible
salt concentration (%)	—	0.15–0.35	c. 0.35	0.35–0.85	—	0.35–0.85	>0.85
conductivity of saturation extract (μmho/cm)	—	4–8	8–10	10–15	—	10–15	>15
Calculated annual soil loss for up and down cultivation on 9% (5°) slope and 22.1 m length (tonne/ha)	0–8	8–31	31–78	78–144	—	144–222	>222
soil depth (cm)	>90	50–90	25–50	<25	—	—	—

*The soil moisture and temperature regime criteria apply specifically to Texas and Oklahoma; the others have more general application.
Source: information from Klingebiel and Montgomery (1961) and Bartelli (1978).

TABLE 5.3
*Limiting value for slope (%) between land
capability classification Classes*

Class	I/II	II/III	III/IV	IV/Worse
Bibby and Mackney (1969) (Britain)	—	12(7°)	19(11°)	47(25°)
Short (1973) (New South Wales)	1	3	20	—
Loxton (1962) (South Africa)	2	5	8	12
Digar and Son (1960) (India)	0.5	1	10	15
Klingebiel (1958)	2	7	12	18
(three examples from	1	5	9	14
United States)	—	1	5	9

Britain, and the slope limits here are set according to the feasibility of using agricultural machinery (see also Table 3.5).

Some Class limits can be justified fairly readily, for example the limits to the use of agricultural machinery (Bibby and Mackney 1969; cf. Curtis *et al.* 1965), but others are more arbitrary. Thus one of the main climatic limitations in Britain is the increase in precipitation with increasing altitude, so that arable cropping becomes impracticable at higher elevations. Thus the lower limit to Class or Grade 4 (Table 5.1) in which arable cropping is just possible is based on rainfall and/or altitude. The Land Use Capability Classification places this limit at 183 m (600 ft) and more than 1270 mm (50 in) annual rainfall (Bibby and Mackney 1969) but the Agricultural Land Classification (MAFF 1966) places it at 328 m (1000 ft) and more than 1320 mm (60 in) annual rainfall. Both are quite reasonable approximations to the actual situation, and neither can be said to be wrong, yet the discrepancies can lead to intense argument unless it is appreciated that these limiting values are only guidelines to assist workers who lack local knowledge.

Where the limiting values for important factors have been established, these may be conveniently applied by means of a 'land judging form' similar to Burnham and McRae's (1974) which is based on the Land Use Capability Classification of the British soil surveys. Rudeforth and Bradley (1972), Rudeforth (1975), and Young and Goldsmith (1977) have described computerized methods of assigning land to Classes on the basis of the limiting values of various criteria.

Modified basic assumptions

It is implicit in many derivatives of the USDA Land Capability Classification that the main assumptions on which the system was founded still apply. However, some of the assumptions, especially those concerning the capability of land for various potential land uses, socio-economic factors, and the permanence of the limitations, are not applicable to specific situations.

The Classes in the Land Capability Classification implicitly assume that the ranked order of land use is for arable crops, pasture, woodland, and recreation/wildlife. Usually land with a capability for horticultural crops (vegetables, soft fruit, tree fruit) is regarded as of superior quality, e.g. Classes (Grades) I, II, or at worst III (Bibby and Mackney 1969; MAFF 1966, 1976). In Romania, however, tree fruits and vineyards tend to be sited on the poorer land and the local land capability classification has reflected this (Carstea 1964):

Class	Superior use
I–IV	Arable (with increasing limitations)
V	Orchard
VI	Vineyard
VII	Pasture
VIII	Hayfield
IX	Woodland
X	Unsuited for vegetal production

Haantjens (1963) points out that land suitable for ordinary cultivation is not necessarily suitable for other forms of land use, e.g. in Malaysia the economy is heavily dependent on tin mining, so Class I is land with mining potential and only Classes II and below consider agricultural or similar land uses (p. 195). Taking an even wider view, the Canada Land Inventory (p. 196) includes parallel soil and land capability/suitability classifications for agriculture, forestry (p. 147), recreation (p. 188), and wildlife, i.e. ungulates and waterfowl (p. 190).

Although the USDA Land Capability Classification is intended to exclude socio-economic factors it does assume a reasonable or moderately high level of management. This may be difficult to assess (p. 9). A good farmer may well get good performances from land of indifferent quality, so that, to the casual observer, the land looks good. On the other hand it is difficult to convince an observer that excellent land, poorly farmed or derelict, really does have an inherently high potential. Particularly in reconnaissance surveys, the evaluator may be influenced by the appearance of the land, and this depends very largely on the level of management (see also p. 14). The problem is particularly acute in developing countries where peasant agriculture exists side by side with more advanced mechanized production. For these cases Steele (1967) has proposed that a separate land capability assessment be made for each of the different farming systems, just as yield predictions are made for more than one level of management in USDA soil surveys (p. 9).

Land capability classification classifies land according to the limitations remaining after all feasible improvements, e.g. drainage, irrigation, stone removal, leaching of salts or exchangeable sodium, and protection from overflow have been made (see p. 57). The problem lies in what is meant by feasible. In Britain, land drainage is an accepted practice, and land, even if undrained, is graded as if a drainage system were installed, but considerable areas of sandy soils remain unirrigated, not because this is technically unfeasible but because local farming practices and economic considerations do not encourage it. In these circumstances it may be useful to make two assessments 'with' and 'without' irrigation.

Advantages and disadvantages of land capability classification

The advantages and disadvantages of land capability classification, the major category system of evaluating land can be compared with those for the main alternatives, i.e. parametric systems, set out on pp. 114–19.

Advantages

(i) Division into a relatively small number of ranked categories is easily understood.

(ii) It is qualitative rather than quantitative. In the present limited state of knowledge of soil/environment/crop interactions this is a realistic approach.

(iii) It is versatile. The nature and relative severity of the limitations which are considered can easily be modified to suit local conditions without materially affecting the basic structure of the system.

(iv) It can be applied easily by an experienced worker, but also, if formal guidelines are established, can be used by less highly trained staff.

(v) It is a general purpose classification which shows a clear distinction between land capable of growing crops and that which is not; while biased towards agricultural use of the land it also includes categories for other forms of rural land use.

(vi) It stresses the likely adverse effects of unwise land use practices on the environment, and thereby helps to encourage sensible soil conservation.

(vii) It reflects the current suitability of the land at the existing level of management, but can also be projected to a higher level of management or to the conditions after major improvements have been carried out.

(viii) The hierarchy of Class, Subclass, and Capability Unit, allows the system to be applied at whatever level is appropriate (p. 86), determined either by the use to be made of the results or the availability of information.

(ix) It is a useful way of relating environmental, soil, and technological information to practical farming.

(x) The results, at whatever level, can be clearly and simply displayed on maps, although it should be recognized that boundaries between different categories, particularly between Classes are often transitional, and lack the sharp dividing line depicted on the map.

(xi) It is very widely used both in developed and in developing countries.

(xii) It gives reasonable and acceptable results which usually match local opinion. The absurdly wrong evaluations which can be produced by following a set formula as in parametric systems (p. 114), are avoided.

Disadvantages

(i) It is subjective. If no limiting values for the various criteria are set then the allocation of land to a particular Class is simply the considered opinion of the evaluator who may or may not be sufficiently experienced to make the correct value judgements. Even where formal guidelines or rules have been established, many of these were arrived at subjectively. However, at least the subjectivity is obvious and not hidden in, for example, a mathematical formula which may appear objective even when highly subjective.

(ii) Interactions between different limiting factors are difficult to take into account, particularly if a set of precise criteria has been established. Should, for example, a tract of land be downgraded if several soil or environmental factors are at levels near the lower boundary of a class, but no single limitation is in itself sufficiently severe to require downgrading? Indeed, Young (1973a), points out that the effect of a particular environmental factor varies according to its interaction with others. He considers that a lack of precise criteria is an actual advantage, because it allows flexibility in assessment. Burnham and McRae (1974) recommend a procedure which includes a subjective review of interactions between factors.

(iii) Division into a few categories is too coarse, particularly when comparing the relative merits of two pieces of land. As it is not a quantitative weighting, the land capability classification does not help in making decisions like 'is the loss to agriculture of 15 hectares of Class I land more serious than the loss of 50 hectares of Class IV land?'

(iv) The implied rank order of potential land uses may give the wrong impression of the true value of land. Class V and VI land may be ideal and much valued for padi rice or livestock rearing respectively.

(v) There is no indication of the suitability of a tract of land for a specific crop. Different crops are so diverse in their requirements that limitations which are critical for some may be insignificant for others. The FAO Framework (p. 48) is more useful in this respect. However, it it possible to make separate suitability classifications for different crops (e.g. Oyama 1965; Hooper and Griffiths 1971). Sometimes the fact that land capability classification is not a productivity rating for specific crops is held to be an advantage (Haantjens 1963).

(vi) The neglect of socio-economic factors means that the classification does not indicate the relative monetary value of the land or its profitability, information vital to planners (Boddington 1978).

(vii) It is negative; it emphasizes the limitations rather than the positive potential of land, and may thus discourage rather than encourage farmers to try new crops and techniques.

(viii) In the original USDA system, Class V was anomalous and often difficult to apply; however, many derivatives of the basic system have abandoned this Class (p. 75).

(ix) It may be difficult to make land capability assessments where soil information is lacking. Indeed, land capability assessments are often the most useful interpretation of a soil map. Soil mapping units, however, are often defined on different criteria from those adopted as guidelines to land capability, or they may extend over an excessive range of non-soil limitations, e.g. climate, slope, flood risk, etc.

Uses of land capability classification

The different levels of Land Capability Classification can be used for different purposes.

Class level

At the Class level land capability classification constitutes a tool for resource inventory or general planning (e.g. Canada Land Inventory 1970; McCormack 1971) to identify the best agricultural land (normally synonymous with Classes I and II) either to protect it against urban or other non-agricultural development (e.g. MAFF 1966, 1974, 1976), or to promote more intensive agricultural development (e.g. Murdoch *et al.* 1976). Originally advice on conservation practices was made at the Class level (e.g. Hockensmith 1947), but with increasing information, advice is now being given at the Capability Unit level, with much greater precision. Land capability classification has been found useful even at the Class level for extensive farming such as rangeland (e.g. Thomas 1962) or sugar cane (Mann 1963).

Subclass level

Where the necessary soil information is provided from a map at 1:200 000 to 1:50 000 the Land Capability assessments are usually at the Subclass level. Many examples can be found in soil memoirs and other reports accompanying soil maps. Some limitations, particularly of climate and relief, apply generally over substantial areas making it possible to assign these to Capability Subclasses, and indeed generalized Capability Units appear even on some small scale maps, e.g. the 1:1 000 000 Land Use Capability Map of England and Wales (Mackney 1979; Burnham 1979).

In the absence of a soil map, an analysis of the landscape into geomorphological units such as land systems and facets may be used as a basis for land capability assessment. The nature of the limitation (i.e. Subclass) if often more easily identified from this than the degree of limitation (i.e. Class) so that land systems may have to be given combined gradings, e.g. IIIw–IVw.

Land capability classification at the Subclass level is most useful to advisory officers to help them to understand the physical environment in which their advice is sought and given. Subclasses tell farm planners the problems to be overcome. Regional and district planners may not require the extra knowledge on the limiting conditions for particular tracts of land, but they may need the greater precision of Subclass mapping.

Capability Unit level

The Land Capability Unit is a grouping of soils, within the same narrow range of environmental conditions, that have about the same response to management and improvement practices and grow a similar range of crops with comparable yields (Klingebiel 1958).

The Capability Unit provides the most specific and detailed information that can be organized within the USDA Land Capability Classification. It covers specific portions of a farm or ranch, (e.g. Figs. 5.2 and 5.3) and can greatly aid detailed farm planning, (Wilkinson 1968, 1977; Hooper 1974a; Mackney 1974a, b). Land capability maps accompanying detailed soil surveys at scales of 1:50 000 or larger usually present Land Capability Units. Allocation of tracts of land to a Class or Subclass will normally follow regionally established guidelines, but grouping of soil-mapping units into Capability Units is a local decision, so that reference to the map legend or report is always necessary.

Capability Units are designated either thus: IIIe-1 or thus: 2w/6, and sometimes the numerical subscripts are applied according to a consistent scheme which is a partial key to some particular problem. For example in California, (USDA 1969).

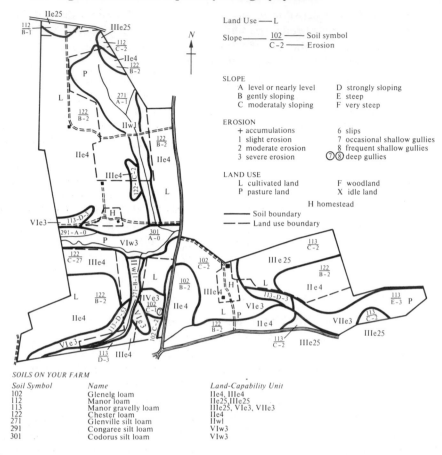

Fig. 5.2. Map of soils and Land Capability Units for a farm in Maryland, prepared by the Soil Conservation Service of the United States Department of Agriculture. The following is a description of one of the map units Glenelg loam — Capability Unit III e 4 and the practices and treatments needed to farm it. (From Stallings (1957), by permission.)

The soils are deep, well drained, easily worked, and hold moisture well. The slopes are moderate but erosion has removed up to ¾ of the original topsoil. The land is suitable for commonly grown crops and responds well to fertilizer. It may be low in potash and may need boron for alfalfa. This land is suitable for rotation cropland. Conservation measures are needed to prevent further damage.

If used for crops: Keep in legume hay at least 2 years out of 4. Use contour cultivation on short slopes or contour strip-cropping on long slopes. Diversions may be needed on longer slopes. Provide safe outlets before diversions are constructed. Seed a winter cover crop, such as rye grass and vetch when land is not in winter grain. Red clover with timothy or orchardgrass is a good hay mixture. Alfalfa or alsike may be added. Lime for the legumes. Fertilize small grain when seeding. Top-dress hay annually with a high potash fertilizer after first cutting. Reinforce manure application with superphosphate.

If used for hay: Reseed by disking in strips across the slope. Reseed as often as necessary to re-establish legumes. Seed to grass-legume mixtures that have a long life. Add ladino clover to mixtures if used for pasture. Fertilize to establish seeding. Top-dress annually with high potash fertilizer after first cutting. Reinforce manure application with superphosphate.

If used for pasture: Lime and fertilize. Top-dress every other year with fertilizer or manure. Mow at least once a year. Control grazing in early spring and late fall. Rotate grazing between fields.

Fig. 5.3. The revised land uses proposed for the farm shown in Fig. 5.2. (From Stallings (1957), by permission.)

0 — a problem or limitation of root penetration caused
by sand and gravel in the substratum
1 — an actual or potential erosion hazard
etc.
8 — a problem or limitation of root penetration caused
by shallow depth of soil over hard bedrock or
hardpan
etc.

Other categoric methods of land evaluation

Prior to the introduction of the Agricultural Land Classification
(Table 5.1) of England and Wales, land was evaluated by a category
system based on the predominant land use together with soil texture
and overall productivity (Stamp 1962; and Table 5.4).

In Scotland, Stamp's emphasis on the cropping potential of land
has been maintained in the categoric systems now used (Coppock
1980). The definitions of the seven categories are:

A+ Category Land — highest quality land capable of
growing all agricultural crops
including intensive market
garden crops.

A Category Land — good fertile land suitable for
growing most crops but with
some restrictions which exclude
it from A + category

B+ Category Land — good land with more limited
cropping potential.

B Category Land — medium land capable of growing average crops of grass, oats,
barley, and roots

B− Category Land — land of less good quality than
medium mostly given over to
grass or for the production of
crops for stock feed

C   Category Land — poor arable land only capable of restricted use, mostly in grass and only cultivated to enable reseeding to take place

D   Category Land — land of little agricultural value owing to severe restrictions of soil, relief, or climate or a combination of these

TABLE 5.4

Land Utilization Survey (1931–38) land classification for Britain

Class	Potential Production Units (arbitrary units)
MAJOR CATEGORY I — Good	
1. First Class land, capable of intensive cultivation	2.0
2. Good general purpose farmland	1.0
2(A)* Suitable for ploughing (mainly arable land)	
2(AG)* Suitable for crops and grass	
3. (G) First Class land, unsuitable for ploughing (first quality grassland)	1.0
4. (G) Good but heavy land (good grassland)	1.0
MAJOR CATEGORY II — Medium	
5. Medium Quality light land	0.5
5(A) Capable of ploughing	
5(G) Unploughable (downland and basic pastures with very shallow soils).	
6. Medium quality general purpose farmland	0.5
6(AG) Grass with some arable	
6(G) Dominantly grassland	
MAJOR CATEGORY III — Poor	
7. (G) Poor quality heavy land (under pasture or deciduous woodland)	0.1
8. (H)*Poor quality mountain and moorland	0.1
9. (H) Poor quality light land (lowland heaths and moors)	0.1
10. (H) Poorest land (saltings, rough marsh pasture, shingle, etc.)	nil

*A denotes mainly arable land; G denotes mainly grassland; H denotes mainly heath similar rough grazing land.
Source: information from Stamp (1962).

The Land Inventory and Monitoring (I and M) Program of the USDA (1975) has recognized the following categories of farmland:

Prime Farmland

Prime Farmland is the land best suited for producing food, feed, forage, fibre, and oilseed crops, and also available for these uses (the land could be cropland, pastureland, rangeland, forest land, or other land, but not urban built-up land, or water). It has the soil quality, growing season, and moisture supply needed to produce sustained high yields of crops economically when treated and managed, including water management, according to modern farming methods.

Unique Farmland

Unique Farmland is land other than Prime Farmland that is used for the production of specific high-value food and fibre crops. It has the special combination of soil quality, location, growing season, and moisture supply needed to produce sustained high quality and/or high yields of a specific crop when treated and managed according to modern farming methods. Examples of such crops are citrus, olives, cranberries, fruit, and vegetables.

Additional Farmland of Statewide Importance

This is land, in addition to Prime and Unique Farmland, that is of statewide importance for the production of food, feed, fibre, forage, and oilseed crops. Criteria for defining and delineating this land are to be determined by the appropriate state agency or agencies.

Additional Farmland of Local Importance

In some local areas there is concern for certain additional farmlands for the production of food, feed, fibre, forage, and oilseed crops, even though these lands are not identified as having national or statewide importance. Where appropriate, these lands are to be identified by the local agency or agencies concerned.

To qualify as Prime Farmland, land must meet the following criteria (summarized by Reganold and Singer 1979; from USDA 1975 and Fenton 1975);

(i) An adequate moisture supply.

(ii) A warm enough temperature regime and long enough growing season for crops adapted to the area.

(iii) A pH of 4.5–8.4 within the root zone.

(iv) A water-table that is maintained at a sufficient depth during the cropping season to allow for crop growth.

(v) An exchangeable sodium percentage of less than 15 and a saturation extract conductivity of less than 4 mmho/cm within the rooting zone.

(vi) Flooding not more often than once in two years.

(vii) A product of the soil erodibility factor, K, and per cent slope of less than 2.0.

(viii) A permeability of at least 0.15 cm/h in the top 50 cm.

(ix) A surface layer with less than 10 per cent rock fragments coarser than 7.5 cm in the longest dimension.

In California, the Soil Conservation Service has added a further criterion for Prime Farmland: a minimum rooting depth of 102 cm.

Category systems and other systems of evaluating land

Relatively few studies have attempted to calibrate categoric systems with actual crop yields or economic returns. In Canada oat yields were found to be related to Capability Classes (Mackenzie 1970), as were gross margins (p. 16) for maize (Patterson and Mackintosh 1976), yet Peters (1977) found considerable disparity in the cereal yields of land placed in the same Capability Class but in different climatic zones. Mathematical models for yield prediction based partly on Capability Class have also been developed in Canada. Hoffman (1975) found that the yield of barley was strongly related to Capability Class and to the nitrogen fertilizer added. Extra terms in the prediction equation relating to growing season, temperature, and to soil clay content imply that insufficient criteria are used to define Capability Classes.

Boddington (1978) has shown (Table 5.5) that the total outputs (p. 16) of particular enterprises in England and Wales are related to Grades in the Agricultural Land Classification (Table 5.1), but observed that Grade (Class) 3 land farmed under grassland, fodder, and feed-roots systems would produce a higher gross output per unit area than Grade (Class) 1 under cereals. This is not, however, an altogether fair comparison, for the Grade 1 land would have given a much larger gross output under vegetables. His figures are,

TABLE 5.5

Total enterprise outputs (£/ha) according to Grade of land in England and Wales

Enterprise	Grade of Land				
	1	2	3	4	5
Wheat and barley	126	126	109	99	NA
Ley legume	141	141	104	74	NA
Roots (mangolds)	153	153	136	124	NA
Green fodder (kale)	247	205	166	148	NA
Industrial crop (sugar beet)	296	296	NA	NA	NA
Grassland	371	274	220	170	49

NA — Not applicable; Grades according to the Agricultural Land Classification (Table 5.1).
    Source: Boddington (1978), by permission.

however, much more realistic than the relative values put to agricultural land of different Grades to assist the Jefferson Committee on route location with regard to environmental issues (1976). MAFF proposed a nominal productivity index of 20 for Grade 1 land, 18 for Grade 2, 10 for Grade 3, 3 for Grade 4, and 1 for Grade 5 (Jefferson 1976).

    In the United States each State may select its own method for defining Prime and Unique Farmland (p. 92; Miller 1979), and so there is some question of the comparability of different evaluation systems. For example, Reganold and Singer (1979) have compared the results of various systems: the USDA Land Capability Classification LCC; p. 68), the parametric Storie Index Rating (SIR; and p. 106) and the I and M definitions (p. 92) for three townships in California (Table 5.6) and found some correspondence between the systems, e.g. land with Storie Index Rating (SIR) above 50 would be rated as Prime land. Similar, reasonably close agreement between Land Capability Classes and SIR has also been reported from California by Singer (1978) and in Alberta (Alberta Institute of Pedology 1974), at least for the better Capability Classes. Parametric systems such as SIR can be converted to category systems by an arbitrary grouping of the scores (p. 120), sometimes specifically to relate to category systems already in use.

TABLE 5.6

Percentage of the land area in three Californian Townships that meets the criteria for Prime Agricultural Land according to six alternative land classification definitions

	Percentage of land area that is Prime Farmland		
Land classification definitions	Citrona Township	Merritt Township	Rumsey Township
LCC Classes I and II	83.8	76.5	8.4
LCC Classes I, II and III with rooting depth ≥ 75 cm	84.8	87.9	8.5
SIR 60–100	48.0	56.7	8.5
SIR 50–100	85.6	75.9	9.8
I & M prime	83.6	76.5	8.4
I & M prime without a rooting depth limitation	84.2	76.5	8.5

LCC — Land Capability Classification; SIR — Storie Index Rating; I & M — Land Inventory and Monitoring Programme.

Source: Reganold and Singer (1979), by permission.

6. Agricultural land capability: parametric systems

Introduction

The division of agricultural land into a small number of categories, as in the USDA Land Capability Classification (p. 68) is inevitably artificial, and users soon come to debate whether an area is 'low 2' or 'top end of Class 3'. A continuous scale of assessment may be more flexible and realistic. One approach would be to grade the land according to its likely yield, as in the Productivity Ratings which are a standard feature of USDA soil reports (see p. 15). Alternatively the various soil and site properties (parameters) that are believed to influence yield can be combined in a mathematical formula. This is the so-called *parametric approach* which is described in this chapter.

Some parametric systems are simple, to the point of naivety; others are extremely complex. Some have been widely accepted, usually because they have been incorporated into legislation on taxation; others have been largely ignored. Parametric systems have also been proposed to evaluate land for non-agricultural uses, e.g. Pipeline corrosion (p. 165) or forestry (Storie and Wieslander 1948). Systems differ in the factors they include and in their mathematical manipulation. Three main kinds of manipulation can be recognized:

$$\text{Additive, e.g.} \quad P = A + B + C$$
$$\text{Multiplicative, e.g.} \quad P = A \times B \times C$$
$$\text{More complex functions, e.g.} \quad P = A \sqrt{(B \times C \times D)}$$

where P is the parametric rating, score, or index, and A, B, C, and D are soil and site properties. These can either be direct values, such as soil depth (cm) or the values can be rated on a scale usually of 0–100 so that for example, soils of total depth 30 cm rate 10, those of 40 cm depth rate 15, and so on.

To apply a parametric system the evaluator must first establish the unit he wishes to assess, e.g. a field, a holding, a map unit, etc.

He then obtains the required data which may involve him in digging one or more soil pits, and sometimes obtaining analytical data (see Chapter 3). He may discover considerable variation in soil and site properties within the area he is assessing, and must choose whether to take average values or values which are representative of the majority of the area. He then converts the raw data to the coding scale, carries out the mathematical operations, and applies the resulting index or score to the entire area. An ideal combination of soil and site properties would be expected to gain the maximum score with progressively lower scores for poorer land.

Additive systems

The numerous additive systems devised in Germany during the 1920s have been reviewed by von Nostitz (1929) and Jacks (1946). For example in Bavaria Fackler (1924) awarded points out of the following totals (see Clarke 1957 for more detail):

Soil conditions		Max. Points
General texture, structure, composition, and humus		30
Quality of the ploughed layer		10
Quality of the subsoil		15
Soil moisture conditions		10
Topography		10
Cultivation, manuring, and fertility		15
	Total	90
Climatic–vegetation complex		
Geographical situation		10
Danger of hail		10
	Total	20
Economics of transport		
Distance from railhead		10
	Total	10
Total possible marks for perfect land	. . .	120

Studies such as this culminated in the legislation (Bodenschätzungagesetz) enacted on 16 October 1934, whereby every field in Germany was to be assessed as part of an extensive land tax reform. The assessment was carried out in two steps (see Weiers and Reid 1974). Firstly the long-term use of every hectare of land was recorded, and then the nature of its soil was described using a separate scheme for arable and for pasture land. Figure 6.1 sets out the second stage of the operation and shows how the information is then used. These descriptions were based on the *nature* of the soil and its *condition* together with either the *mode of origin* of arable soils or the *climatic and water conditions* of pasture land.

After every hectare of land had been described the appropriate arable or pasture evaluation framework was applied, to produce, respectively, a *soil* or *pasture base figure*. Jacks (1946) and Weiers and Reid (1974) present the two evaluation frameworks, but neither publication makes it clear just how the various base figures were established.

The base figures were related to a national standard (Hauptstütz-punkte) of 100 points awarded to land belonging to Frau Else Haberhauffe of Bickendorf, near Magdeburg. This land is now in East Germany, and a new standard of comparable quality has been established near Hildesheim in West Germany. The classification of other land is expressed as a percentage of the national standard through a set of regional and local standards.

The base figures in the evaluation frameworks refer to land with flat or slightly uneven topography, an annual average temperature of 8°C, an annual average rainfall of 600 mm, and market conditions corresponding to those in central Saxony in 1934 (20–50 ha farms). Where, as is usually the case, the conditions vary from these, points are added to, or subtracted from the evaluation framework figures to give, respectively, the final *arable figure* or *pasture figure*. Detailed instructions for these adjustments are laid down in the 1934 legislation. Weiers and Reid (1974) give an example.

The *yield index* for each field can then be calculated (Fig. 6.1). It is claimed that this index correlates well with actual yields (Nieschlag 1974). Further adjustments can also be made to the yield index for marked differences in soil quality within a field, losses of agricultural land, costs of drainage and ditch maintenance, risk of hailstorms, newly reclaimed areas, abnormal incidence of pests, weeds and bird damage, regular long periods of flooding, and extremely light or extremely heavy soils.

The average *adjusted yield index* per hectare for a farm, known popularly as the Bodenpunkte, is often used to describe land quality in the sale particulars of a farm. A sample of the prices asked in 1974 for farms in the Federal Republic of Germany showed the relatively

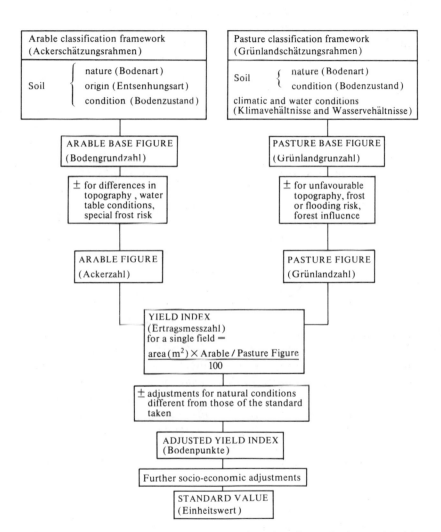

Fig. 6.1. The German system of land classification. (From Weiers and Reid (1974), by permission.)

narrow range of 270 to 440 DM per hectare per unit of the Bodenpunkte (Weiers and Reid 1974). The most usual rent charge was 4 to 6 DM per hectare per year per unit of the Bodenpunkte.

Beckel (1962) noted that 'since the system is not wholly in line with modern soil science, attempts have been made to supplement this assessment survey'. However, the system is so enshrined in German legislation that it would be very difficult to overhaul it radically. Valuation of the land in terms of money value per hectare, e.g. for taxation purposes, is ultimately derived from the adjusted yield index, suitably modified by the addition or subtraction of points for a variety of economic factors, including farm size, buildings, industrial influences, regional price and wage conditions, mineral rights, etc. (see Weiers and Reid 1974).

Similar soil rating methods have been developed in Russia (e.g. Blagovidov 1960; Gavrilyuk 1967, 1977; Taichinov 1971; Hooper 1974*b*). There the quality of a given piece of land is related to a standard taken as 100 points by adding points for soil features such as genetic soil type, humus content, thickness of the topsoil, texture and fertility, and site factors such as topography and drainage. The product prices credited to State and Collective Farms are inversely related to the mean point rating of the land belonging to each farm.

Since 1962 an elaborate additive system has been developed in Romania (Teaci 1970; Teaci and Burt 1964, 1974; Teaci, Burt, Voiculescu, and Munteanu 1974; Teaci, Tutunea, Burt, Predel, and Munteanu 1974). Detailed maps of soil, topography and climatic data have been used to compile maps of '*Homogenous Ecological Territories*' (TEOs) at 1:50 000. Each TEO comprises a single soil type and lies within a defined range of topographic and climatic properties. A TEO is comparable to a Land Capability Unit (p. 87). Each TEO is homogenous within itself, but differs in one or more respects from all others on the map.

Points on a scale of 0 to 100 are awarded to each TEO according to its suitability to grow each of 24 common crops. A maximum of 50 points is awarded for the quality of the soil itself, by reference to an extensive collection of tables relating crop performance to soil type (Table 6.1). Empirical curves (Fig. 6.2) relate crop yields to significant and measurable soil and site properties, e.g. temperature, precipitation, slope, surface waterlogging, and groundwater influences. Correction tables (e.g. Table 6.2) derived from these indicate points to be added to or subtracted from the soil points for each crop.

TABLE 6.1

*An extract from the score sheet of three
'Homogenous Ecological Territories' (TEOs)
for typical crops in Romania*

	TEO reference number and soil type		
	119	184	701
	Typical		
	Leached	Degraded	Pseudogleyed
Crop	Chernozem	Chernozem	Planosol
Pasture	43	46	29
Apples	42	26	0
Vines	48	18	0
Wheat	42	43	14
Maize	43	45	9
Potatoes	41	45	8
Vegetables	35	49	0

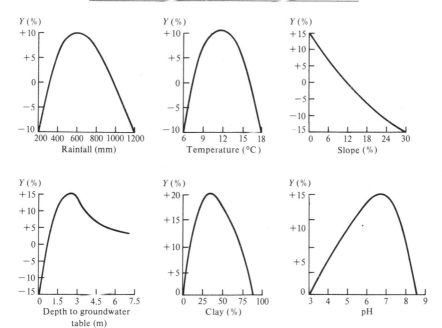

Fig. 6.2. Some examples of the empirical curves used in the Romanian
parametric land classification system to relate crop yields (in these examples, maize) to soil and site properties. Y is the percentage increase or
decrease in yield. (Adapted from Teaci and Burt (1974), by permission.)

TABLE 6.2

Corrections applied to basic score for TEO 119 (Typical Leached Chernozem) in an area south-west of Bucharest, Romania (see Table 6.1)

		Corrections for					
Crop	Basic score	Tempera- ture	Precipi- tation	Slope	Surface water- logging	Ground water	Final Score
Pasture	43	0	−10	13	0	0	46
Apples	42	−5	−7	10	0	0	40
Vines	48	9	2	12	0	0	71
Wheat	42	10	−5	10	0	0	58
Maize	43	10	−3	8	0	0	58
Potatoes	41	0	−5	6	0	0	42
Vegetables	35	10	0	5	0	0	50

The system is used to rationalize the distribution of crops on Collective and State Farms in Romania so that maize, for example, will be encouraged in those areas where the land classification score suggests it will grow best. Conversely, permission to plant orchards and vineyards (regarded as relatively undemanding and unprofitable crops) will only be given where the score suggests that arable crops will be unsuitable.

Other Eastern European countries use more or less elaborate additive systems (e.g. Geczy 1964; Garbouchev, Trashliev, and Krastanov 1974; Teaci and Burt 1974; Riquier 1974; Krastanov and Kabakchiev 1975).

In assessing land capability in Papua New Guinea, Haantjens (1963) first used a simple modification of the conventional UDSA Land Capability Classification (p. 79) but later (Haantjens 1965, 1969; Bleeker 1975) developed a more radical modification which is, in effect, an additive parametric system. Each of 14 environmental factors is given a rating from 0 (little or no limitation) to 4, 5, or 6 (severe limitation) according to its 'individual suitability' for each of four types of land use (annual crops, tree crops, improved pastures, and padi). These are then combined by an arbitrary summation process designed so that a single very low rating or a combination of moderately low ratings give the same general result.

There has been very little use of additive systems in the United States. Miller (1924) and Berger, Hole, and Beardsley (1952) proposed additive systems, but these have received little attention. An additive system is now used in Canada. A multiplicative system based on the Storie Index (see p. 113) had been used in Saskatchewan for many years (Mitchell 1940, 1950; Bowser 1940; Freeman 1940), but in time it appeared that the ratings did not relate well to long-term yields of wheat, the main crop of the region (Moss 1972). So Moss (1972) proposed an additive system for non-irrigated land in Saskatchewan (but see p. 126 for irrigated land). He offered no justification of the change from multiplicative to additive manipulation of the factors. The system is:

$$\text{Final rating} = \text{Soil Rating} \ - \text{Landscape Factor}$$
$$= (C + T + P) - L.$$

Where the maximum points are 40 for C (the climatic factor), 40 for T (the soil texture and organic matter), and 20 for P (the genetic soil profile and related features), as described below:

Climate (C)

Soil zone	Rating
Gray Wooded (podzolic) zone	40 – 35
Black Gray (Transition) area	40 – 35
Black Soil zone	40 – 25
Dark Brown Soil zone	22 – 17
Brown Soil zone	15 – 5

Texture and organic matter (T)

Soil texture	Rating
heavy clay	40*
silty clay	35
clay	32
silty clay loam	27 – 30†
clay loam	25 – 28
sandy clay loam	20 – 25
silty loam	20 – 24
loam	17 – 20
very fine sandy loam	13 – 17
fine sandy loam	10 – 13
sandy loam	5 – 7
loamy sand	3
sand	1

*Lower ratings may be required for heavy clay soils in the more humid areas — notably Black–Gray clays.

†The higher ratings for texture are suggested for the heavier types, e.g. 30 for heavy silty clay loam.

Soil organic matter	*Rating*
Black soils (except clays) with C ratings of 30 or more	10
Black soils with C ratings of 25 or less	5
Black clay and silty clay	5
Transition Black–Dark Brown soil areas	5
Dark Gray soils	10 – 5
Dark Gray Wooded	5 – 2
Gray Wooded, Degraded Brunisol, Poizol	0
Dark Brown and Brown soils	0
All zones — heavy clay soils, eroded soils, Regosolic and Gleysolic soils	0

The soil organic matter rating is added only where the soil texture rating alone does not give good agreement with the crop yields. The combined rating should not exceed 40.

Where subsoil textures differ from the topsoil by two grades or more (see below) the original rating for texture is modified by averaging ratings for topsoil and subsoil.

Grade	*Textures*
1	Sands
2	Loamy sands
3	Sandy loam and fine sandy loam
4	Very fine sandy loam, loam, silty loam
5	Sandy clay loam, clay loam, silty clay loam
6	Clay, silty clay
7	Heavy clay

Soil profile (P)

Kind of soil

Chernozemic (Dark–Coloured Grassland) profiles

Orthic (hard columnar or prismatic), Calcareous (Calcareous earth or columnar calcareous), and Rego-Calcareous (high lime) profiles — on mid to lower slopes, and well to moderately drained

With Ca horizon (lime layer) below 30 cm	20
With Ca horizon (lime layer) at 30 cm to 17.5 cm	19 – 10

Above soil types with thin profiles, occurring on arid (dry) crests and upper slopes of knolls and ridges — 5 – 1

Rego-Chernozemic clay (cloddy granular clays) — 20 – 18

Massive hard clay (including 'Loose Top' clay)

Moderately developed, hard	15 – 10
Strongly developed, very hard	5

Eluviated and Solodic Chernozemic (degraded and Solodic) — 17 – 14

Solonetzic (hard, poorly structured) profiles of grassland and forest	*Rating*
Solod	15 – 10
Solonetz and Solodized Solonetz	10 – 5
Eroded Solodized Solonetz ('burn-outs')	3 – 1
Alkaline Solonetz	1

Luvisolic, Degraded Brunisolic and Podzolic profiles (Degraded Black, Gray Wooded, and Podzol)	
Dark Gray Chernozemic (slightly degraded Black)	18
Dark Gray Wooded (moderately-strongly Degraded Black)	16 – 10
Gray Wooded (Gray Podzolic) and Degraded Brunisol (Podzolic Sand)	7 – 5
Low Humic Eluviated Gleysol (Depression or 'Bluff' Podzol)	5 – 2
Podzol	1

Other profiles	
Regosolic (weakly developed, immature)	5 – 1
Eroded, all A horizon removed, to B horizon removed	5 – 1
Gleysolic (chiefly meadow, slough bottom, and shallow peat)*	1
Organic (deep peat or bog or 'muskeg')*	1
Soils with loose, single grain, structureless condition	1

*These soils, when drained, are classified according to profile features.

Where landscape features (topography, drainage and salinity, stoniness, erosion and wooded cover) are favourable, no deductions are made from the soil rating. Where there are unfavourable features, tentative guidelines are given which will reduce the final rating to 30 or less if the conditions are very unfavourable, and make corresponding smaller reductions if the problems are not so severe or if the soil rating is already below 30. If the landscape features make the land completely unsuitable for agriculture, the landscape rating is made equal to the basic rating to give a final rating of zero.

This is a particularly clear example of the way most parametric systems are adjusted to lend apparently objective support to the subjective judgement of the evaluator.

There are two additive systems for rating land according to its suitability for irrigation. In Yugoslavia Didic (1964) gave soil depth, texture, porosity, moisture held at field capacity, permanent wilting percentage, permeability, infiltration rate and pH scores between 1 and 4. Somewhat confusingly, the scores were low when the factor was favourable, and high when unfavourable, so that the final additive index was lowest for the land most suitable for irrigation and highest for unsuitable land.

In India, Mehta, Mathur, and Shankara-Narayan (1958) assessed the suitability of land for irrigation by evaluating certain properties of the topsoil, the subsoil, and the substratum. The scores for three of the properties were summed over the whole profile, while the others were averaged. The results of this were then added to produce a single index figure, as shown in Table 6.3.

Additive parametric schemes for assessing the suitability of land for padi rice have also been proposed (Rossell 1950a; Hernandez 1955).

Multiplicative systems

The best-known multiplicative system for rating the quality of land is the Storie Index Rating which originated in California. This first appeared in 1933, but has subsequently been revised and reprinted on several occasions (Storie 1933, 1937, 1944, 1948, 1953, 1955, 1964a, 1976, 1978). Adaptations of the system have been used in many other parts of the world.

As originally conceived (Storie 1933) the Storie Index Rating (SIR) is given by

$$\text{SIR} = \underset{\substack{\textit{Character of} \\ \textit{soil profile}}}{A} \times \underset{\substack{\textit{Texture of} \\ \textit{surface soil}}}{B} \times \underset{\substack{\textit{Miscellaneous} \\ \textit{factors (such as} \\ \textit{drainage, alkalinity,} \\ \textit{steep slopes)}}}{C.}$$

Later, Storie (1944) introduced a new factor C to evaluate slope and the original factor C became factor X (miscellaneous factors that can be modified by management), as that the SIR became

$$\text{SIR} = \underset{\substack{\textit{Character of} \\ \textit{soil profile}}}{A} \times \underset{\substack{\textit{Texture of} \\ \textit{surface soil}}}{B} \times \underset{\substack{\textit{Slope}}}{C} \times \underset{\substack{\textit{Miscellaneous} \\ \textit{factors}}}{X.}$$

TABLE 6.3
An additive parametric system used in India

Factor	Maximum possible score for topsoil	Maximum possible score for subsoil	Maximum possible score for substratum	Manipulation	Maximum possible score for profile
Soil texture	8	7	5	Add	20
Total soluble salts	10	8	7	Add	25
Permeability	0	13	7	Add	20
pH	15	15	15	Average	15
Exchangeable sodium	10	10	10	Average	10
Non-capillary porosity	10	10	10	Average	10
					100

Source: information from Mehta *et al.* (1958).

Each factor is scored as a percentage but multiplied as a decimal. The final index is expressed as a percentage. Where more than one property is considered as in factor X, each is also scored as a percentage, then all are multiplied together as decimals and expressed as the combined percentage for that factor. All derivatives of the Storie system use this convention.

The most recent revision (Storie 1978) gives the following ratings for each factor:

FACTOR A — Rating on character of physical profile	per cent
I Soils on recent alluvial fans, flood plains, or other	
secondary deposits having undeveloped profiles	100
x shallow phases (on consolidated materials) 60 cm deep	50 – 60
x shallow phases (on consolidated materials) 90 cm deep	80
g extremely gravelly subsoils	80 – 90
s stratified clay subsoils	80 – 95
II Soils on young alluvial fans, flood plains, or other	
secondary deposits having slightly developed profiles	95 – 100
x shallow phases (on consolidated material) 60 cm deep	50 – 60
x shallow phases (on consolidated material) 90 cm deep	70
g extremely gravelly subsoils	80 – 95
s stratified clay subsoils	80 – 95
III Soils on older alluvial fans, alluvial plains or	
terraces having moderately developed profiles	
(moderately dense subsoils)	80 – 95
x shallow phases (on consolidated material) 60 cm deep	40 – 65
x shallow phases (on consolidated material) 90 cm deep	60 – 70
g extremely gravelly subsoils	60 – 90
IV Soils on older plains or terraces having strongly	
developed profiles (dense clay subsoils)	40 – 80
V Soils on older plains or terraces having hardpan	
subsoil layers	
at less than 30 cm	5 – 20
at 30 to 60 cm	20 – 30
at 60 to 90 cm	30 – 40
at 90 to 120 cm	40 – 50
at 120 to 180 cm	50 – 80
VI Soils on older terraces and upland areas having dense	
clay subsoils resting on moderately consolidated or	
consolidated material	40 – 80

VII   Soils on upland areas underlain by hard igneous
       bedrock
at less than 30 cm	10 – 30
at 30 to 60 cm	30 – 50
at 60 to 90 cm	50 – 70
at 90 to 120 cm	70 – 80
at 120 to 180 cm	80 – 100
at more than 180 cm	100

VIII Soils on upland areas underlain by consolidated
       sedimentary rocks
at less than 30 cm	10 – 30
at 30 to 60 cm	30 – 50
at 60 to 90 cm	50 – 70
at 90 to 120 cm	70 – 80
at 120 to 180 cm	80 – 100
at more than 180 cm	100

IX   Soils on upland areas underlain by softly consolidated
       material
at less than 30 cm	20 – 40
at 30 to 60 cm	40 – 60
at 60 to 90 cm	60 – 80
at 90 to 120 cm	80 – 90
at 120 to 180 cm	90 – 100
at more than 180 cm	100

FACTOR B — Rating on basis of surface texture	*per cent*
Medium textured:	
very fine sandy loam	100
fine sandy loam	100
loam	100
silt loam	100
sandy loam	95
loamy fine sand	90
silty clay loam	90
clay loam	85
Heavy textured:	
silty clay	60 – 70
clay	50 – 60
Light or coarse textured:	
coarse sandy loam	70 – 90
loamy sand	80
very fine sand	80

fine sand	65
sand	60
coarse sand	30 – 60

Gravelly:

gravelly fine sandy loam	70 – 80
gravelly loam	60 – 80
gravelly silt loam	60 – 80
gravelly sandy loam	50 – 70
gravelly clay loam	60 – 80
gravelly clay	40 – 70
gravelly sand	20 – 30

Stony:

stony fine sandy loam	70 – 80
stony loam	60 – 80
stony silt loam	60 – 80
stony sandy loam	50 – 70
stony clay loam	50 – 80
stony clay	40 – 70
stony sand	10 – 40

FACTOR C — Rating on basis of slope	*per cent*
A — Nearly level (0 to 2 per cent)	100
AA — Gently undulating (0 to 2 per cent)	95 – 100
B — Gently sloping (3 to 8 per cent)	95 – 100
BB — Undulating (3 to 8 per cent)	85 – 100
C — Moderately sloping (9 to 15 per cent)	85 – 95
CC — Rolling (9 to 15 per cent)	85 – 95
D — Strongly sloping (16 to 30 per cent)	70 – 80
DD — Hilly (16 to 30 per cent)	70 – 80
E — Steep (30 to 45 per cent)	30 – 50
F — Very steep (45 per cent and over)	5 – 30

FACTOR X — Rating on conditions other than those in factors A, B, and C	
	per cent

Drainage:

well drained	100
fairly well drained	80 – 90
moderately waterlogged	40 – 80
badly waterlogged	10 – 40
subject to overflow	Variable

Alkali:

alkali free	100
slightly affected	60 – 95
moderately affected	30 – 60
moderately to strongly affected	15 – 30
strongly affected	5 – 15

Nutrient (fertility) level:

high	100
fair	95 – 100
poor	80 – 95
very poor	60 – 80

Acidity: according to degree   80 – 95

Erosion:

none to slight	100
detrimental deposition	75 – 95
moderate sheet erosion	80 – 95
occasional shallow gullies	70 – 90
moderate sheet erosion with shallow gullies	60 – 80
deep gullies	10 – 70
moderate sheet erosion with deep gullies	10 – 60
severe sheet erosion	50 – 80
severe sheet erosion with shallow gullies	40 – 50
severe sheet erosion with deep gullies	10 – 40
very severe erosion	10 – 40
moderate wind erosion	80 – 95
severe wind erosion	30 – 80

Microrelief:

smooth	100
channels	60 – 95
hogwallows	60 – 95
low hummocks	80 – 95
high hummocks	20 – 60
dunes	10 – 40

An example of the calculation of the SIR for the Altamont soil map unit in California is:

Factor A: Altamont series brown upland soil, shale
parent material, bedrock at 90 cm,
profile group VIII   70 per cent
Factor B: clay loam texture   85 per cent
Factor C: rolling topography   90 per cent
Factor X: moderate sheet erosion with shallow
gullies   70 per cent

Index Rating = $0.70 \times 0.85 \times 0.90 \times 0.70 = 0.37$, reported as 37 per cent.

A soil map can be annotated with SIRs, if necessary weighted according to the areal proportion of different soils within compound map units. SIR ratings can also be converted to ranked categories. (p. 120).

The Storie Index Rating has been extensively used in California (e.g. Weir and Storie 1937; Edwards *et al.* 1970) particularly for taxation purposes (Storie and Weir 1942; Storie and Harradine 1950; Storie 1954). In other areas it may have to be modified to include factors which are not important in California. Inclusion of a factor for climate is common, for example in Hawaii (Nelson 1963; Olson 1974) and India (Shome and Raychaudhuri 1960). In New Zealand, Leamy (1962, 1974) has included a factor for management level, and for the humid tropics Sys and Frankart (1972) and Frankart and Sys (1974) include factors for soil colour and for the development of an organic rich topsoil.

Sometimes there is an apparent increase in the number of factors which are considered. This is usually because soil and site properties included with the miscellaneous (X) factors in the basic Storie Index Rating are drawn out as separate factors, e.g. salinity (Bowser 1940; Omar and El-Kalei 1969; Borden and Warkentin 1974; Sys and Verheye 1974; Sys 1979).

For development projects the FAO (Bramao and Riquier 1967; Riquier *et al.* 1970) has proposed an Index of Soil Productivity.

Index of Soil Productivity
$$= P \times T \times (N \text{ or } S) \times O \times A \times M \times D \times H$$
where P = effective soil depth;
T = texture and structure of A horizon;
N = base status;
S = soluble salts content;
O = organic matter of A_1 horizon;
A = mineral exchange capacity and nature of clay in B horizon;
M = reserves of alterable minerals in B horizon;
D = drainage;
H = soil moisture content.

Complex parametric systems

Some systems combine the additive and multiplicative approaches Clarke (1950, 1951, 1957) proposed a Profile Value (P) and claimed that was proportional to wheat yields in the Cotswold Hills (Oxfordshire):

$$P = V \times G$$
$$= (\Sigma (D \times T)) \times G,$$

where D is the depth in inches of each horizon and T a value for texture, ranging from 3 for gravel to 20 for a medium loam. These are summed over all the horizons in a profile to a total depth of 75 cm (30 inches) to give the profile texture value V. G is a drainage factor ranging from 1.0 for a soil with perfect drainage to 0.5 for a soil with gleying at 22.5–30 cm (9–12 inches). This system was inadequately tested.

The original procedure for assessing Saskatchewan soils (Mitchell 1940, 1950; Freeman 1940) was:

Index = $(A_1 + A_2 + A_3) \times B \times (C_1 + C_2 + C_3 + C_4)$

A_1 = Texture   (40) ⎫
A_2 = Structure   (30) ⎬ 100 − Factor A (Profile)
A_3 = Natural fertility (30) ⎭

B = Topography   100 − Factor B (Topography)

C_1 = Climate   (25) ⎫
C_2 = Salinity   (25) ⎪
C_3 = Stoniness   (25) ⎬ 100 − Factor C (Various)
C_4 = Tendency to   (25) ⎪
      wind erosion   ⎭

This has been replaced (p. 102) by a purely additive system.

At first sight a system proposed for New Mexico by LeVee and Dregne (1951) seems to be a simple multiplicative system:

$$\text{Land Rating} = \begin{array}{c}\text{Profile Rating} \\ \text{(adjusted for} \\ \text{associated soil} \\ \text{factors)}\end{array} \times \begin{array}{c}\text{Slope} \\ \text{Rating}\end{array} \times \begin{array}{c}\text{Erosion} \\ \text{Rating}\end{array} \times \begin{array}{c}\text{Special} \\ \text{Factor} \\ \text{Rating}\end{array}$$

in which each Rating is expressed as a percentage. The Profile Rating is, however, obtained by summing values for topsoil, subsoil and, in some cases, substratum, then multiplying the sum by values for a number of associated soil factors (some of which have values in excess of 100 per cent). Harris (1949) has proposed a similar combined additive and multiplicative system for Arizona.

The relatively simple multiplicative system proposed by Riquier and co-workers (Bramao and Riquier 1967; Riquier et al. 1970; p. 112) has subsequently (Riquier 1972) been developed into an extremely complex mathematical model involving Mitscherlich yield functions.

By comparison, the 'square root' system of Strzemski (1972) is extremely simple:

$$\text{Index} = A\sqrt{(ps. pc. pr. pa.)}$$

where A = an empirical coefficient;
    ps = soil;
    pc = climate;
    pr = relief;
    pa = water conditions.

Advantages and disadvantages of parametric systems

The advantages and disadvantages of parametric systems may be compared with those set out on pp. 83–6 for land capability classifications, the main category system of evaluating agricultural land.

Advantages	*Comments*
(i) Easy to apply consistently, even by non-specialists (Berger et al. 1952; LeVee and Dregne 1951; Leamy 1962)	A strong point in favour of parametric systems but the Storie Index needs a thorough knowledge of soil morphology and geology (Singer, Tanji, and Snyder 1979)
(ii) Attractively simple (Gibbs 1966; Riquier et al. 1970)	But many other systems, e.g. the USDA Land Capability Classification (p. 68) or the FAO Framework (p. 48) are not substantially more difficult to comprehend
(iii) Quantitative, accurate and specific (Mitchell 1940; Singer et al. 1979)	May give a misleading impression of accuracy which subsequently leads to a loss of confidence in the system (Gibbs 1966)

(iv)   Reduced   subjectivity
(Leamy 1962; Teaci *et al.* 1974)

True, as regards the actual application of the system once established, but as great, if not greater, subjectivity in the choice of factors to be considered, the values assigned to them and the mathematical manipulation to give the results required (Storie 1933; Gavrilyuk 1967; Riquier *et al.* 1970; Riquier 1972)

Some important factors may be forgotten or deliberately omitted (LeVee and Dregne 1961; Olson 1974). Much experimentation is needed to minimize subjectivity during the setting up of the system (Garbouchev *et al.* 1974; Gibbs 1966; Rosell 1950a; Millette and Searl 1969; Sys and Frankart 1972; Teaci *et al.* 1974)

(v) Easily adapted, e.g. if the ratings do not give sensible results they can be modified by altering the choice of factors, the weighting given to them or the mathematical manipulation (Riquier *et al.* 1970)

In reality, the great weakness of parametric systems. There is nothing 'fundamental' about them, they have been designed and modified so as to give the 'right' answer. Some might argue, however, that so long as a suitable answer is produced, the contrived method of producing it does not matter

(vi) Positive rather than negative features are stressed (Riquier *et al.* 1970; Bridges 1974)

Yet land use choices are usually made on negative grounds, i.e. a limitation or limitations exist which prevent complete freedom of action

(vii) Based on soil properties and, in most cases, other environmental factors, leaving out the vexed questions of management level and other socioeconomic factors (Mitchell 1940; Shome and Raychaudhuri 1960; Millette and Searl 1969; Riquier 1972; Garbouchev *et al.* 1974; Krastanov and Kabakchiev 1975; Teaci and Burt 1974)

This tacitly assumes that the empirical relationships on which the choice of factors, their weighting, etc. are themselves free from management and socio-economic bias. If required, management factors can be incorporated (e.g. Leamy 1962, 1974; Weiers and Reid 1974). Some workers regret the absence of such factors in the basic systems (e.g. Mitchell 1940; LeVee and Dregne 1951)

(viii) Allows the likely benefits of various improvements to the soil or land to be assessed (Millette and Searl 1969; Bramao and Riquier 1972; LeVee and Dregne 1951)

The criticism of spurious accuracy again applies. Other systems can take improvements into account, e.g. in the USDA Land Capability Classification land can be assessed with and without the provision of irrigation

(ix) Takes into account the combined effects of various factors

A criticism of categoric capability systems is that each limiting factor is usually taken as acting independently. However, a simple 'addition' or 'multiplication' of factor levels is probably too naive

(x) Amenable to data bank or other computerized manipulation (Smyth 1970*b*; Garbouchev *et al.* 1974; Singer *et al.* 1979)

So are other systems (e.g Rudeforth and Bradley 1972)

(xi) Extremely useful (as a 'sliding scale') for taxation and related purposes. Farmers are said to like it, as an apparently fair

Where parametric systems have been widely adopted, it is because they were chosen for a taxation or related purpose.

and equable method of tax assessment (Mitchell 1940, 1950; Freeman 1940; Rosell 1950*b*; Storie (1954); Riquier *et al.* 1970; Weiers and Reid 1974)

Once enshrined in legislation, modification is extremely difficult

(xii) Helpful in regional development programmes or land resource inventories (Bowser 1940; Leamy 1962; Bramao and Riquier 1967; Riquier *et al.* 1970; Krastanov and Kabak-chiev 75; Vink 1975)

No more helpful than category systems unless unusually well founded on much research data

(xiii) Can be averaged over any required area, e.g. field or farm (Storie 1933, 1978; Berger *et al.* 1952; Leamy 1962; Riquier *et al.* 1970)

But difficult to depict on a map as scores ranging from 0–100. For cartographic representation the scores have to be divided into ranges (p. 120) to provide categories to appear on the map

(xiv) Can indicate the suitability of soil or land for specific crops (e.g. Teaci *et al.* 1974; Frankart and Sys 1974; Bramao and Riquier 1967; Riquier 1972; Millette and Searl 1969)

Crops vary in their requirements (LeVee and Dregne 1951; Krastanov and Kabachiev 1975) so that systems must make separate evaluations for each crop (Teaci *et al.* 1974)

Does not help with practical farming problems (Beckel 1962; although see Sys and Frankart 1972)

(xv) Popular for irrigation projects (Storie 1964*b*; Bowser and Moss 1950; Canada Department of Agriculture 1964; Leamy 1964; Borden and Warkentin 1974; Bowser and Moss, in Moss 1972; Sys and Verhaye 1974; and p. 126)

Probably not so popular as methods based on the USBR approach (p. 127)

Probably the most significant of the various advantages listed above are that parametric systems are attractively simple, appear to be objective, are easily applied by non-specialists and have proved popular for taxation or related purposes. Their main disadvantage is that the apparent objectivity and precision are illusory. Parametric systems are artefacts. Even the most elaborate systems (e.g. Riquier 1972; Teaci *et al.* 1974) assume relationships between crop behaviour, soil and site parameters that are still very imperfectly understood. Less elaborate systems have less justification, and that they seem to give reasonable results is a triumph of the ingenuity of the workers who have developed them. At best they are only valid in a limited area. In many cases parametric systems are mathematical expressions of subjective opinion. Unfortunately once a system has been adopted its subjective origins are soon forgotten. However, if the system gives reasonable answers and an acceptable ranked order of land then perhaps its theoretical imperfections can be overlooked. The choice is then between an additive multiplicative or a more complex approach.

The main virtue of a multiplicative system is that, as in reality, the least favourable factors dominate the final result whereas in additive systems quite severe limitations may not be given due weight (Storie 1933; Bowser 1940; Marin-Laflèche 1972). Storie (1933) points out that land on which the soil has:

Factor A — excellent profile conditions   100 per cent
Factor B — excellent surface soil conditions   100 per cent
Factor C — bad alkali accumulation   10 per cent

has the very low index of 10 per cent, i.e. the severe alkali accumulation dominates the quality of the soil, rendering it wholly unproductive for plants. On an additive basis, assuming each factor was equally weighted the score would be the equivalent of

$$\frac{100 + 100 + 10}{3} = \frac{210}{3} = 70 \text{ per cent}$$

which is a respectable score that would not give a true indication of the serious limitation.

One way out of this apparent dilemma is, of course, to 'weight' the factors in an additive system so that really important limitations do significantly influence the final result, and this is advocated by Rossell (1950*a*) and Taichinov (1971). Garbouchev *et al.* (1974) and

Krastanov and Kabakchiev (1975) describe additive systems where, if any one factor is scored zero then the whole index must be reported as zero, however good the other factors are.

Promising future developments appear to be either the introduction of more complex factors into the formula (e.g. Riquier 1972) or better calibration of each factor against crop performance as in the Romanian system (Teaci and co-workers). This system (p. 100) has the additional benefit of allowing separate assessments for each important crop, but the considerable disadvantages that it requires large amounts of experimental data to establish the system.

For the moment, however, multiplicative systems appear to give more realistic results and they have undoubtedly proved more popular than additive systems. A suitable local modification of the Storie Index would appear to be the best (p. 106). The factors to be included however, and the values ascribed to the different levels of each factor need to be determined locally (see Nelson (1963) and Leamy (1962) for good examples of modifications).

Calibration of parametric systems

The true test of any indirect land evaluation system is how well it can predict actual crop performance (p. 18). The limited investigations which have been carried out to relate parametric indices to crop yields have tended to justify them. Snyder and Weekes (1956) showed that apple yields in California are related to the Storie Index, land with SIR of 55 giving only half the yield of land of SIR 100. Sys and Frankart (1972) showed a close correlation between their parametric soil capability index and yields of cocoa ($r = 0.98$) and cotton ($r = 0.93$) in the Congo Basin, and Frankart, Sys, and Verheye (1972) presented similar results for rice yields in Thailand ($r = 0.98$). Bramao and Riquier (1967) quote a correlation ($r = 0.83$) between peanut yields and a multiplicative index (p. 112) while Riquier et al. (1970) give several examples of crop yields well correlated with their more complex index.

Multivariate analysis can be used to optimize a parametric system. It would be easier to test an additive system in which both the choice of variables and their weighting could be adjusted to give the best correlation with the yield of the most important crop or some other measure of agricultural success.

Conversion of parametric scores to ranked categories

It is quite common to convert the continuous scale of ratings from parametric methods into a limited number of range classes, even though this seems to nullify one of the main advantages (continuous scale) claimed for parametric methods. It may be done deliberately to relate parametric indices to a category system already in use (e.g. Hernandez 1955; Berger *et al.* 1952; LeVee and Dregne 1971), or to indicate the suitability of land for a specific crop or crops (e.g. Bramao and Riquier 1967; Sys and Frankart 1972; Storie and Wieslander 1948) or a specific purpose e.g. irrigation (Bowser and Moss 1950; Leamy 1962; Didic 1964; Moss and Bowser, in Moss 1972; Sys and Verhaye 1974; Borden and Warkentin 1974), or simply to give a general indication of the significance of a particular score result (Bowser 1940; Mitchell 1950; Rosell 150*a*; Storie 1954, 1976; Cardoso 1968; Millette and Searl 1969; Omar and El-Kalei 1969; Alberta Institute of Pedology 1974; Singer 1978; Reganold and Singer 1979; and p. 94).

Six soil grades have been set up in California (Storie 1978) by combining soils with the following ranges of Storie Index Rating (p. 106):

Grade I (excellent): Soils that rate between 80 and 100 per cent and which are suitable for a wide range of crops, including alfalfa, orchard, truck, and field crops.

Grade 2 (good): Soils that rate between 60 and 79 per cent and which are suitable for most crops. Yields are generally good to excellent.

Grade 3 (fair): Soils that rate between 40 and 59 per cent and which are generally of fair quality, with less wide range of suitability than Grades 1 and 2. Soils in this grade may give good results with certain specialized crops.

Grade 4 (poor): Soils that rate between 20 and 39 per cent and which have a narrow range in their agricultural possibilities. For example, a few soils in this grade may be good for rice but not good for many other uses.

Grade 5 (very poor): Soils that rate between 10 and 19 per cent are of very limited use except for pasture, because of adverse conditions such as shallowness, roughness, and alkali content.

Grade 6 (non-agricultural): Soils that rate less than 10 per cent include, for example, tidelands, riverwash, soils of high alkali content, and steep broken land.

Reducing the appearance of precision in a parametric index is particularly useful when indices are to be generalized on a map, over areas within which there are bound to be variations in land attributes.

7. The evaluation of land for irrigation

Irrigation methods and project design

The main methods of irrigation are:
(i) Gravity flow via pipelines and open ditches.
(ii) Air-borne or sprinkler methods with water under pressure.
(iii) Trickle irrigation.
(iv) Special techniques, such as subsurface irrigation.

Whatever method is chosen, it must ensure minimal losses of water during transport and application, maintenance of the long-term productivity of the land by preventing erosion, soil salinization or the raising of the ground-water table, and the maximum economic return.

Thus the design of a major irrigation project needs a multidisciplinary team including:

(i) Hydrologists and water engineers to investigate the sources and quality of the irrigation water.

(ii) Engineers to plan distribution networks, the levelling and grading of the land, drainage systems, and in major schemes, perhaps the construction of large dams and reservoirs. The area which is irrigable from a given source is called a command area.

(iii) Soil surveyors to provide information about the suitability of the land and the consequences of any engineering works.

(iv) Climatologists to predict the crop needs for irrigation and to calculate irrigation schedules.

(v) Agronomists, soil chemists, and soil physicists to plan the cropping of the irrigated land and predict, and if possible prevent, adverse changes due to the irrigation.

(vi) Economists to appraise the relative costs and benefits of the scheme as a whole or certain parts of it.

(vii) Sociologists to ascertain what help the indigenous or introduced population will need in order to cope with the changes in their lifestyle.

(viii) Planners and politicians, since many schemes are undertaken for social and political reasons although in strict economic terms the benefits may never repay the costs.

Many textbooks and monographs deal with irrigation in general (e.g. US Bureau of Reclamation 1953; Israelson and Hansen 1962; Zimmerman 1966; Hagan, Haise, and Edminster 1967; Hagan, Houston, and Allison 1968; Kovda, van den Berg, and Hagan 1973; Withers and Vipond 1974; FAO 1979; Stern 1979; Hall, Hargreaves, and Cannell 1979), or with specific aspects such as the economics (Carruthers 1968; Clark 1970; Bergmann and Boussard 1976; Carruthers and Clark 1981), technology (Olivier 1972; Booher 1974; Hudson 1975; Pair, Hinz, Reid, and Frost 1975), climate (Blaney and Criddle 1950; Olivier 1961; FAO/World Bank 1976), and methods for soil analyses (Richards 1954; Loveday 1974).

This chapter deals more specifically with the role of the soil surveyor in evaluating land for irrigation, and how to present the information to other members of the team or to decision makers.

Data required

Table 7.1 lists the physical and chemical data collected by a soil surveyor and his colleagues and which has a bearing on the suitability of the land for irrigation. The balance between rainfall and evapotranspiration determines the overall need for water and also the scheduling of water applications. An indication of the variability of the climate allows calculation of the safety margin that must be included in the design of the system.

Much of the soil information needed would be gathered during a normal soil survey, with its supporting laboratory checks (e.g. of field estimates of texture by laboratory analysis of particle size distribution) or can be collected if specified in advance (e.g. Robertson and Mitchell 1976; and p. 23).

Measurements on the movement and retention of water will be linked to the measurements by hydrologists and drainage engineers. Measurements of the soluble salts in the soil and in the water to be used for irrigation may guide the choice of system, e.g. gravity irrigation versus sprinkler application, choice of crops tolerant of the present or anticipated salinity, and the design of drainage schemes.

The relief of the area will be a major factor in its suitability for irrigation; minor relief can be modified by grading and levelling. The soil surveyor can help the irrigation engineer by gathering

TABLE 7.1

Soil and site information required to assess the suitability of land for irrigation

Climate	Soil	Drainage and hydrology	Topography and vegetation
Rainfall	Field	Field	Macrorelief
Potential evapo-transpiration	Texture	Profile morphology	Microrelief
Frost risks	Structure	Depth to water-table	Erosion hazard
Storms	Stoniness	Infiltration rate	Existing vegetation (especially shrubs and trees)
Temperature	Arrangement of horizons	Hydraulic conductivity	Position and accessibility
Length of growing season	Depth of rooting zone	Surface drainage and outlets	Flood hazard
Seasonal variability	Consistence		
		Laboratory	
	Laboratory	Water quality	
	Particle size distribution	Hydraulic conductivity	
	Bulk density and porosity	Moisture retention and available moisture capacity	
	Structural stability		
	Organic matter content		
	CEC and base saturation		
	Electrical conductivity		
	pH		
	Soluble and exchangeable cations especially sodium and magnesium		
	Nutrient levels including possible toxicities		
	Sulphate and carbonate		
	Effect of leaching		
	Clay mineralogy		

information on microrelief such as gilgai, on the soil profiles which might result after grading, on obstructions such as trees and shrubs which have to be cleared, and on erosion hazards.

Irrigation may cause profound changes such as clay migration, damage to the soil structure and changes in the water-table, as well as chemical changes, particularly in the kind and distribution of salts.

Simple interpretation of soil survey information

If a soil map and supporting data are already available, it will be simplest to evaluate the irrigation potential of each soil map unit, as in Table 7.2 from an Australian soil survey report. USDA soil survey reports rate map units either favourable or unfavourable for irrigation depending on the presence or absence of restrictive features that affect design, layout, construction, management, or performance of an irrigation system (USDA 1978a) and may allocate each map unit to an irrigation design group. Separate capability groupings (p. 67) and yield predictions (p. 7) may be provided for dryland or irrigated use.

The FAO Framework for Land Evaluation (p. 48) can be applied to the selection of land for irrigation (Purnell 1978, 1979), when Suitability Classes S1, S2, S3, and S4 are for irrigable land with increasing degrees of limitation, and N1 and N2 for land temporarily and permanently non-suitable. Purnell (1978) suggests the following Subclass notation:

a — Alkali problems
d — Effective depth of soil
e — Erosion hazard
g — Gravelliness, stoniness (surface or subsoil)
h — Soil reaction (pH)
i — Slow intake
m — Available moisture holding capacity
q — Texture and tilth
r — Rockiness
s — Soil limitations in general
t — Topography (slope)
v — Vertic properties, swelling and cracking clays
w — Wetness, drainage requirement, oxygen availability
z — Salinity

TABLE 7.2

A summarized assessment of the irrigation potential of the soils of the Jernargo District, New South Wales, Australia

Soil series	Intrinsic properties	Surface drainage	Slope	Command-ability*	Associated microrelief
Burganbigil	Good	Good	Long; moderate gradient	Good	Smooth
Purdanima	Good; highly permeable	Excellent	Short and steep; variable gradient	Doubtful	Uneven but no gilgais
Thulabin sandy loam	Very good	Very good	Short and steep; variable gradient	Doubtful in many cases	Uneven but no gilgais
Thulabin loam	Very good	Very good	Long; moderate gradient	Usually possible	Smooth
Tuppal	Fair	Poor; sometimes occluded	Very low gradient	Good	Usually with gilgais
Wandook	Poor	Occluded	Very low gradient	Good	Usually with gilgais
Billabong	Poor	Fair	Long; low gradient	Good	Usually smooth
Riverina	Poor	Poor	Very low gradient	Good	Occasionally with gilgais
Mundiwa	Fair to poor	Poor; sometimes occluded	Long; very low gradient	Good	Occasionally with gilgais
Willbriggie	Fair	Fair	Long; low gradient	Good	Usually with gilgais
Coree	Fair	Poor; sometimes occluded	Long; very low gradient	Good	Usually with gilgais
Yooroobla	Very good	Fair	Long; low gradient	Good	Highly gilgaied
Wunnammurra	Very good	Fair to poor	Very low gradient	Good	Highly gilgaied

*Commandibility = the ease with which irrigation water can be brought to the site.
Source: Churchward and Flint (1956), by permission.

Such assessments, however, usually do not take into account the availability of water, or any economic analyses of the likely costs and benefits.

Parametric methods

An element of apparent objectivity can be introduced by the parametric approach (Chapter 6), in which each important soil and site property is given a numerical rating. An overall rating is produced by adding or multiplying the separate ratings. The parametric systems proposed by Bowser and Moss (1950), Mehta *et al.* (1958; and p. 106), Desaunettes (1960), Storie (1964*b*), Didic (1964; and p. 105), Canada Department of Agriculture (1964), Bowser and Moss, in Moss (1972), Sys and Verheye (1974), Borden and Warkentin (1974), and Sys (1979) can be used to assess land for irrigation, sometimes with conversion to ranked categories (p. 120). For example Moss and Bowser's scheme for western Canada which is, in effect, a modified Storie Index (p. 106), is:

Overall Rating $= P \times T \times G \times D \times E \times F \times (Sa \times St)$
where P = Soil profile factor;
　　　 G = Geological deposition;
　　　 T = Soil texture;
　　　 D = Drainage;
　　　 E = Degree of erosion;
　　　 F = Fertility;
　　　 Sa = Salinity and alkalinity;
　　　 St = Stoniness.

As with the simple interpretation of soil maps (p. 124) such parametric systems usually only answer the question 'could this land be irrigated?' and not 'should this land be irrigated?' Having derived a parametric index for irrigation suitability, the Canada Department of Agriculture (1964) proceeds to consider factors such as surface relief, vegetation cover, irrigation pattern, earthmoving costs, costs of the distribution system, drainage, groundwater, climate, and economic investigations of farm practices, before final selection of the land actually to be irrigated.

The Irrigation Suitability Classification of the United States Bureau of Reclamation (USBR)

This system (USBR 1953), is the best example of a system which takes the economic aspects of an irrigation scheme into account in evaluating land for irrigation. Maletic and Hutchings (1967) and FAO (1974, 1979) give good reviews and discussions.

Each area of land (usually a soil mapping unit) is labelled on a map with a symbol which conveys important information in coded form. A typical mapping symbol is explained in Fig. 7.1.

The *Land Class* is defined as a 'category of land having similar physical and economic attributes which affect the suitability of land for irrigation'. The criteria of the Land Classes are set for each individual irrigation project according to the local physical and economic situation, so that Land Classes are not universally similar (see Tables 7.3–7.5). The economic attributes of a piece of land are summed up in the *payment capacity,* which is the 'residual available to defray the cost of water after all other costs have been met by the farm operator' (USBR 1953).

Land Classes 1, 2, and 3 have respectively the highest, intermediate and lowest irrigation suitability and payment capacity. Class 4 is used, with appropriate suffixes, to indicate special-use land, e.g. pasture, fruit, rice, or truck (i.e. vegetable) farming or

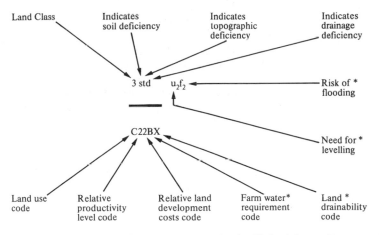

Fig. 7.1. A typical mapping symbol used in the United States Bureau of Reclamation's Irrigation Suitability Classification. (See text for explanation.) *These symbols are optional.

land with particular difficulties which can, however, be economically overcome. Class 5 is a temporary designation for land requiring further special investigation before final allocation to another Class and Class 6 is for land unsuited to irrigation.

In this classification, *arable land* is 'land which, in adequate sized units and if properly provided with the essential improvements of levelling, drainage, irrigation facilities, and the like, would have a productive capacity, under sustained irrigation, sufficient to meet all production expenses, including irrigation operation and maintenance costs and a reasonable return on the farm investment; to repay a reasonable amount of the cost of project facilities; and to provide a satisfactory level of living for the farm family'. *Irrigable land* is 'the arable land under a specific project for which a water supply is or can be made available and which is provided with or planned to be provided with irrigation, drainage, flood protection, and other facilities as necessary for sustained irrigation'. It excludes those portions of the arable land needed for non-productive uses, e.g. rights of way or land which is not feasible to irrigate because of location, accessibility, etc.

The definitions and descriptions of the six Classes are:

Class 1   Arable lands of Class 1 are those particularly suitable for irrigation farming, being capable of producing sustained and relatively high yields of a wide range of climatically adapted crops at reasonable cost. They are smooth lying with gentle slopes. The soils are deep and of medium to fairly fine texture with mellow, open structure allowing easy penetration of roots, air, and water and having free drainage yet good available moisture capacity. These soils are free from harmful accumulations of soluble salts or can be readily reclaimed. Both soil and topographic conditions are such that no specific farm drainage requirements are anticipated, minimum erosion will result from irrigation, and land development can be accomplished at fairly low cost. These lands potentially have a relatively high payment capacity.

Class 2   Arable lands of Class 2 comprise those that are moderately suitable for irrigation farming, being measurably lower than Class 1 lands in productive capacity, adapted to somewhat narrower a range of crops, more expensive to prepare for irrigation, or more costly to farm. They are not so desirable nor of such high value as lands of Class 1 because of certain correctable or non-correctable limitations. They may have a lower available moisture capacity, as indicated by coarse texture or limited soil depth; they may be only slowly permeable to water because of clay layers or compaction in the subsoil; or they also may be moderately saline, which may limit productivity or involve moderate costs for leaching. Topographic limitations include: uneven surface requiring moderate costs for levelling, short slopes requiring shorter length of runs, or steeper slopes necessitating special care and greater costs to irrigate and prevent erosion. Farm drainage may be required at a moderate cost or loose rock or woody vegetation may have to be removed from the surface. Any one of the limitations may be sufficient to reduce the lands from Class 1 to Class 2, but frequently a combination of two or more of them is operating. The Class 2 lands have intermediate payment capacity.

Class 3   Arable lands of Class 3 are suitable, but approaching marginality, for irrigation development and are of distinctly restricted suitability because of more extreme deficiences in the soil, topographic or drainage characteristics than those described for Class 2 lands. They may have good topography, but the inferior soils restrict crop adaptability, require larger amounts of irrigation water or special irrigation practices, and demand greater fertilization or more intensive soil improvement. The topography may be uneven, saline concentration moderate to high, and drainage restricted but correctable at relatively high costs. Generally, a greater risk may be involved in farming Class 3 lands than the better Classes of land, but under proper management they are expected to pay adequately.

Class 4   Limited arable or special-use lands of Class 4 are included in this Class only after economic and engineering studies have shown them to be tillable. They may have an excessive specific deficiency or deficiencies that can be corrected at high cost, but are suitable for irrigation because of present or contemplated intensive cropping, such as for vegetable and fruits. They may have one or more excessive, non-correctable deficiencies that limit their use to meadow, pasture, orchard, or other relatively permanent crops, but still be capable of supporting a farm family and meeting water charges if operated in units of adequate size or in association with better lands. The deficiency may be inadequate drainage, salt content that requires extensive leaching, unfavourable position allowing periodic flooding or making water distribution and removal difficult, rough topography, excessive quantities of loose rock on the surface or in the flow zone, or cover such as timber. The magnitude of correctable deficiency is sufficient to require outlays of capital in excess of those permissible for Class 3 but in amounts shown to be feasible because of the specific utility anticipated. Subclasses other than those devoted to a special crop use may be included in this class, such as those for sub-irrigation and sprinkler irrigation which meet general arability requirements. Also recognized in Class 4 are suburban lands that do not meet general arability requirements. Such lands can pay water charges as a result of income derived either from the suburban lands and other sources or from other sources alone. The Class 4 lands may have a range in payment capacity greater than that of the associated arable lands.
    The designations for the special-use categories are:

$$4P \quad — \quad \text{pasture}$$
$$4F \quad — \quad \text{fruit}$$

4R — rice
4V — truck farming
4H — suburban developments
4S — sprinkler irrigation
4U — sub-irrigation

Class 5   Non-arable lands of Class 5 are non-arable under existing conditions, but have a potential sufficient to warrant tentative segregation for
special study before the classification *(sic)* is completed. They may also be
lands in existing projects whose arability is dependent upon scheduled
project construction or land improvements. They may have a specific soil
deficiency such as excessive salinity, very uneven topography, inadequate
drainage, or excessive rock or tree cover. In the first instance the land
deficiency or deficiencies are of such kind and magnitude that special
agronomic, economic, or engineering studies are required to provide adequate information (such as for extent and location of farm and project
drains, or probable payment capacity under the anticipated land use) for
completing the classification *(sic)* of the lands. The designation Class 5 is
tentative and must be changed to the proper arable class or Class 6 until the
land classification *(sic)* is completed. In the second instance, the effect of the
deficiency or the outlay necessary for improvement is known, but the lands
are suspended from an arable Class until the scheduled date of completion
of project facilities and land development, such as project and farm drains.
In all instances, Class 5 lands are segregated only when the conditions in the
area require consideration of such lands for competent appraisal of the
project possibilities, such as when an abundant supply of water or shortage
of better lands occurs, or when problems related to land development,
rehabilitation, and resettlement are involved.

The status of Class 5 land can be shown thus:

5   — Pending investigation
5 ( )   — Pending reclamation
5d ( )— Pending reclamation (drainage problems)
5f ( ) — Pending reclamation (flooding problems)
5i ( ) — Isolated, pending investigation or reclamation
5h ( )— Pending investigation or reclamation (high position)
5l ( ) — Pending investigation or reclamation (low position)

The brackets will contain the likely Class (or Subclass) after the investigation or reclamation has been carried out, e.g. 5d (1).

Class 6   Non-arable lands of Class 6 include those considered non-arable
under the existing project or project plan because of failure to meet the
minimum requirements for the other Classes of land; arable areas definitely
not susceptible to delivery of irrigation water or to provision of project
drainage; and Classes 4 and 5 land, when the extent of such lands or the
detail of the particular investigation does not warrant their segregation.
Generally, Class 6 lands comprise steep, rough, broken, or badly eroded
lands; lands with soils of very coarse or fine texture; lands with shallow soils

over gravel, shale, sandstone, or hardpan; or lands that have inadequate drainage and high concentrations of soluble salts or sodium. With some exceptions, Class 6 lands do not have sufficient payment capacity to warrant consideration for irrigation.

Particular varieties of Class 6 land are designated thus:

6i — Isolated position
6h — High position
6l — Low position
6w — Water rights

Not all Classes need to be used in evaluating a particular area, and modifications to the Class numbering may be required. For example land suited to padi rice would normally have to be placed in Class 4 of the basic system, but the USBR (1967) used a modified system in south-east Asia using two basic diversified crop Classes (1 and 2) and two basic wetland (padi) rice Classes (1R and 2R) with one Class (6) to identify the non-arable land.

Subclasses of Classes other than Class 1 show the reason or reasons why the areas are placed in a Class lower than 1. The Subclasses are s, t, d, st, td, and std, where 's' represents soil deficiencies, 't' topographic deficiencies, and 'd' drainage deficiencies. The 'deficiencies' may be appraised further and if so the notation below elaborates the nature of the problem. If desired a subscript numeral relating to the appropriate Land Class level can be added.

Soil appraisals:

k — shallow depth to coarse sand, gravel or cobbles
b — shallow depth to relatively impervious substrata
z — shallow depth to a concentrated zone of lime
v — very coarse texture (sands, loamy sands)
l — moderately coarse texture (sandy loams, loams)
m — moderately fine texture (silt loams, clay loams)
h — very fine texture (clays)
e — poor structure
n — poor consistence
q — poor available moisture capacity
i — poor infiltration
p — poor hydraulic conductivity
r — stoniness
y — poor soil fertility
a — salinity and alkalinity

Topographic appraisals:

g — slope
u — surface
j — irrigation pattern
c — brush or tree cover
r — rock cover

Drainage appraisals:

f — needs surface drainage — flooding
w — needs subsurface drainage — water-table
o — drainage outlet needed

The present *land use,* knowledge of which may be useful in any economic analysis of the project, is shown by the following codes:

C — irrigated cultivated
L — non-irrigated cultivated
P — irrigated permanent grassland
G — non-irrigated permanent grassland
B — brush or timber
H — suburban or homestead
W — waste or miscellaneous
ROW — right of way

The basic Land Class is decided by taking into account the *relative land development costs.* These may be appraised separately and shown by an appropriate class number (1, 2, 3, 4, or 6). A pair of numbers, the first relating to productivity, the second to land development costs, e.g. '22' in the mapping symbol shown (Fig. 7.1) is placed after the land-use code.

The estimated *farm water requirement* can be shown by the following codes:

A — low
B — medium
C — high

The following codes are used for *drainability* within the 1.5–3.0 m depth of soil plus substrata:

X — good drainage
Y — restricted drainage
Z — poor or negligible drainage

So the mapping symbol in Fig. 7.1, i.e.

$$\frac{3\ \text{std}}{\text{C22BX}}\ u_2f_2$$

can be seen to mean: This is land marginal in its suitability for irrigation (3), with problems associated with soil (s), topography (t), and drainage (d). In particular the mapping unit would need to be levelled (u_2), and is subject to flooding (f_2). The land is at present used for irrigated cultivation (C), and the potential productivity is at an intermediate Class 2 level (2), although development costs will be high (2). The farm water requirement is medium (B), and soil and substrata drainage is free (X).

The most difficult part of applying the USBR Irrigation Suitability Classification is to define the limits of the major classes. Maletic and Hutchings (1967) discuss the problem but give no practical advice. Indeed it is difficult to set any universal guidelines, since each irrigation scheme is different and requires its own individual classification. 'What needs to be avoided is any generalized specifications of ideal soil and land requirements for irrigation. These could be seriously misleading. This structure is not intended to discourage the evaluator from attempting to develop and quantify his own *local* criteria for assessing suitability. On the contrary, a clear statement of these criteria is likely to be the best measure (short of successful irrigation) of the merit of his work and his main contribution, given suitable caution, to general experience in this field' (Smyth, Eavis, and Williams 1979). Probably the best approach is to study the classifications established in similar areas and to make such informed modifications as seem necessary. Tables 7.3 to 7.5 give examples from three contrasting irrigation schemes to illustrate the differences in the determining factors for USBR Land Classes which have been applied in the mainland United States (Maker, Bailey, and Anderson 1970), Hawaii (Maletic and Hutchings 1967), and New Zealand (Griffiths 1975). Further examples are given in Maletic and Hutchings (1967), Western (1978), and FAO (1979).

Level of investigation and map scales

Soil surveys for irrigation projects can be undertaken at various levels of intensity (Table 3.9), according to the planning stage which the project has reached. At all stages the soil surveyor must know

TABLE 7.3
Detailed specifications for Irrigation Suitability Classes in the Pacific Southwest basin, United States

Property	Irrigation Suitability Class			
	1	2	3	4
Soil				
Surface texture	loamy very fine sand to clay loam	loamy sand to clay; peat; muck	medium sand to clay	medium sand to clay
Available water capacity of top 120 cm (cm)	>15	11.5–15	7.5–11.5	6–7.5
Effective depth (cm)	100	75–100	50–75	25–50
Salinity (mmho/cm)	<4	4–8	8–12	12–16
Severity of sodic conditions;	Slight	Moderate	Moderate	Moderate
percent area affected	<5	5–15	15–25	25–35
Permeability (cm/h)	0.5–12.5	0.1–12.5	0.1–25	Any
Max volume of gravel (%)	15	35	55	70
Max volume of cobbles (%)	5	10	15	35
Distance apart of rock outcrops (m)	60	30	25	10
Topography (including land development items)				
Stone removal (m³/ha)	25	60	125	175
% slope (mod-severe erosion)	<2	2–5	5–10	10–20
(slight erosion)	<4	4–10	10–20	10–20
Surface levelling or amount of tree cover	Light	Medium	Medium heavy	Medium heavy
Drainage				
Depth to water table during growing season (cm)				
Loam or finer	>150	100–150	50–100	25–50
Sandy	>125	75–125	50–75	25–50
Surface drainage	Good	Good	Restricted	Restricted
Depth to drainage barrier (m)	>210	180–210	150–180	45–150
Air drainage	No problem	Minor	Restricted	Restricted

Class 6 (non-irrigable) includes land which does not meet the minimum requirements for other Classes.
Land unsuited to gravity irrigation may be considered for sprinkler irrigation; designation is by 'S', e.g. 3–S.
Severely eroded soils will be downgraded one class; less severely eroded soils may be downgraded one class, depending on other conditions.
Specifications as representative of the conditions after the land has been developed for irrigation. Each individual factor represents a minimum rquirement, and, unless all other factors are near optimum, two or more interacting deficiencies may result in land being placed in a lower class.
Source: modified from Maker *et al.* (1970).

TABLE 7.4

*Detailed specifications for Irrigation Suitability Classes,
Kokee Project, Hawaii*

| Property | Irrigation Suitability Class | | |
	1 Arable	2 Arable	3 Arable
Soil			
Texture	Sandy loam to silty clay	Sandy loam to permeable clay	Loamy fine sand to moderately permeable clay
Depth to basalt or coral formation (cm)	>90	>60	>45
Depth to strongly gleyed layer or marl (cm)	No gleyed layer present	>60	>30
Depth to red, yellow, or grey weathered rock	>90	>60	>30
Exchangeable sodium (%)	15	15	10–15 (depending on soil)
Salinity (mmho/cm)	4	8	8
Topography			
Surface slope (%)	0–2	2–12	12–20
Need for land levelling;	Minor	May be required	Required
Maximum depth of cuts (cm)	—	<7.5	<15
Width of field (m)	>9	>9	May be <9
Minimum length of run (m)	90	45–90	22.5–45
Altitude (m)	<300	300–525	300–525
Rock (Vol % in root zone)	0–5	5–15	15–20
Costs of clearing vegetation ($/ha)	<36	36–72	72–108
Drainage			
Natural internal drainage	Well	Well–Moderately well	Moderately well
Flood risk	None	Infrequent	Frequent
Drain spacing (m)	180	60–180	24–60
Controlled depth of water table (m)	1.2	0.6–1.2	0.6–1.2

Class 6 (non-arable) includes land which does not meet the minimum requirements for other classes.
Source: modified from Maletic and Hutchings (1967), by permission.

what information he has to gather and must establish soil mapping
units compatible with the irrigation suitability classes to be employed. A general purpose soil survey carried out without regard to
the purpose may have map units and soil boundaries which do not
match the irrigation suitability categories.

At the *Pre-investment* or *Project Appraisal* stage, a reconnaissance soil survey at scales around 1:100 000 will produce general
information about the whole of a large project area and identify
smaller areas which seem to have special development potential. A
representative profile description and basic chemical data (e.g.
organic matter, pH, and soluble and exchangeable salts) are collected for each map unit. Complementary information is collected
on topography, groundwater levels, and water quality. Together
these allow a general selection of areas of potentially arable (irrig-

TABLE 7.5
Detailed specifications for Irrigation Suitability Classes in New Zealand

Property	Irrigation Suitability Class			
	1 Highly suitable	2 Suitable	3 Moderately suitable	4 Marginally suitable
Soil				
Permeability class of profile	Moderate	Moderately	Slow to rapid	Very slow to very rapid
Infiltration class	Moderate	Moderately slow to moderately rapid	Slow to rapid	Very slow to very rapid
Minimum depth to impermeable layer (cm)	120	90	60	30
Minimum available water in root zone (cm)	13	7.5	5	2.5
Minimum effective rooting depth (cm) for average texture of profile	75 very fine sandy loam or finer	45 very fine sandy loam or finer / 60 sandy loam 90 sand	30 very fine sandy loam or finer / 45 sandy loam or sand	15 very fine sandy loam or finer / 25 sandy loam 30 sand
Maximum stones (% by volume)	0	20	40	60
Maximum total salts (%)	0.15	0.3	0.7	0.7
Topography (t)				
Maximum slope (%) surface	3.5 (2°) even	5.2 (3°) if even / 3.5 (2°) if rough	8.8 (5°)	21.3 (12°)
Drainage (d)				
Overall drainage class (natural or altered)	Well drained	Moderately well to well drained	Imperfectly to somewhat excessively drained	Poorly to excessively drained

Class 5 (unsuitable) includes land which does not meet the minimum requirements for other Irrigation Suitability Classes.
Source: Griffiths (1975), by permission.

able) land, but may not be enough for assessments of local differences in its suitability or the possibility of its improvement. At this level, field-studies will be minimal, and there will be considerable reliance on existing data or indirect sources of information. Some preliminary decisions can be made about the irrigation methods, water suitability, and drainage factors.

Mitchell's (1976) study of the irrigation potential of soils in Botswana illustrates this stage, as do the land classification maps of various counties in New Mexico, at scales around 1:500 000 by Anderson and colleagues. Figure 7.2 is a block diagram from one of their reports (Maker *et al.* 1970) to which land assessments for irrigation according to the specifications in Table 7.3 have been added. At this scale map units may comprise more than one suitability Class. The Mohave–Stellar Association, for example, is denoted 2/1/3 and the report states:

> This association has the best potential in the county for expansion of irrigated land. A very high percentage of the soils is well suited for use as cropland under irrigation. About 42 per cent of the land in this general soil area is in irrigation land Class 2; 29 per cent is in Class 1; 19 per cent is in Class 3; 7 per cent in Class 4; and only 3 per cent is non-irrigable Class 6

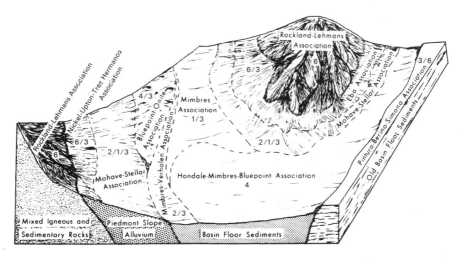

Fig. 7.2 . A diagrammatic presentation of soil association and landscape relationships in Luna County, New Mexico, with the USBR Irrigation Suitability Classes appropriate to each association. Based on a soil survey map at 1:500 000. (Adapted from Maker *et al.* (1970), by permission.)

land. If provided with essential improvements of levelling and irrigation systems, and with the application of good farming practices, the land in this unit has sufficient productive capacity to support sustained irrigation.

The next stage, the *Feasibility Stage* involves more detailed mapping of the more promising areas, (for example in Fig. 7.2 the Mimbres, the Mohave–Stellar, the Mimbres–Verhalen, and possibly the Pintura–Berino–Simona Associations). Map scales between 1:25 000 and 1:10 000 are appropriate. Comprehensive chemical and physical data will be collected for the soils of each map unit.

The feasibility study is to answer the question 'is the project worthy of construction?' and so must include the necessary studies of the topography, the hydrology, and the economics of the scheme, as well as the engineering proposals for land regrading, supply and distribution of the water and drainage schemes.

Once the decision to proceed with the project has been made, still more detailed soil surveys (at scales of 1:5000 to 1:2000) will need to be made for the *Design and Execution* stage. The field surveys and the accompanying field and laboratory tests and observations need not be carried out on the entire area, but will be restricted to those zones where special problems exist. Details of the distribution network can be completed, e.g. the canal size and the amounts of water to be supplied.

8. The evaluation of land for forestry

Introduction

Much timber production in the past has been extractive, simply removing trees of economic value from existing forests. Depletion of forest resources and, in many areas, the emergence of alternative land uses means that future timber production will require the deliberate allocation of land to forestry. New planting or the retention of woodland should be preceded by an evaluation of the area as potential forest. The safest evaluation is based on the measured performance of the timber species on analogous sites. There is an extensive technical literature on forest mensuration (e.g. Husch, Miller, and Beers 1972), so what follows is no more than a summary.

Assessing tree growth

Site Index

The best measure of forest productivity is the volume of useful timber produced on a unit area in a given time. Tree height is much easier to measure, and, with certain reservations, height growth is correlated with volume growth. Assessments of *Site Index* are based on the height attained at a specific *index age*. In the United States the index age is 50 years for relatively short lived species east of the Great Plains, but 100 years for long lived species (mainly hardwoods), and more generally in the west. Site Indices may be assessed from stands a few years younger or older than the index age with the aid of height:age curves for each species, preferably in the same region (e.g. Fig. 8.1). The measured trees should be free growing, uninjured, and never less than 20 years old. A decision must be made whether to measure a sample of the biggest (dominant) trees or all that reach canopy level (dominant and co-dominant). Within limits, tree height is not much affected by spacing within the stand, but it is best to choose stands which are fully stocked, of even age, and not disturbed by uneven thinning, undue competition, severe fires, heavy grazing, storm damage, or heavy attacks of pests or

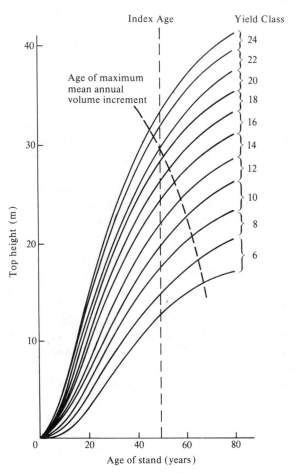

Fig. 8.1 General Yield Class Curves for Sitka spruce in Great Britain. Yield class measures the incremental growth ($m^3ha^{-1}a^{-1}$) and 50 years is the Index age for the Site Index. (See text for explanation.) (Adapted from Hamilton and Christie (1971). Crown Copyright. Reproduced by permission of the Controller of H.M. Stationery Office.)

diseases. Carmean (1975) gives Site Index curves for species important in the United States. The volume yield of an area fully stocked with trees of normal shape may be determined from its Site Index by means of a yield table for the species. This presupposes a particular rotation length.

Optimum rotation length

The *optimum rotation length* will give the maximum yield, measured as mean annual volume increment per unit area of land, and maximum returns, in the absence of exceptional factors such as a high risk of loss by windblow or disease, or a considerable premium for large logs. Because the height of typical trees of a given species is well correlated with timber volume an optimum rotation length for a tree species can be calculated from its particular height: age curve (e.g. Table 8.1). Soil and climate factors influence the rate of growth and hence the optimum rotation length, giving a range from 45 to 68 years for Sitka spruce in Britain and 75 to 118 years for beech.

Yield Class and Production Class

These are used in Britain instead of Site Index (Hamilton and Christie 1971). *Yield* is the mean annual increment of the volume of stemwood of more than 7 cm overbark at the optimum rotation length. *Yield Classes* are defined for each species by dividing the total range of yield into steps of 2 m³/ha. A standing crop can be assigned to its Yield Class at any age by measuring only the height of a sample of trees and then referring to a family of height:age curves (e.g. Fig. 8.1). The Yield Class depends very much on soil and site conditions. For oak, one of the slowest growing British trees, it ranges from 4 to 8 m³/ha, while for grand fir *(Abies grandis)*, one of the fastest growing, it ranges from 14 to 30 m³/ha. The average yield of all hardwoods in Britain is about 5.0 m³/ha, and of conifers about 9.5. The average conifer species yields about 3.5 m³/ha in Scandinavia, and 18.0 m³/ha in New Zealand. Yields from tropical plantations may reach 50 m³/ha or more (Johnson 1975). In Canada, it is worth harvesting crops which produce a marketable yield of only 1 m³/ha, but in Britain about 6 m³/ha is needed for economic viability, because of planting costs.

Production Class is a more accurate measure of forest productivity, and involves measurements of tree girth (normally at breast

TABLE 8.1

The relationship of height at 50 years (Site Index for the conifers). Yield Class, and optimum rotation length for poor, average, and good stands of forest trees commonly planted in Britain

Species	Stand quality	Site Index, i.e. height at 50 years (m)	Yield Class (m³/ha)	Optimum rotation length (years)
Conifers				
Scots pine	Poor	11.0	4	90
(*Pinus sylvestris*)	Average	16.0	8	77
	Good	22.3	14	66
Corsican pine	Poor	13.0	6	70
(*P. nigra* var.	Average	22.0	14	57
maritima)	Good	27.3	20	53
Sitka spruce	Poor	13.5	6	66
(*Picea sitchensis*)	Average	21.0	14	57
	Good	32.5	24	46
Deciduous trees				
Oak	Poor	14.5	4	90
(*Quercus robur* or	Average	20.0	6	78
petraea)	Good	24.0	8	68
Beech	Poor	13.0	4	106
(*Fagus sylvatica*)	Average	17.0	6	98
	Good	24.5	10	79

Source: information from Hamilton and Christie (1971).

height 137 cm from the ground), as well as height. Standard volume tables may be used to calculate the volume of individual trees from these two measurements. For fully stocked, unthinned stands, tables of Production Class give timber volume per hectare. Allowances can be made for thinning, and to take account of the form of the trees, i.e. trunks which taper abnormally.

Environmental factors affecting forest productivity

Introduction

If enough natural or semi-natural vegetation survives, it is possible to assess the integrated effects of soil and site conditions from this, and to define categories of land suitability (e.g. Anderson 1961; Burger 1972). In the long run it may be more helpful to relate timber production to parameters of climate, soil, etc., as in the assessment of land for agriculture (Toleman 1974). It is usually necessary to use a separate relation for forestry. For example, the forester regards cultivation as a possible means of improving land rather than a regular necessity, so that boulders, rock outcrops and steep slopes do not necessarily debar forestry. Trees may be extracted by winching, etc., from terrain too difficult for the mechanical harvesting of agricultural crops. On the other hand trees are a perennial crop and so the growth of a number of years is at risk from relatively rare crises, such as storms, untimely frosts or a period of soil waterlogging, which in agriculture would destroy the product of only one season. Again, the delay in securing a return from the costs of establishment means that these are carried forward at compound interest. Thus foresters are often reluctant to incur the expense of drastic modifications of soil conditions, and may prefer to adapt planting or management to make the best of existing circumstances.

Active interest in the evaluation and classification of forest land began more than 50 years ago, notably in Finland. It was then concerned with the selection of the most appropriate tree species for particular sites. However, species are chosen in the expectation of an economic yield, and the species considered most suitable is likely to produce the highest volume of good quality timber. Therefore evaluation is now concerned with predictions of yield. Table 8.2 summarizes the soil and climatic factors affecting the selection of some economic tree species in Britain, and draws attention to the most relevant aspects of climate and soil. Rennie (1962) gives a more general review, and Carmean (1975) one for the United States.

Climate

Temperature is important; growth is slight below 5 °C, increases to about 28 °C, and declines above 28 °C. Temperature often determines the length of the growing season, 4 months with a mean temperature above 10 °C being about the minimum for economic forestry. In Lat 53.50 N in Alberta, where only about 70 days are frost free, lodgepole pine grows at a rate of about $1.5 m^3 ha^{-1} a^{-1}$ and the optimum rotation is 100 to 200 years (Dumanski, Wright, and Lindsay 1973). In the humid tropics and subtropics, growth can proceed almost all the year round, and *Pinus caribbea* may yield up to $40 m^3 ha^{-1} a^{-1}$ in a rotation of 30 years or even less (Lamb 1972,

TABLE 8.2

Soil and climate factors affecting the selection of tree species for forestry in Great Britain

Species	Yield class (m³/ha)	Timber quality	Soil depth	Topsoil reaction	Soil drainage	Climatic zone	Annual rainfall	Exposure	Other factors
Grand fir	12–26	G	D	A–B	F	H	W	S	Fr
Western hemlock	10–20	G	M	AA–B	F–WW	C	D–W	E	Fr Cv
Sitka spruce	6–18	G	S	AA–B	F–P	CC	W	EE	Fr Cv
Western red cedar	10–22	D(E)	S	A–BB	F–W	H	W	W	
Douglas fir	8–22	E	D	A–B	F	H	W	S	
Norway spruce	6–18	G	M	A–B	F–WW	C	D–W	E	Cv
Corsican pine	4–18	F	M	AA–B	FF–W	H	D–W	E	Sc
Hybrid larch	4–14	G–E	S	AA–B	F–W	CC	D–W	EE	
Scots pine	4–12	G	S	AA–B	FF–WW	CC	D	E	
Hybrid poplar	4–12	S	M–D	M–DB	F–W	H	D–W	S	Sc
European larch	2–12	E	M	A–B	F	C	D–W	EE	Sc
Lodgepole pine	4–10	F	S	AA–A	FF–P	CC	D–W	EE	Sc
Beech	4–8	E	M	A–BB	F	C	D–W	E	Fr
Ash	4–8	S	M	B–BB	F	H	D–W	S	
Oak	2–6	G	S–M	A–B	F–W	H	D–W	E	

Timber quality: E — Excellent; G — Good; F — Fair to Good; S — Special purpose. *Soil depth:* S — <20 cm; M — 20–50 cm; D — > 50 cm. *Topsoil reaction* (pH): AA — <4.2; A — 4.2–5; B — 5–7; BB — calcareous. *Soil drainage:* EF — Excessively drained sand, gravel, or scree; F — Well or imperfectly drained loam, silt, or clay; W — Mineral gley soil, but actual surface seldom waterlogged; MW — Marshy for much of the year, with or without thin peat; P — peat > 40 cm thick. *Climatic zone:* H — Lowlands; C — Hill land (240–420 m in England and Wales, 120–240 m in Scotland); CC Highland — (240–450 m in Scotland). *Annual rainfall:* D — Below 900 mm (35 in); W — Above 900 mm (35 in). *Exposure:* EE — Severely exposed; E — Moderately exposed; S — Sheltered. *Other factors:* Fr — Damaged by severe frost; Cv — Presence of heather checks growth; Sc — suitable for sea coast.

1973). *Eucalyptus grandis* yields up to 70 m³ha⁻¹a⁻¹ in east and central Africa, although yields of 20–30 m³ha⁻¹a⁻¹ are more typical of *Eucalyptus* species worldwide. The yields of tropical rain forest are also high, but species are mixed and productivity is less than in nearby plantations (Dawkins 1959). Freedom from frost is essential for many tropical and subtropical species: the high yielding *Pinus radiata, Pinus pinaster*, and most eucalypts will not stand severe frost.

Adequate rainfall is also important. Near the Californian coast the Site Index of Douglas fir increases 1.5 m for each 250 mm rise in mean annual precipitation (Zinke 1959). Few useful trees can stand prolonged and severe moisture stress, and drought is commonly accompanied by damaging fires. Potential timber production varies in rough proportion to Paterson's (1956) climatic index (I), particularly in northern Europe where

$$I = \frac{T_v PGE}{T_a\ 1200},$$

where T_v is the mean temperature (°C) of the warmest month, P the annual precipitation (mm), G the length of the growing season (months), E a factor based on latitude (or specifically the total annual radiation expressed as a percentage of that at the Poles), and T_a the mean annual range in temperatures (°C) between the coldest and warmest month. However, a formula which takes no account of other more local climatic factors or of soil conditions can be only very approximate.

Exposure to wind is a hazard in many parts of the world, whether through occasional hurricanes, or through the tattering and distorting effects of the persistent strong winds of maritime or elevated sites near west coasts in latitudes higher than 40°. Exposure can vary greatly over short distances and is greatest on summits and ridges. An experienced observer can grade sites according to their degree of exposure to the wind. The 'topex' method adds together the angles between the visual horizon and horizontal at the eight points of the compass (Pyatt 1977) and so is greatest for the most sheltered site. A more reliable quantitative method sums the loss in weight of standard cotton flags exposed in standard holders for 12 two-month periods (Lines and Howell 1963). This technique has proved invaluable in the Scottish Highlands, where exposure commonly determines the economic tree line. Liability to wind-throw depends on many other factors; shallow soil and especially waterlogged soils make crops particularly vulnerable. Some species such as Douglas fir are very sensitive, others such as Sitka spruce and lodgepole pine are very resistant, while gappy or newly thinned crops are in special danger. Thus exposed land may only be suitable for short rotations without thinning, which limits its uses to pulp or chipboard.

Soil

Unless nutrient deficiencies are severe, soil physical conditions appear to be more important than chemical properties. This applies particularly to conifers. The most significant factor is available water-holding capacity, which is affected by the depth of the rooting zone, and the soil texture and stone content. Indicators of drainage conditions are important, e.g. depth to mottling, depth to water-table, subsoil permeability, and depth of peat. The bulk density or porosity of subsoils, which are related to ease of rooting and to permeability, are occasionally significant.

The commonest nutrient deficiency is of phosphate, but in peaty or coarse textured soils in humid climates the lack of combined nitrogen and/or potassium is sometimes a significant limitation. Adequate magnesium and calcium are important for some broad-leaved trees, while very high Mg:Ca ratios (associated with serpentine rock) may be detrimental. Minor element deficiencies (e.g. Zn) and toxicities (e.g. Cr, Ni) are rarely of more than local importance. While yields are commonly greater on soils of high pH, calcareous soils are often detrimental.

Surface soil organic matter content is sometimes significant, and humus type or degree of podzolization has proved significant for some broad-leaved species. Spurr and Barnes (1973) and Carmean (1975) have discussed the factors mentioned above.

Forest land evaluation systems

Introduction

Though land evaluation for forestry is analogous to evaluation for agriculture, there are several important differences. Yield estimates are easier to measure (cf. Chapter 2), and a single estimate sums the growth of a number of years, thus allowing for climatic variability. A full economic evaluation of long rotations is highly speculative, since it is impossible to predict timber prices in 50 or 100 years time.

Tree crop suitability

Yield estimates are easily made if suitable stands of trees exist in the area, but there may be a few or no stands and the success of indigenous trees has little predictive value for exotic species. In this case the forester will have to examine the soil and climatic conditions on the site or in each soil-mapping unit (e.g. Table 8.2) in order to recommend the tree species likely to be successful, and to make other suggestions on the hazards, or the need for ground preparation, etc. of a particular site or map unit. Such information may be included in a soil survey report (cf. Mackney and Burnham 1966; and most USDA soil reports). In some regions preferred species have been listed by soil series, e.g. Limstrom (1963) for the central United States. Stevens and Werts (1971) considered that correct species selection in Wisconsin could produce a 60 per cent increase in sawtimber yield.

Category systems of forest land evaluation

Because it is relatively easy to obtain data on the performance of timber trees, the classes of category systems are nearly always calibrated, at least approximately, in terms of either Site Index or of the expected volume of timber production. Thus the sharp distinctions in agricultural land evaluations between systems based on categories (p. 67) or parametric indices (p. 96) do not apply. The performance ranges of categories may be specified nationally (e.g. in Canada) or regionally (e.g. in the United States).

The Canada Land Inventory *Land Capability Classification for Forestry* (McCormack 1967; and Table 8.3) has a structure similar to the Soil Capability Classification for Agriculture (p. 75) and assessments for recreation (p. 189) and wildlife habitat (p. 190). The classification for forestry has seven *Capability Classes* which indicate the inherent ability of land to grow commercial timber, Class 1 being the best and Class 7 unable to yield timber in commercial quantities. Each Class has a *Productivity Range* based on the mean annual increment of the best species or group of species adapted to the site at or near rotation age and expressed as the gross merchantable volume down to a minimum diameter of 10 cm in normal, fully stocked stands, not including thinnings, bark, or

TABLE 8.3
The Canada Land Inventory Land Capability Classification for Forestry

Classes

Class	Degree of limitations	Usual productivity ($m^3ha^{-1}a^{-1}$)
1	None important	>7.8
2	Slight	6.4–7.7
3	Moderate	5.0–6.3
4	Moderately severe	3.6–4.9
5	Severe	2.2–3.5
6	Very severe	0.8–2.1
7	Preclude commercial forestry	<0.7

Subclasses

Local climate	Soil moisture	Permeability and depth of rooting	Other soil factors
A — drought	M — too dry	R — restriction by bedrock	E — actively eroding soils
H — frost	W — too wet	D — restriction by dense or compact layers	F — low soil fertility
U — exposure	Z — intricate pattern of wet organic soils and bedrock	Y — intricate pattern of shallowness, compaction or other restriction to rooting	I — periodically inundated areas
C — two or more factors	X — other intricate soil patterns		K — permafrost layer present
			L — high levels of carbonates
			N — excessive soluble salts or other toxic constituents
			P — stoniness
			S — a combination of soil factors

Indicator species
A maximum of two indicator species is denoted by a letter code, e.g. rP — red pine; w S — white spruce; b S — black spruce, etc.

Source: information from McCormack (1967).

branch wood. Good management is assumed, but location, access, distance to markets, size of units, ownership, and present state are not considered. Present cover or production is taken into account, but together with any evidence that this is unrepresentative of true potential. Classification is based on the natural state of the land without improvements such as fertilization or drainage.

The *Capability Subclass* shows the kind(s) of limitation affecting tree growth and applies to all Classes except 1. Up to two, or occasionally three, symbols may be used. The normal regional climate is considered in assigning to a Class but has no particular Subclass notation.

Map symbols conveying information about Class, Subclass, and Index Species are denoted thus:

$$2M$$
$$rP$$

which denotes Capability Class 2 due to insufficient soil moisture (M). Well managed red pine (rP) is expected to yield 6.4–7.7. $m^3ha^{-1}a^{-1}$. Two, or exceptionally three, Classes may occur in combination, with the relative proportion of each indicated to the nearest 10 per cent thus:

6	4
3RM	7W
wS	bS

This denotes a complex of 60 per cent class 3 land affected by limitations of shallowness to bedrock (R) and insufficient soil moisture (M) on which well-managed white spruce (wS) is expected to yield 5.0–6.3 m^3/ha.a, and 40 per cent Class 7 land with wet soils (W) on which black spruce (bS) would yield less than 0.7 m^3/ha.a (cf. p. 189 and p. 190).

USDA soil survey reports routinely interpret map units in terms of *Woodland Suitability* (USDA 1967; Lemmon 1970). *Woodland Suitability Classes* indicate levels of potential soil productivity, and are based on the average Site Index of an indicator tree species or forest type suited to the area and kind of soil. Class 1 is the highest. The range of Site Indices within each Class (Table 8.4) is specified by foresters for each species or forest type within a given region, often for one or a group of Land Resource Areas, as defined by Austin (1965). The ranges in Site Index are narrow enough for the

Classes to be useful in forest management. Normally five Woodland Suitability Classes are sufficient, but the number is not mandatory, and it may be convenient to use more or fewer Classes for a particular species of forest type in a particular region.

Subclasses are based on selected soil properties associated with moderate or severe hazards or limitations in woodland use or management. Lemmon (1958) distinguished nine elements important to growth and management to which soil properties are relevant: potential productivity; species suitability; suitability for special woodland products (e.g. turpentine, Christmas trees); seedling mortality; erosion hazard; windthrow hazard; plant competition; equipment limitations; hazards from specified pests and diseases. The soil and site limitations relevant to each of these elements can then be rated as *slight, moderate,* or *severe,* on the criteria given in USDA (1967), and the single most significant to the growth or management of woodlands is used to designate the Subclass. The symbols used to denote Subclass limitations and their order of priority are:

x — rockiness (or stones >2.54 cm diameter)
w — wetness including flood risk
t — toxic substances (excessive alkalinity, acidity, salts, etc.)
d — limited rooting depth
c — clayey soil
s — sandy soil
f — stoniness (stones <2.54 cm diameter)
r — slope or relief pattern
o — slight or no restrictions owing to soil or topography, but climatic restrictions may apply.

Subclass notations follow the Class figure thus:

1o, 2w, etc.

The lowest level of the classification, the *Woodland Suitability Group* (WSG), serves local and regional needs and is comparable to the agricultural Capability Unit (p. 87). It groups together soil mapping units that can be treated alike by a forester and will give a similar performance. This will be shown by the achievement of similar ratings when evaluated in terms of the nine previously mentioned elements. The notation for a WSG is in the form 4sl, 2o3, etc.

TABLE 8.4
Range of Site Index (m) within Woodland Suitability Classes in the United States

Indicator species or forest type	Woodland Suitability Class				
	1 Very High	2 High	3 Moderately High	4 Moderate	5 Low
Douglas fir	>56.6	56.6–47.6	47.5–38.3	38.2–29.1	<29.1
Loblolly pine } Sweetgum }	>29.0	29.0–26.1	26.0–23.1	23.0–20.0	<20.0
Upland oaks	>26.0	26.0–23.1	23.0–20.0	19.9–17.0	<17.0

Source: Lemmon (1970), by permission.

When placing soil mapping units into WSGs it generally appears necessary to divide series into phases in terms of slope, climate, rockiness, etc. If phases have not been mapped, soil series or complexes may be placed in the single most appropriate WSG. Land types not expressed as soil series may be placed in a WSG or left unclassified. More than one WSG may be assigned to a soil association, but it must then be stated to which WSG each of the components of the association is assigned.

USDA reports also give, for each map unit, an assessment of management concerns, rating the land *slight, moderate,* or *severe* in respect of erosion hazard, equipment limitation, seedling mortality, and plant competition. The Site Index of important trees already growing on the land and recommended trees to plant is also given.

Using soil and other maps as a basis for forest land evaluation

Maps to show the distribution of many of the factors influencing the capability of land for forestry either exist, or could easily be made in many areas. These include topographic factors such as altitude, climatic factors, existing vegetation, and soil. Because some relevant factors are soil properties or are environmental characteristics affecting soil formation, a soil map may be the most informative single analysis of the landscape for forest use. However the soil series is not an ideal mapping unit since many series do not differ much in forest capability, while some show excessive intra-class variability. There are at least three ways of dealing with this situation (cf. p. 36):

(i) Begin by producing a general purpose soil map, but try to divide soil series with excessive silvicultural variability into suitable phases, according to depth, etc. Then consolidate mapping units of equal capability for forestry. The soil map provides the boundaries, so only a special legend is needed. This is the USDA Woodland Suitability approach (p. 149).

(ii) Draw up a specific land capability classification for forestry, and then combine soil, topographic, climatic, and vegetation information from maps, air photographs, and ground check to draw a specific land capability map for forestry. This has been done in the Canada Land Inventory approach (p. 147).

(iii) Prepare special soil maps whose legend has been drawn up with forestry in mind and superimpose other criteria known to be important, e.g. climatic region, elevation, class of estimated exposure to wind, abundance of heather. Define Broad Site Groups on combinations of these criteria. Then draw up tables of the predicted yields and recommended silvicultural practices for each. This is the procedure of the British Forestry Commission (Toleman and Pyatt 1974; Toleman 1974; Pyatt 1977; also Table 8.5).

Procedures (ii) and (iii) require collaboration between foresters and soil scientists. A general purpose soil surveyor is likely to find procedure (i) most appropriate, and can attempt the task at either of two levels:

(i) Describe the typical and limiting soil and site conditions of each of his general purpose mapping units to a forester with experience in the area; use the mapping units as pigeonholes for the forester's subjective judgements on suitable species and treatments and probable yields.

(ii) Measure trees in sample plots that cover as many combinations of species and mapping unit as possible; use the information collected as 'bench marks' (cf. p. 8) to guide subjective estimates for the missing categories.

Yield prediction using equations

If the yield of trees and the main environmental variables can both be quantified at a number of sites, the techniques of multiple correlation can be used to examine how they are interrelated (Kendall 1975; Van de Geer 1971).

The yield of a particular species is the dependent variable. The chief problem is to identify the most informative independent

TABLE 8.5

Expected average yields of broad site groups in southern Scotland, increment in $m^3ha^{-1}a^{-1}$

Soil type Tree species	Brown earth SS	Peaty ironpan soil and intergrades to brown earth SS	LP	Surface water gley SS	Peaty gley and flushed peat SS	Basin peat and hill peat SS	LP
Altitudinal zone (m)							
0–215	16	14	10*	18	14	13	11
215–380	14	11	9	15	12	10	8
Over 380	12	10	8	13	11	7	7

SS — Sitka spruce *Picea sitchensis* (Queen Charlotte Island provenance); LP — Lodgepole pine *Pinus contorta* (South Coastal provenance).

Notes

1. Dry, infertile soils, low rainfall and dominance of heather are factors that favour the choice of *Pinus* (in category marked *P. nigra (maritima)*).
2. Values are for moderately exposed mid slope positions. For sheltered lower slopes and valleys add up to 2 m³. For exposed ridge tops and plateaux subtract up to 2 m³.
3. Prediction covers all lithologies except Carboniferous shales and clay tills on which surface water gley and peaty gley values should be reduced by up to 2 m³.

Source: Toleman (1974). Reproduced from Technical Bulletin 30, Ministry of Agriculture, Fisheries and Food, by permission of the Controller of H.M. Stationery Office.

(environmental) variables, transform them if necessary so that their relationship to yield is linear, and then to weight them so that their combination explains as much of the variation in yield as possible. If significant, the resulting equation can be used to predict the yield that might be obtained from a site as yet unforested, provided the necessary environmental variables can be measured or estimated (cf. p. 18). Page (1970) and Carmean (1975) have discussed procedures for setting up a yield prediction system (cf. p. 156).

(i) The first decision is the size of the study area. It may be possible to explain a high proportion of the variation in yield in small areas with data on a small number of site properties from comparatively few sample plots. Nevertheless, there may be inexplicable discrepances even between the equations for small areas that are not widely separated. Over a very large area there is often a very wide range in many different soil and site properties, including some, such as day length, that could be neglected in small areas. The development of prediction equations for large areas requires many and widely scattered plots. Although more soundly based, the equations may appear to explain a lower proportion of the variation in yield. In general it is better to consider the whole of a medium sized region with reasonable coherence in terms of geology, topography, and climate, such as the 10 000 km² of north and central Wales, than to examine small blocks of, say, 10 km². Yield prediction within a region may be improved by calculating separate equations for markedly different categories of land, such as peat.

(ii) The tree species examined must be represented in the study area by enough stands of acceptable age (for conifers in Britain between 20 and 80 years) over virtually the full range of site conditions.

(iii) The sample plots should cover the full range. It is important to include some 'crop failures' and some exceptionally good crops, involving ideally the full range of conditions of all kinds and in all combinations. If possible, the best procedure is to stratify all available plots and select randomly between those that represent the same combination of characters, but in some areas suitable woodland may be too scarce.

(iv) The selection of variables to be measured or assessed will be a compromise, guided by the time and resources available. Priority should be given to factors which can be assessed on the site, e.g. soil depth, texture, slope, and aspect. The characters should be quantified, and the recording procedure standardized. Even such properties as position on slope, soil structure, drainage, degree of podzolization, and of humification of peat can be categorized to give numerical values. For example, soil drainage classes might be assigned the values ; 0 — very poor; 1 — poor; 2 — imperfect; 3 — moderate; 4 — good. Subjective judgements, e.g. of exposure to wind, can be ranked similarly, 0 for the most exposed. Every variable must be estimated at every site.

(v) Height and age are probably adequate measures of tree performance, although it will be necessary to establish standard height/age curves if this has not been done already for the species in the same or a similar region. Volume can be estimated from Yield Class on a standard curve. Better still, Production Class can be estimated from the basal area of unthinned stands (Hamilton and Christie 1971), but this is likely to prove too laborious for many sites.

(vi) Some properties, e.g. the nature of organic layers, pH, or degree of podzolization may have been affected by the tree crop itself. Page (1968, 1970) recommends calculating the relationship of these to the age of the forest; the field values are then corrected to zero time. Such corrections may be desirable if the prediction equations are to be used to guide planting on bare ground, but they are not worth making unless they have a substantial bearing on the result of the exercise. It is important to assess exposure as if there were no trees in the area.

(vii) Multiple correlation assumes linear relationships, so the values for each characteristic should be examined to see if they need transformation. Aspect will certainly need to be transformed (Carmean 1975), ideally with an allowance for slope. Other interactions can be allowed for, e.g. depth may be corrected by an appropriate reduction for the volume of stones.

(viii) A matrix of simple correlation coefficients between all possible pairs of variables will reveal the relationships between topographic soil and climatic factors. It may be possible to substitute an easily measured factor, e.g. elevation, for another which has a more direct influence on growth, such as temperature or exposure. The interaction of factors may give 'feedback' correlations which need not reflect a causal connection (Ferrari 1966).

(ix) The multiple correlation can then be modified stepwise by the omission of variables which have a very small effect, possibly with some discrimination in favour of the more easily assessed parameters.

(x) The final equation selected is tested on a new, preferably random, sub-set of sites from the same population to determine the proportion of the variation in tree growth that it can explain.

Once prediction equations have been produced and tested, they may be used to investigate unforested land. The prediction equation can be applied to an array of points, and isopleths interpolated to produce yield-prediction maps (Page 1970). To map a large area it would be necessary to limit the equation to variables that could be estimated at a large number of sites, e.g. from maps and air-photographs.

Carmean (1975) has presented an admirable review of soil-site studies in the United States, arranged by tree species and region. Among others there have been similar studies in Scotland on Scots pine (Adu 1968; Blyth 1974) and Sitka spruce (Malcolm 1971), in England on Corsican pine (Fourt, Donald, Jeffers, and Binns 1971), and for three species in Wales (Hetherington and Page 1965; Page 1970). Two of Page's equations for topheight (m) at 50 years (H) are:

(i) Douglas fir

$$H = 15.32 - 0.27 \ x_1 + 1.50 \ x_2 + 0.05 \ x_3 + 0.03 \ x_4 + 0.65 \ x_5$$
$$= 4.64 \ x_6 + 1.00 \ x_7$$

(74.5 per cent of the total variation in topheight accounted for)

(ii) Japanese larch

$$H = 5.56 - 0.04 \ x_1 + 1.35 \ x_2 + 0.04 \ x_4 + 0.66 \ x_5$$
$$+ 1.6 \ x_7 + 3.40 \ x_8$$

(84.0 per cent of the total variation in topheight accounted for)

where x_1 = elevation (m);
  x_2 = texture of soil at 15–30 cm depth on the following scale: clay or peat — 1, silty clay — 2, clay loam — 3, loam — 4, sandy loam — 5;
  x_3 = percentage slope;
  x_4 = percentage of distance from ridge line to valley bottom;
  x_5 = soil series mapping units ranked as follows:
    1 Denbigh (deep brown earth),
    2 Cymmer and Cymmer–Peris (brown podzolic soils),
    3 Ynys, Ynys–Pentir, and Cegin (gleys and peaty gleys),
    4 Manod (brown podzolic soil intergrading to podzol),
    5 Powys and Powys–Bangor (shallow brown earths),
    6 Hiraethog and Hiraethog–Bodafon (peaty podzol),
    7 Caron (deep peat);

x_6 = Bulk density at 2.5 cm depth;
x_7 = Shape of slope as follows:
    1 Convex,
    2 Straight,
    3 Concave.
x_8 = pH at 30 cm depth (1:2.5 soil:water)

Economic measures of forest productivity

The economic return from managing or establishing an area of forest can be calculated from the costs of planting (if required) and future management and extraction, together with the future prices of products if these can be estimated. The inputs needed from the evaluator of forest land would be: choice of species; the Site Index or the Yield Class likely to be achieved; site restrictions on rotation length, e.g. liability to disease or windthrow after a certain time; and site advantages or limitations which may require that the assumed cost of operations be adjusted for items like the cost of access roads. Even when all these inputs are supplied, however, the result of the analysis largely depends on accurate prediction of the interest payable on capital invested and the discount to be applied to future cash returns (Linnard and Gane 1968).

Even if the assumptions are sound, such calculations are essentially notional when applied to isolated small parcels of land which cannot be managed at standard costs. They would show the lowest Site Index or Yield Class likely to be profitable under particular economic conditions, and thus predict whether forestry would be profitable on particular soil and site conditions. They are indispensable for predicting the overall success of a large forestry project (Watt 1972), and have been used to calculate the area of land that could profitably be afforested in Britain (CAS 1980) and to discuss the allocation of land between agriculture and forestry (Maxwell, Sibbald, and Eadie 1979).

Economic analysis is much less speculative when the management objective is to maintain a steady production from a forest estate that already contains much standing timber in various stages of growth. In this case land evaluation must predict volume yields and optimum rotation lengths, from which the annual volume which can be harvested on a sustained basis (allowable cut) can be calculated. The management planning needed to forward such a policy is called forest regulation, and is described by Davis (1966), who uses the term 'soil rent' as a measure of the profitability of forestry on a specified area.

Environmental factors and forest management

The estimation of potential yield is only one aspect of forest planning (Davis 1966; Johnston, Grayson, and Bradley 1967; Lloyd and Clark 1979). Bennema and van Goor (1975) mention a number of other factors that are affected by soil or site conditions and are important in management. These include the effect of topography on the size and shape of management units and on the convenience of logging. Topography and soil factors affect road construction (p. 173) and the need for and cost of terrain preparation such as drainage and the disruption of soil pans. Climate affects fire hazard, climate, soil and previous vegetation affect weed problems, seedling mortality and the incidence of pests and diseases. Some conditions, such as 'heather check', and 'replant' problems are specifically related to the previous vegetation. Finally, soil, site, and climatic conditions all influence the risk of soil erosion after disruptive forestry operations. USDA soil reports conventionally list the main forestry management limitations for each map unit.

Non-commodity uses of woodland

The value of woodland to the community often extends well beyond timber production (Echelberger and Wagar 1979). The protection of vulnerable catchments against water erosion, which also prevents excessive siltation of rivers and reservoirs, is often an important benefit. Trees also act as a windbreak, to check wind erosion and shelter farm stock, crops, and more vulnerable trees. Woodlands frequently enhance the scenic value of a landscape, provide opportunities for recreation and support wildlife, whether for exploitation by sportsmen or for conservation (p. 186).

Non-commodity uses are especially important in areas of low wood-producing potential and to owners of small areas of woodland, to whom timber may be as irrelevant as the carcass value of a pet animal. The owners and managers of larger areas have been under increasing pressure to consider the scenic implications of their activities (Litton 1974; Crowe 1978). Litton advocates the identification of areas of visual vulnerability as part of forest land evaluation. The visual effect of the change seen from a particular viewpoint through an entire rotation can be simulated by a computer (e.g. Myklestad and Wagar 1976).

9. The evaluation of land for non-agricultural purposes

Introduction

Land has many uses other than the production of food and timber, and evaluation of land for these purposes has become common during the last decade. There has been special emphasis on civil engineering, recreational and amenity uses, and waste disposal.

The main approaches in non-agricultural evaluations are:

(i) Quantitative classifications of soil materials for the evaluation of specific sites or projects, mainly in civil engineering (e.g. Klingebiel 1967; Holtz 1969; USDA 1971; and pp. 159–66).

(ii) Rating schemes for the interpretation of soil-map units according to their suitabilities or limitations for specific purposes. All recent USDA soil survey reports include non-agricultural interpretations of the map units following standard schemes described by USDA (1968, 1971, 1978a), Olson (1973), and Bartelli (1978). Similar evaluations are also being applied in Britain (e.g. Hartnup and Jarvis 1973; Jarvis and Mackney 1979; Jarvis, Hazelden, and Mackney 1979), and in other countries especially the Netherlands (e.g. Westerveld and Van den Hurk 1973; and pp. 166–87).

(iii) Land resource surveys for non-agricultural purposes, e.g. in the Canada Land Inventory (CLI 1965/70) and pp. 187–90.

Quantitive classifications of soil materials for the civil engineer

The two *engineering soil classifications* most generally used are those of the American Association of State Highway (and Transportation) Officials (AASHO 1961; Bartelli 1978) and the so called 'Unified Soil Classification System' of the United States Army Corps of Engineers (Table 9.1). The British Soil Classification System for Engineering (British Standards Institute 1976; Hartnup and Jarvis 1979) is similar to the Unified system. The Unified system is based on organic matter content, a particle size analysis using 4-mesh (5mm) and 200-mesh (0.75mm) sieves and measurements of liquid and plastic limits (United States Department of Defence 1968; Olson 1973;

TABLE 9.1
*The 'Unified Soil classification System' for
civil engineers*

Description	Code
Highly organic soils (Peat and Muck)	Pt
Coarse-grained soils (over 50% coarser than 0.074 mm)	
Gravel (% particles greater than 5 mm exceeds % particles between 5 mm and 0.074 mm)	
Less than 5% finer than 0.074 mm	
Well graded	GW
Poorly graded	GP
More than 5% finer than 0.074 mm	
Fines mostly silt	GM
Fines mostly clay	GC
Sand (% particles between 5 mm and 0.074 mm exceeds % particles greater than 5 mm)	
Less than 5% finer than 0.074 mm	
Well graded	SW
Poorly graded	SP
More than 5% finer than 0.074 mm	
Fines mostly silt	SM
Fines mostly clay	SC
Fine-grained soils (over 50% finer than 0.074 mm)	
Low-organic silts (liquid limit is greater than (20 + 4/3 Plasticity Index):	
Low plasticity (liquid limit below 50% moisture by weight)	ML
High plasticity (liquid limit above 50% moisture by weight)	MH
Low-organic clays (liquid limit is less than (20 + 4/3 Plasticity Index):	
Low plasticity (liquid limit below 50% moisture by weight)	CL
High plasticity (liquid limit above 50% moisture by weight)	CM
Organic-rich silts and clays	
Silts and clays of low plasticity (liquid limit below 50% moisture by weight)	OL
Clays of higher plasticity (liquid limit above 50% moisture by weight)	OH

Notes:
1. 'Well graded' means a wide distribution of particle sizes with no 'gap' or excess in any grade.
2. Plasticity index = liquid limit − plastic limit.
3. The determination of liquid limit and plasticity index is described in standard textbooks of soil mechanics (e. g. Jumikis 1967) and by Olson (1973).
4. A CL–ML intergrade is recognized for soils with a liquid limit below (20 + 4/3 Plasticity Index) but above 10% and Plasticity Index between 4 and 7.
Source: adapted from United States Department of Defence (1968), by permission.

Tice 1979). Some of the data required are not usually included in the reports of agriculturally oriented soil surveys, but Olson (1973) gives guidelines for interpreting the information commonly available.

Brink *et al.* (1981) discuss the use of soil survey for engineering purposes. Thornburn (1966), Allemeier (1973), and McGown and Iley (1973) give examples of the use of agricultural soil survey information in highway engineering.

Table 9.2 shows how the engineering properties and most appropriate uses of soils are related to the Unified soil groups. These have been ranked according to their suitability for each use. Estimates of other soil properties such as permeability and shrink–swell potential can also be derived from the Unified system. Where these are particularly important, however, they must be evaluated separately, for example permeability (Table 9.3) when assessing the suitability of land for septic tank drainage (p. 178). Permeability Classes or the major layers in all USDA mapping units are usually estimated by analogy with actual determinations made on a few 'bench-mark soils' (p. 38).

In civil engineering the properties of clayey subsoils need special consideration (Chen 1975), especially in vertisols or other swelling clay soils as in South Australia (Aitchison 1973). The volume changes are affected by the amount of moisture change, and hence by climate, and in dry climates shrinkage may reach a depth of 2 m, and may affect utilities and fences as well as buildings (Brink *et al.* 1981). The main soil factors are the amount of clay present and its nature. The two commonest quantitative expressions for the shrink–swell behaviour of soil are the coefficient of linear extensibility (COLE) used by soil scientists, and the potential volume change (PVC) used by engineers, as in the United States Federal Housing Administration. The USDA (1971) has devised an interpretative system using five shrink–swell classes (Table 9.4).

Cast iron and steel can corrode in contact with soil (Argent and Furness 1979), and classifications of *potential corrosivity* have been developed, despite the difficulty of weighting the different factors involved. An additive points system (Table 9.5) has been devised by the Cast Iron Pipe Research Association in the United States (Smith 1968), but it involves tedious measurements. The simpler USDA rating system (Table 9.6) is based on texture, drainage, resistivity, and total acidity. Soil maps can be interpreted to give the

TABLE 9.2
Engineering uses for various types of soils

Unified Soil Group (Table 9.1)	Permeability when compacted	Shearing strength (†)	Compressibility (†)	Workability as a constructional material	Relative desirability for various uses*				
					Rolled earth dams			Canal sections	
					Homogenous embankment	Core	Shell	Erosion resistance	Compacted earth lining
GW	Pervious	E	N	E	—	—	1	1	—
GP	Very pervious	G	N	G	—	—	2	2	—
GM	{Semi pervious to impervious	G	N	G	2	4	—	4	4
GC	Impervious	G-F	VL	G	1	1	—	3	1
SW	Pervious	E	N	E	—	—	3A	6	—
SP	Pervious	G	VL	F	—	—	4A	7A	—
SM	{Semi pervious to impervious	G	L	F	4	5	—	8A	5B
SC	Impervious	G-F	L	G	3	2	—	5	2
ML	{Semi pervious to impervious	F	M	F	6	6	—	—	6B
CL	Impervious	F	M	G-F	5	3	—	9	3
OL	{Semi pervious to impervious	P	M	F	8	8	—	—	7B
MH	{Semi pervious to impervious	F-P	H	P	9	9	—	—	—
CH	Impervious	P	H	P	7C	7	—	10	8C
OH	Impervious	P	H	P	10	10	—	—	—
Pt	—	—	—	—	—	—	—	—	—

*In ranked order: 1—best; 14—poorest. A—gravelly; B—erosion critical; C—volume change critical.
†When compacted and saturated; E—Excellent; G—good; F—Fair; P—Poor; N—Negligible; VL—Very Low; L—Low; M—Moderate; H—High.
Source: Holtz (1969), by permission.

TABLE 9.2 continued

Unified Soil Group (Table 9.1)	Permeability when compacted	Foundations		Roadways		
		Seepage important	Seepage not important	Fills frost heave possible		Surfacing
				yes	no	
GW	Pervious	—	1	1	1	3
GP	Very pervious	—	3	3	3	—
GM	Semi pervious to impervious	1	4	4	9	5
GC	Impervious	2	6	5	5	1
SW	Pervious	—	2	2	2	4
SP	Pervious	—	5	6	4	—
SM	Semi pervious to impervious	3	7	8	10	6
SC	Impervious	4	8	7	6	2
ML	Semi pervious to impervious	6	9	10	11	—
CL	Impervious	5	10	9	7	7
OL	Semi pervious to impervious	7	11	11	12	—
MH	Semi pervious to impervious	8	12	12	13	—
CH	Impervious	9C	13C	13C	8C	—
OH	Impervious	10	14	14	14	—
Pt	—	—	—	—	—	—

TABLE 9.3
USDA Permeability Classes

Permeability Class	Hydraulic conductivity in/h	cm/h	Typical texture
Very rapid	>20	>60	Coarse sand, gravel
Rapid	6.3–20	16–50	Loamy sand
Moderately rapid	2.0–6.3	5–16	Sandy loam
Moderate	0.63–2.0	1.6–5.0	Well structured silt loam, loam and occasionally clay loam
Moderately slow	0.2–0.63	0.5–1.6	Loamy, silty, or clayey soils in appropriate structural condition
Slow	0.063–0.2	0.16–0.50	Silty or clayey soils with poor structure
Very slow	<0.063	<0.16	Silty or clayey materials lacking vertically oriented voids; strongly cemented hardpans

Source: information from USDA (1971).

TABLE 9.4
USDA Shrink–swell Classes

Class	Typical textures	Coefficient of liner extensibility (COLE)	Potential volume change (PVC)
Very low	All sands and loamy sands; sandy loams, loams and silt loams with clay which does not swell much (e.g. dominated by kaolinite)	<0.01	<1.0
Low	Other sandy loams, loams and silt loams; clay loams and clays with a weakly swelling clay content	0.01–0.03	1.0–2.0
Moderate	Clay loams and clays of mixed clay mineralogy	0.03–0.06	2.0–4.0
High	Clay loams and clays with a large percentage of montmorillonite or other strongly swelling clay minerals	0.06–0.09	4.0–6.0
Very high	Very strongly swelling	>0.09	>6.0

Source: information from USDA (1971).

most suitable route for underground pipelines (e.g. Haans and Westerveld 1970).

The *corrosion of concrete* in soils is favoured by acid conditions, and the presence of salts, especially sulphates (Table 9.7). In acid conditions (lower than pH 6) special techniques such as low-water concrete mixes with supersulphated cements are recommended (Building Research Establishment 1981). The salts giving rise to the corrosion of concrete may derive from subsoil materials used in its manufacture (Fookes and Collis 1975*b*), or from the surrounding soil and groundwater. The effects include cracking caused by crystal

TABLE 9.5
CIPRA soil test evaluation for corrosivity of cast iron

Soil property	Range	Points* (to be added)
Resistivity (ohm/cm)	<700	10
	700–1000	8
	1000–1200	5
	1200–1500	2
	1500–2000	1
	>2000	0
pH	0–2	5
	2–4	3
	4–6.5	0
	6.5–7.5	0†
	7.5–8.5	0
	>8.5	3
Redox potential	>100mV	0
	50–100 mV	3.5
	0–50 mV	4
	Negative (−)	5
Sulphides/sulphates	Significant	3.5
	Trace	2
	Negative	0
Moisture	Poor drainage, continuously wet	2
	Fair drainage, generally moist	1
	Good drainge, generally dry	0

*A total of ten points indicates that the soil is certain to be corrosive to ferrous pipe.

†If sulphides or sulphates are present and low or negative redox results are obtained, 3 points should be given for this range.

Source: Smith (1968); reprinted from *Journal American Water Works Association*, Volume 60, by permission. (Copyright 1968, the American Water Works Association.)

TABLE 9.6

USDA ratings for the corrosivity of uncoated steel in soil

Corrosivity	Typical soils	Total acidity meq/100g soil	Resistivity ohm/cm	Conductivity mmho/cm
Very low	Excessively drained sands and loamy sands	<4	>10 000	<0.1
Low	Well drained sandy loams, loams, silt; imperfectly drained sands and loamy sands	<8	>5000	<0.2
Moderate	Well drained clay loams; moderately well drained loams, silt loams and silts; imperfectly drained sandy loams; very poorly drained soils (including peats and mucks)	<16	>2000	<0.4
High	Well drained and moderately well drained clays; all moderately well, imperfectly, and poorly drained soils other than clays and categories mentioned above	<16	>1000	<1.0
Very high	Imperfectly, poorly and very poorly drained clays; mucks and peats	<16	>1000	<1.0

Source: information from USDA (1971).

growth and the expansion of corroded steel reinforcing rods. Deterioration of concrete due to the specific action of sulphates is extremely common in arid areas (Fookes and Collis 1975*a*,*b*; Anon 1975: Fookes 1978), but it can occur also in sub-humid climates, such as Alberta (Lindsay, Scheeler, and Twardy 1973). Even in England certain clay subsoils (e.g. of the Evesham series) contain enough soluble sulphate for concrete to be severely attacked (Corcoran, Jarvis, Mackney, and Stevens 1977).

Interpretations of soil-maps for non-agricultural purposes

USDA interpretations allocate soil map units to broad categories either according to their *suitability* or to the degree of their *limitations* (as *slight, moderate, severe* or rarely *very severe*) for a particular purpose.

The most recent set of tables (USDA 1978*a* replacing USDA 1971) list criteria for each property in descending order of estimated

TABLE 9.7

Requirements for concrete exposed to sulphate attack in near neutral groundwater

Class	Concentrations of sulphates expressed as SO_3			Type of cement	Requirements for dense fully compacted concrete	
	Total SO_3 in soil (%)	SO_3 in 2:1 water:soil extract (g/l)	In groundwater (g/l)		Minimum cement content (kg/m³)*	Maximum free water/cement ratio*
1	Less than 0.2	Less than 1.0	Less than 0.3	Ordinary Portland Cement (OPC) Rapid Hardening Portland Cement (RHPC)—or combinations of either cement with slag‡ or pfa§ Portland Blastfurnace Cement (PBFC) OPC or RHPC or combinations of either cement with slag or pfa PFBC	Plain concrete† 250 Reinforced concrete 300 330	0.70 0.60 0.50
2	0.2 to 0.5	1.0 to 1.9	0.3 to 1.2	OPC or RHPC combined with minimum 70% or maximum 90% slag†† OPC or RHPC combined with minimum 25% or maximum 40% pfa†† Sulphate Resisting Portland cement (SRPC) OPC or RHPC combined with minimum 70% or maximum 90% slag OPC or RHPC combined with minimum 25% or maximum 40% pfa	310 290 380	0.55 0.55 0.45
3	0.5 to 1.0	1.9 to 3.1	1.2 to 2.5	SRPC	330	0.50
4	1.0 to 2.0	3.1 to 5.6	2.5 to 5.0	SRPC	370	0.45
5	Over 2	Over 5.6	Over 5.0	SRPC + protective coating	370	0.45

*Inclusive of content of pfa or slag.
†When using strip foundations and trench fill for low-rise buildings in Class 1 sulphate conditions further relaxation in the cement content and water/cement ratio is permissible.
‡Ground granulated blastfurnace slag.
§Pulverized fuel ash.
††Per cent by weight of slag/cement or pfa/cement mixture.
Source: Crown Copyright. Reproduced from Building Research Establishment Digest 250 (1981), by permission of the Controller of H.M. Stationery Office.

importance. The properties of a map unit are first tested against the criteria for land with *slight limitations*, and to be placed in that category, all the criteria have to be met. If any properties fail to meet the criteria for slight limitations the values for *those properties only* are tested against the appropriate criteria for *moderate limitations*. If any also fail these, then the map unit is rated as having *severe limitations*. For clarity the severe limitations column gives, for all properties, the criteria which would result in a grading of severe, although in practice many properties of a map unit rated severe would have values which only merited a slight or moderate rating. The main *restrictive feature* causing downrating to moderate or severe is usually reported by a key phrase. Thus, for example, the rating of a vertisol map unit for shallow excavations (Table 9.8) might be reported 'severe; cutbacks cave'. In all the examples given, it is assumed that permafrost is absent although its presence causes severe limitations (USDA 1978*a*) or makes the land unsuited for many purposes unless special techniques are used (Linell and Tedrow 1981).

The main non-agricultural purposes for which interpretations are made include:

(i)   use of soils as constructional materials (pp. 168–70);
(ii)   building site development (pp. 171–4);
(iii) waste disposal (pp. 175–81);
(iv)   recreational and amenity uses (pp. 181–6);
(v)   wildlife habitats (pp. 186–7).

Soils as constructional materials

In USDA soil survey reports each map unit is rated *good, fair,* or *poor* as a suitable source of *roadfill* and *topsoil* (USDA 1978*a*). Important factors are soil depth, texture, drainage, and slope.

Roadfill is used to construct low embankments (less than 2 m high), and the ratings reflect the ease of excavating and working the material, and its expected performance when compacted and adequately drained.

The possible stabilisation of the soil with lime or cement is not usually considered, though information on its suitability for stabilisation (Kezdi 1979) may be given in the descriptions of each soil series. USDA reports usually contain estimates of the engineering properties for each horizon, which may be substantially different. When evaluating soil material as roadfill it is assumed that there will

TABLE 9.8

Soil and site limitations for shallow excavations

Property	Degree of limitation			Restrictive feature
	Slight	Moderate	Severe	
Depth to bedrock (cm)				depth to rock
hard	>150	>100	<100	
soft	>100	>50	<50	
Depth to cemented pan (cm)				cemented pan
hard	>150	>100	>100	
soft	>100	>50	<50	
Texture				
sandy soils or silts	Any except silt*, sand†, loamy sand†, gravel	Any except sand†, loamy sand†, or gravel	Sand†, loamy sand, or gravel	cutbanks cave
clayey soils	Any except clay or silty clay	Clay or silty clay	—	too clayey
Soil order	Any except vertisols	Any except vertisols	Vertisols	cutbanks cave
Bulk density (g cm⁻³)	<1.8	>1.8	—	dense layer
Unified soil group (Table 9.1)	Any except OL, OH, Pt	Any except OL, OH, Pt	OL, OH, Pt	excess humus
Stones over 7.5 cm diameter (weight %)‡	<25	<50	>50	large stones
Ponding	None	None	Yes	ponding
Depth to high water table (cm)	>200	>75	<75	wetness
Flooding	None, rare or protected	common	—	floods
Slope (%)	<8	<15	>15	slope

*If the site is loess, rating should remain slight.
†Including fine or coarse sands or loamy sands.
‡Weighted average to 100 cm.
Source: adapted from USDA (1978*b*), by permission.

be mixing of different soil horizons. Soils rated *good* for roadfill are deep, coarse-grained, with low shrink–swell potential, low potential liability to frost action and few stones; the water-table is below 1 m and slopes are gentler than 15 per cent. Soils rated *fair* may be shallower, have a lower strength (as indicated by AASHTO classification, see p. 159) or suffer other limiting features such as moderate shrink-swell potential, wetness, or stoniness. If there is less than 1 m depth of suitable soil, the entire soil is rated *poor*.

Ratings for suitability as a source of *topsoil* (not necessarily an organic-rich A horizon) reflect the ease of excavation and spreading, the ability of the material to support plant life and the damage that could result at the area from which it is extracted. Soils rated *good* have at least 40 cm of fertile, friable, loamy, relatively stone-free material at the surface and occur on gentle slopes without a wetness limitation which would hinder excavation. Soils rated *fair* may have less favourable textures (e.g. loose sands or firm clays), be only 20–40 cm thick or contain appreciable amounts of stones or soluble salts. *Poor* soils have more pronounced adverse features, such as steep slopes, poor drainage, or shallowness, are too stony, sandy, clayey, or humose, or may be too acid or contain excess sodium.

Ratings of *probable* or *improbable* (USDA 1978*a*) express the likelihood of obtaining useful quantities of *sand* or *gravel* in or below the soil as indicated by soil texture and stoniness, particularly of the subsoil. The ratings do not necessarily imply that commercially valuable deposits underlie the map unit, and do not take into account ease of excavation or the ease of restoring the site after excavation.

USDA soil reports also rate map units according to their limitations for constructing *pond reservoirs, embankments, dikes, and levees*, and *aquifer-fed excavated ponds*. For these purposes, properties such as permeability, drainage, soil depth, soil stability, and slope have to be considered (USDA 1978*a*). Other *water management* features for which USDA assessments of soil map units can be made are for *drainage* (though not for the design of suitable artificial drainage systems, see p. 58), *irrigation* (p. 124), and the construction of *grassed waterways* and *terraces and diversions* (USDA 1978*a*).

Building site development

Tables 9.8, 9.9, and 9.10 set out the limitations that affect *shallow excavations* and the *construction of dwellings* (with or without basements), *small commercial buildings,* and *local roads and streets.* A *slight limitation* means that conditions are favourable for the specified use and the limitations, if any, are easily overcome. The effects of *moderate limitations* can be overcome or modified by special planning, design or maintenance, but *severe limitations* are so severe that the use is either unfeasible or requires a major increase in construction effort, a special design or intensive maintenance. In USDA soil survey reports it is customary to indicate both the degree and kind of limitation. Thus the limitations of a map unit for dwellings without basements might be rated 'severe; shrink– swell, low strength, wetness'.

The digging of *shallow excavations* for pipelines, sewers, telephone and power transmission lines, basements, open ditches, and cemeteries is affected by depth to and hardness of bedrock or pan, soil bulk density, stoniness and the tendency of the soil to cave in. Depth to seasonal water table, flooding and slope may obstruct the use of machinery (Table 9.8).

Dwellings and *small commercial buildings,* less than three stories high usually have foundations resting on undisturbed soils. The capacity of these to support load and resist settlement is influenced by wetness, flood risk, plasticity, texture, and shrink–swell potential. Wetness also affects the ease of excavation, together with slope, depth of bedrock and content of stones and boulders. Table 9.9 gives the USDA criteria for *buildings without basements,* and a similar ranked order of criteria, though with more restrictive limits applies to *small commercial buildings.* Depth to bedrock or cemented pan is given more significance for *dwellings with basements* but the criteria are otherwise similar to those for dwellings without basements. Other features not included in the ratings may also have to be considered, for example, the potential corrosivity of steel and concrete (p. 165) and the provision of septic tank drainage (p. 175). Specific on-site investigations (see Brink *et al.* 1981) are required to make detailed designs of foundations, and to locate individual buildings and utility lines, for which general interpretations of soil map units are not sufficiently precise.

Local roads and streets have an all-weather surface capable of carrying light to medium traffic throughout the year. They consist of

TABLE 9.9

Soil and site limitations for dwellings without basements

Property	Degree of limitation			Restrictive feature
	Slight	Moderate	Severe	
Flooding	None or protected	None or protected	Rare or common	Floods
Ponding	None	None	Yes	Ponding
Depth to high water-table (cm)	>75	>45	<45	Wetness
Shrink–swell potential (Table 9.4)	Low	Moderate	High	Shrink–swell
Unified soil group (Table 9.1)*	Any except OL, OH, Pt	Any except OL, OH, Pt	OL, OH, Pt	Low strength
Slope (%)	<8	<15	>15	Slope
Depth to bedrock (cm)				Depth to rock
hard	>100	>50	>50	
soft	>50	>50	—	
Depth to cemented pan (cm)				Cemented pan
thick	>100	>50	<50	
thin	>50	<50	—	
Stones over 7.5 cm diameter (weight %)†	<25	<50	>50	Large stones

* Of thickest layer between 25 and 100 cm.
† Weighted average to 100 cm.
Source: adapted from USDA (1978*b*), by permission.

TABLE 9.10

Soil and site limitations for local roads and streets

Property	Degree of limitation			Restrictive feature
	Slight	Moderate	Severe	
Depth to bedrock (cm)				Depth to rock
hard	>100	>50	<50	
soft	>50	<50	—	
Depth to cemented pan (cm)				Cemented pan
thick	>100	>50	<50	
thin	>50	<50	—	
Soil strength*	High	Moderate	Low	Low strength
Ponding	None	None	Yes	Ponding
Depth to high water-table (cm)	>75	>30	<30	Wetness
Slope (%)	<8	<15	>15	Slope
Flooding	None	Rare	Common	Floods
Susceptibility to frost action	Low	Moderate	High	Frost action
Shrink–swell potential (Table 9.4)	Low	Moderate	High	Shrink–swell
Stones over 7.5 cm diameter (weight %)†	<25	<50	>50	Large stones

*Of thickest horizon between 25 and 100 cm; USDA (1978b) gives more precise criteria based on AASHTO classification (p. 159).
†Weighted average to 100 cm.
Source: adapted from USDA (1978b), by permission.

a *subgrade* of the underlying soil material, a *base* of gravel, crushed rock fragments or soil stabilized with lime or cement, and a flexible or rigid *surface* of asphalt or concrete (Brink *et al.* 1981). The limitations of Table 9.10 refer mainly to the subgrade.

Other countries have less formal systems for assessing the suitability of land for building. In the Netherlands, for example, urban expansion onto naturally wet clay and peat soils with low bearing capacity has required building sites to be raised 1–2 m by the spreading of sand (Haans and Westveld 1970; Westerveld and Van den Hurk 1973). Around Utrecht, the following standards for land suitable for building were set (De Kievit 1970):

(i) Groundwater below 1 m depth either naturally or by artificial lowering.

(ii) For land not meeting requirement (i), elevation with sand was required, by 1 m for sandy and clayey soils and 1.5m for peaty soils where subsidence of the surface due to compression of the peat was expected.

Soil and groundwater maps (Fig. 9.1A and 9.1B) were used to decide which sites should be raised. Raising was considered unnecessary for all soils with water-table classes 3–6 and the majority of sand, transitional and river levee soils with water table classes 1 and 2; the standards could be met by lowering the groundwater levels. Raising with sand was required for back-swamp or peat soils in water table classes 1 and 2, or where the high groundwater levels were caused by underground seepage. With a map of depth to underlying sand (Fig. 9.1C) it was possible to estimate for each soil mapping unit the foundation depths required, and the costs of foundations and of road and sewer construction. The final map of soil suitability for building sites (Fig. 9.1D) was based on the cost per hectare of preparing land for building (at 1968–69 price levels); the costs on the least suitable land may be double those on the most suitable.

Haans and Westerveld (1970) and Westerveld and Van den Hurk (1973) give other examples of this problem-oriented approach, including studies of the siting of farm roads and buildings, pipeline construction and the planning of lakes, playing fields, buildings, and roads in areas of urban expansion. Soil survey information has proved particularly useful in countries with frequent earthquakes (e.g. Rodriguez 1962; Northey 1973; Milne and Northey 1974).

Waste disposal

Except in very cold or very arid climates, most soils provide a suitable natural environment for *biodegradation of organic materials* applied as a liquid or slurry, or for *burying solid waste* material, but intelligent site selection is vital. A reduction in the failure rate of septic tank drainage schemes has been claimed as the most important non-agricultural benefit of soil surveys (Bender 1971; Zayach 1973).

Disposal of liquid wastes A *septic tank absorption field* comprises a subsurface pipe system that distributes the effluent from a septic tank into the soil. Absorption of the effluent is influenced by the soil permeability, the depth to seasonally high water table, the depth to bedrock or pan, and the susceptibility to flooding (Bouma 1971, 1973, 1974, 1979; Beatty and Bouma 1973). Other factors affecting installation include stoniness, depth to bedrock or pan, and slope which, if excessive, may produce lateral seepage and surfacing of the effluent (Table 9.11). The depth of the distributor pipe is assumed to be 60 cm so that only soil between 60 cm and 2 m depth is considered in making the ratings.

Soil permeability is very variable over short distances, so that soil-map interpretations have often proved more useful than the limited number of on-site tests that is usual. Nevertheless, calibration of mapping units still involves permeability measurements. These are often made by a 'falling head' method, where water is poured down an auger hole and the rate of fall measured (Olson 1964; Witwer 1966), but a 'constant head' method gives less variable results (Bouma 1971). Both give much higher values than the saturated hydraulic conductivity measured in the laboratory (e.g. the Uhland core method used by the USDA) or in the field by a double-tube method (Bouma 1971).

In practice the actual rate of percolation of effluent into soil horizons may be less than 5 per cent of the legally recognized values measured by infiltrating water into auger holes because of the formation of organic slurries and slaking of soil materials caused, for example, by water softener effluents. The USDA (1971, 1978*a*) specifically warns that field percolation tests made by local health departments should be interpreted with caution, and are reliable only if the soil under test is at or near field capacity.

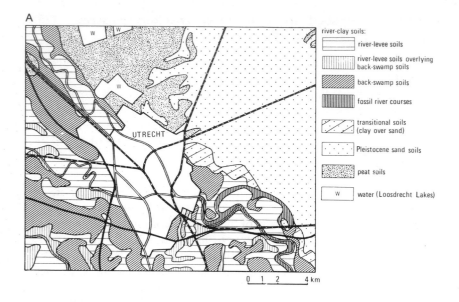

river-clay soils:

river-levee soils

river-levee soils overlying back-swamp soils

back-swamp soils

fossil river courses

transitional soils (clay over sand)

Pleistocene sand soils

peat soils

W water (Loosdrecht Lakes)

0 1 2   4 km

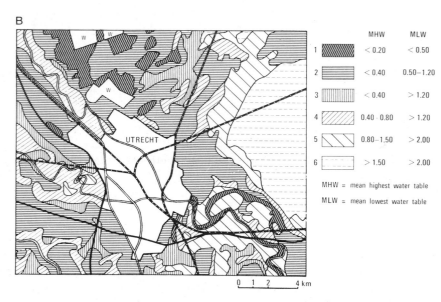

		MHW	MLW
1		< 0.20	< 0.50
2		< 0.40	0.50–1.20
3		< 0.40	> 1.20
4		0.40–0.80	> 1.20
5		0.80–1.50	> 2.00
6		> 1.50	> 2.00

MHW = mean highest water table

MLW = mean lowest water table

0 1 2   4 km

Fig. 9.1. Soil and derived maps of the 'Midden Utrecht' area, Netherlands (original map scale 1:50 000). A — Soil map; B — Map of water-table classes (water-tables in m below surface); C — Map of depth to Pleistocene sand (m below surface); D — Map of suitability for building sites, based on costs of making soils suitable for building, at 1968–69 prices (Dfl 1000 = approx. US $280). (From Westerveld and van den Hurk (1970), by permission.)

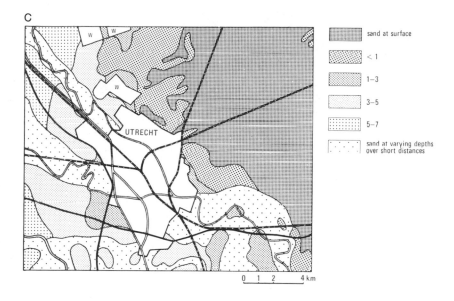

C

	sand at surface
	< 1
	1–3
	3–5
	5–7
	sand at varying depths over short distances

UTRECHT

0 1 2   4 km

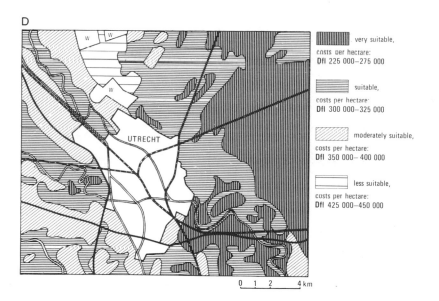

D

UTRECHT

0 1 2   4 km

very suitable,
costs per hectare:
Dfl 225 000–275 000

suitable,
costs per hectare:
Dfl 300 000–325 000

moderately suitable,
costs per hectare:
Dfl 350 000– 400 000

less suitable,
costs per hectare:
Dfl 425 000–450 000

TABLE 9.11

Soil and site limitations for septic tank absorption fields

Property	Degree of limitation			Restrictive feature
	Slight	Moderate	Severe	
Flooding	None or protected	Rare	Common	Floods
Depth to bedrock (cm)	>180	>100	<100	Depth to rock
Depth to cemented pan (cm)	>180	>100	<100	Cemented pan
Ponding	None	None	Yes	Ponding
Depth to high water-table (cm)	>180	>120	<120	Wetness
Permeability (cm/h)				
60–150 cm:	>5	>1.5	<1.5	Percs slowly
All layers below:	<15	<15	>15	Poor filter
Slope (%)	<8	<15	>15	Slope
Stones over 7.5 cm diameter (weight %)	<25	<50	>50	Large stones

*Weighted average to 100 cm.
Source: adapted from USDA (1978*b*), by permission.

An alternative to septic tank drainage is a *centralized sewage disposal* facility from which the wastewater may also be dispersed by land irrigation. American experience suggests that forested land may provide ideal surface conditions for the absorption of wastewater (Sopper 1979), for ploughed land tends to seal at the surface. Extremes of soil permeability and impermeability must be avoided, since the effluent must infiltrate and not pond or run off, yet must be retained within the biologically active layer of the soil long enough for adequate renovation. Bender (1971), Parizek (1973), Wells (1973), Hall, Wilding, and Erikson (1976), Bartelli (1978), Sopper (1979), and van Volk and Land (1979) have discussed in some detail the soil and site properties that affect effluent disposal. Suitable soils should:

(i) Be at least 1 m thick without restrictive layers such as fragipans; underlying substrata should be free of coarse water-conducting channels.

(ii) Have high surface infiltration capacity and moderate subsoil permeability.

(iii) Be well drained to moderately well drained.

(iv) Have moderate to high moisture-holding capacity.

(v) Be slightly acid to moderately alkaline in reaction (pH 6.5–8.2).

(vi) Have medium to high organic matter levels in the surface horizon.

(vii) Have slopes of 4 per cent and occur on landscape positions where the movement of surface and subsurface water in the form of run off and seeps does not present a hazard to the overall water quality in the drainage basin (Hall *et al.* 1976).

Similar considerations apply to the evaluation of land for the *disposal of animal slurries*, mainly from pigs or cattle kept without bedding (Richardson 1976; Norstadt 1979; Lea 1979). Agricultural use of the land must not be prejudiced (Pollock 1979), so that soils with an unstable structure should be avoided (Berryman 1970).

Sewage can also be treated in shallow ponds where aerobic bacteria decompose the solid and liquid wastes. These *sewage lagoons* are commonly 1–2 m deep with cut slopes or embankments of compacted, relatively impervious soil material, so that the main limitations (Table 9.12) relate to soil permeability and depth, through flood risk and slope also affect the construction and functioning of the lagoon.

TABLE 9.12
Soil and site limitations for sewage lagoons

Property	Degree of limitation			Restrictive feature
	Slight	Moderate	Severe	
Permeability of layer 30–150 cm (cm/h)	<1.5	<5	>5	Seepage
Depth to bedrock (cm)	>150	>120	<120	Depth to rock
Depth to cemented pan (cm)	>150	>120	<120	Cemented pan
Flooding*	None or protected	None or protected	Rare or common	Floods
Slope (%)	<2	<7	>7	Slope
Unified soil group (Table 9.1)	Any except OL, OH, Pt	Any except Pt	Pt	Excess humus
Ponding	None	None	Yes	Ponding
Depth to high water-table (cm)†	>150	>105	<105	Wetness
Stones over 7.5 cm diameter (weight %)‡	<20	<35	>35	Large stones

* If floodwater will not enter or damage the sewage lagoon (low velocity and depth <150 cm) disregard flooding.
† If floor of sewage lagoon has slowly permeable material at least 120 cm thick, disregard wetness.
‡ Weighted average to 50 cm.
Source: adapted from USDA (1978b), by permission.

Boersma (1979) has reviewed the particular problems of the disposal of thermal effluents on land.

Disposal of solid wastes   *Sanitary landfill* is a method of disposing of solid waste by placing refuse in successive layers either in excavated trenches (trench-type) or on the surface of the land (area-type). The waste is spread, compacted, and covered daily with thin layers of soil. The main considerations relevant to land evaluation for *trench-type landfills* (Table 9.13) refer to the risk of polluting the groundwater (special hydrologic investigations may be needed), the ability of the land to withstand heavy vehicular traffic, and the ease of excavation (Loughry 1973; Loughry and Lacour 1979). Soil from the site is used as intermediate and final cover and its texture and consistence, which determine the workability both wet and dry, are also rated.

For *area landfills* soil depth and depth to water-table can be less, and the factors such as soil texture which influence the ease of excavation in trench-landfills can be ignored. *Daily cover for landfill* is usually imported to the site. It should be easy to excavate and handle. Loamy or silty soils free of stones and boulders are best since clayey soils are difficult to handle and sandy soils may be easily eroded (USDA 1978*a*). The final soil cover should be suitable for plant growth (ideally topsoil), and the borrow area should be capable of revegetation.

Recreational and amenity uses of land

The map units in USDA soil survey reports are rated according to the degree and nature of restrictive limitations such as flooding, wetness, and slope, that can affect their suitability for a number of recreational uses such as *camp areas, picnic areas, playgrounds*, and *paths and trails* (Montgomery and Edminster 1966; USDA 1968, 1978*a*). Site-specific features such as the location, accessibility, size and shape of the area, and its scenic quality, are not considered, nor its suitability for providing ancillary facilities like septic tank drainage (p. 175). These USDA rating schemes have been adapted for British conditions by Palmer and Jarvis (1979) and George and Jarvis (1979), and Tables 9.14, 9.15, and 9.16 are examples.

Camp and picnic sites   Land evaluation for *camp and picnic sites* must consider its ability to bear heavy foot traffic. Camp sites must

TABLE 9.13
Soil and site limitations for trench-type sanitary landfills

Property	Degree of limitation			Restrictive feature
	Slight	Moderate	Severe	
Flooding	None	Rare	Common	Floods
Depth to bedrock (cm)	>180	>180	<180	Depth to rock
Depth to cemented pan (cm)				
thick	>180	>180	<180	
thin	>180	<180	—	Cemented pan
Permeability of bottom layer (cm/h)*	<5	<5	>5	Seepage
Ponding	None	None	Yes	Ponding
Depth to high water-table (cm)				
apparent	>180	>180	<180	Wetness
perched	>120	>60	<60	
Slope (%)	<8	<15	>15	Slope
Texture				
clayey soils*†‡	Any except clay loam, sandy clay, silty clay loam, silty clay or clay	Any except silty clay or clay	Any including silty clay or clay	Too clayey
sandy soils‡	Any except loamy sand, sand or gravel	Any except sand or gravel	Any including sand or gravel	Too sandy
Unified soil group (Table 9.1)†	Any except OL, OH, Pt	Any except OL, OH, Pt	OL, OH, Pt	Excess humus
Stones over 7.5 cm diameter (weight %)§	<20	<35	>35	Large stones
Sodium adsorption ratio (Great Group)	<12 (any)	<12 (any)	>12 (natric, sodic)	Excess sodium
pH	>3.6	>3.6	<3.6	Too acid
Salinity (mmho/cm)	<16	<16	>16	Excess salt

*Disregard in all Aridisols except Salorthids and Aquic intergrades and all Torric great groups of Entisols except Aquic.
†If kaolinitic, rate one class better if experience confirms.
‡Thickest layer between 25 and 150 cm.
§Weighted average to 100 cm.
Source: adapted from USDA (1978b), by permission.

TABLE 9.14

Suitability of land for camp and caravan sites in Great Britain

Property	Well suited	Moderately well suited	Poorly suited	Unsuited*
Soil wetness class (Table 3.7)	I and II; III in drier areas†	I–III; IV in drier areas†	I–IV	V or VI
Air capacity (%)	>20 to 50 cm; >15 to 80 cm;	>10 to 50 cm; >5 below 50 cm	>5; <5	>5; <5
Hydraulic conductivity K (m/day) K(m/day)	>1	>0.1	>0.01	<0.01
Dryness subclass (Table 3.8)	a or b	a–c	a–d	—
Retained water capacity in topsoil (%)	<30	<45	<50	>50
Topsoil texture	Sandy loam; loam; silt loam; loamy sand	As well suited plus clay loam; sandy clay loam; silty clay loam; compact sand	As moderately well suited plus sandy clay; silty clay and clay (each with <45% clay); loose sand; all humose soils	Clays with <45% clay; peat
Volume of stones (%)	<16	<36	<70	>70
Rock outcrops (%)	<2	<10	<50	>50
Flood hazard	None	None	Not more than twice during season of use	More often than twice during season of use
Slope (%)	<5(3°)	<12(7°)	<27(15°)	>27(15°)
Exposure	Very sheltered	Moderately or very sheltered	Moderately exposed or more sheltered	Exposed or very exposed

*Land with any property whose value exceeds the limits of the poorly suited class should be rated 'unsuited'.
†With less than 700 mm mean annual rainfall.
Source: adapted from George and Jarvis (1979), by permission.

TABLE 9.15

Suitability of land for golf course fairways in Great Britain

Property	Well suited	Moderately well suited	Poorly suited	Unsuited*
Soil wetness class (Table 3.7)	I and II	I–III; IV in drier areas†	I–IV	V and VI
Air capacity (%)	>20 to 80 cm; depth	>10 to 50 cm; >5 below 50 cm	>10 in topsoil can be 10 below	<10 in topsoil
Hydraulic conductivity K(m/day)	>1	>0.1	>0.01	<0.01
Dryness subclass (Table 3.8)	a or b	a–c	a–d	—
Retained water capacity in topsoil (%)	<30	<45	<55	>55
Topsoil texture	Sandy loam; fine and medium loamy sand and sand; silty clay loam	As well suited plus coarse loamy sand and sand; sandy clay loam; clay loam; silty clay loam; silt loam	As moderately well suited plus sandy clay; silty clay and clay each with <45% clay ; All humose soils	Sandy clay, silty clay and clay each with >45% clay peat
Volume of stones (%)	<6	<16	<36	>36
Rock outcrops (%)	None	<2	<10	>10
Flood hazard	None	Not more than twice per year; <3 days on each occasion	Not more than five times per year; <3 days each occasion	More than five times per year
Slope (%)	Mostly 0–5 (0–3°)	Mostly 0–12 (0–7°)	Mostly 0–19 (0–11°)	Mostly >19 (>11°)

*Land with any property whose value exceeds the limits of the poorly suited class should be rated unsuited.
†With less than 700 mm mean annual rainfall.
Source: adapted from Palmer and Jarvis (1979), by permission.

TABLE 9.16
Suitability of land for winter playing fields in Great Britain

Property	Well suited	Moderately well suited	Poorly suited	Unsuited*
Soil wetness class (Table 3.7)	I	I–III; IV in drier areas†	I–IV	V and VI
Air capacity (%)	>20 to 80 cm; depth	>10 to 50 cm; >5 below 50 cm	>10 in topsoil can be <10 below	<10 in topsoil
Hydraulic conductivity K(m/day)	>1	>0.1	>0.01	<0.01
Depth to rock (cm)‡	>100	>75	>50	<50
Retained water capacity in topsoil (%)	<30	<45	<55	>55
Topsoil texture	Sandy loam; with >70% sand); fine and medium loamy sand and sand	As well suited plus coarse loamy sand and sand: sandy loam (with <70% sand); loam	As moderately well suited plus silty clay loam; sandy clay silty clay and clay (each with <45% clay); all humose soils	Clays with >45% peat
Volume of stones (%)	<1	<6	<16	>16
Rock outcrops (%)	None	<2	<10	>10
Flood hazard	None	Once in 2 years or less; 3 days on each occasion	Not more than twice per year; 3 days on each occasion	More than twice per year
Slope (%)	0–1.8 (0–1°)	0–2.5 (0–1.5°)	0–5.2 (0–3°)	>5.2 (>3°)

*Land with any property whose value exceeds the limits of the poorly suited class should be rated unsuited.
†Wetness Class IV soils in areas with less than 700 mm mean annual rainfall, if subsoil permeability is moderate or rapid.
‡Depending on rock type; soft rocks at depth impose less limitations.
Source: adapted from Palmer and Jarvis (1979). by permission.

also cope with vehicular traffic and may require site preparations such as levelling for tent and parking areas, and stabilizing roads and intensively used areas. The best soils have good drainage, are stone-free, absorb rainfall readily but remain firm, and are not dusty when dry (USDA 1978a; George and Jarvis 1979). For camp sites or parking areas on picnic sites the land should not have steep slopes nor be excessively stony (Table 9.14). The actual siting of camp and picnic sites also takes aesthetic values and broad recreational possibilities into account. Thus the approach of the Canada Land Inventory (p. 188) may be more realistic.

Parks and extensive play areas   Foot traffic is lighter and better distributed, but there is still a risk of soil erosion. Where it is concentrated, as on golf fairways and informal paths, a strong turf cover throughout the year is desirable, if possible without irrigation. Thus the most suitable land (see Table 9.15) should have soils which are not loose or droughty, nor ill-drained, for wet surfaces are very easily damaged and fine-textured topsoil adheres to footwear. Mowing and other maintenance operations will generally be mechanized, so rocky or very stony soils should not be grassed, but should be used for decorative planting.

Intensive play areas   The requirements for *intensive play areas* such as athletic fields, football pitches, tennis courts, and cricket pitches are more rigorous than for extensive play areas (Beard 1973; USDA 1978a; Escritt 1979; Palmer and Jarvis 1979). A level surface is essential, and may have to be produced artificially. Desirable soil attributes (see Table 9.16) are:

(i) Minimum tendency to compaction. The ideal soil is an artificial mixture of 85–90 per cent medium sand (0.1–0.5 mm) and 10–15 per cent clay with an adequate humus content.

(ii) Good infiltration and percolation. A high water-table can be advantageous so long as it can be controlled and is never within 30 cm of the surface.

(iii) Freedom from toxic chemicals.

(iv) Adequate moisture and nutrient retention.

Wildlife habitats

The USDA (1972) has prepared a general system for interpreting soil maps in terms of *wildlife habitat*. The procedure begins by rating soil mapping units on a four point scale: 1 — good, 2 — fair, 3 — poor, and 4 — very poor, for each of the eight habitat elements: A — grain and seed crops, B — domestic grasses and legumes, C — wild herbaceous plants, D — hardwood trees, E — coniferous plants, F — shrubs, G — wetland plants, and H — shallow water areas. Then a score is produced for each of the four major kinds of habitat: openland, woodland, wetland, and rangeland, by adding the numerical ratings for the relevant habitat elements, applying the following weighting:

Openland = $(3 \times A) + (3 \times B) + (3 \times C) + (D, E, \text{or} F)$
Woodland = $(2 \times B) + (2 \times C) + (6 \times D)$
Wetland   = $(5 \times G) + (5 \times H)$
Rangeland = $(5 \times C) + (5 \times F)$

Thus the openland score for a map unit which was rated poor (3) for grain and seed crops, good (1) for domestic grasses and legumes, good (1) for wild herbaceous plants, and very poor (4) for hardwood trees, coniferous plants, shrubs, wetland plants, and shallow water areas would be $(3 \times 3) + (3 \times 1) + (3 \times 1) + (4) = 19$. The scores can be converted to an objective rating for each habitat element according to: Good 10–14, Fair 15–24, Poor 25–34, Very Poor 35.

Thompson (1979) has reviewed the value of soil surveys to nature conservation in England and Wales, and presents tables showing the soil conditions associated with the natural occurrence of native trees and shrubs. For habitat surveys in remote areas a soil survey may be disproportionately costly and, for some purposes, an inappropriate starting point.

Natural resource surveys

Some forms of land evaluation for non-agricultural purposes are not significantly linked to soil maps.

Mineral potentiality

Maps of mineral resources can be compiled from prospection records and geological maps and reports. These are specially important where the minerals are likely to be won by open-pit mining. The following categories are used in Malaya (Panton 1970):

(i) Probable mining land as deduced from prospecting results and geological evidence.

(ii) Area under mining lease or certificate, or area in which active mining is taking place.

(iii) Possible mining land as deduced from geological evidence.

(iv) Area which on geological evidence might contain mineral deposits.

(v) Area for which no geological or other information is available.

(vi) Non-mining land.

Capability for informal recreation

The Canada Land Inventory (CLI) includes a scheme for the assessment of Capability for Recreation (Cressman and Hoffman 1968; CLI 1969). The seven Classes are based on the 'sustainable quantity of recreation per unit area' (Sinclair, Ambrose, Baker, McNeice, and Van der Meer 1973). Class 1 has the highest capability for outdoor recreation, Class 7 the lowest (cf. pp. 75 and 147). Twenty-five Subclasses indicate the dominant kind of recreational use:

A — Land providing access to water affording opportunity for angling or viewing sport fish.

B — Shoreland capable of supporting family beach activities. In high-class units, this will include family bathing. In Classes 4 and 5, the activities may be confined to dry land due to cold water or other limitations.

C — Land fronting on and providing direct access to waterways with significant capability for canoe tripping.

D — Shoreland with deeper inshore water suitable for swimming or boat mooring or launching.

E — Land with vegetation possessing recreational value.

F — Waterfall or rapids.

G — Significant glacier view or experience.

H — Historic or pre-historic site.

J — Area offering particular opportunities for gathering and collecting items of popular interest.

K — Shoreland or upland suited to organized camping, usually associated with other features.

L — Interesting landform features other than rock formations.

M — Frequent small water bodies or continuous streams occurring in upland areas.

N — Land (usually shoreland) suited to family (or other recreational) lodging use.

O — Land-affording opportunity for viewing wildlife.

P — Areas exhibiting cultural landscape patterns of agricultural, industrial, or social interest.

Q — Areas exhibiting variety, in topography or land and water relationships, which enhances opportunities for general outdoor recreation such as hiking and nature study or for aesthetic appreciation of the area.

R — Interesting rock formations.

S — A combination of slopes, snow conditions, and climate providing downhill skiing opportunities.

T — Thermal springs.

U — Shoreland fronting water accommodating yachting or deep-water boat tripping.

V — A vantage point or area which offers a superior view relative to the Class of the unit(s) which contain it, or a corridor or other area which provides frequent viewing opportunities.

W — Land affording opportunity for viewing wetland wildlife.

X — Miscellaneous features with recreational capability.

Y — Shoreland providing access to water suitable for popular forms of family boating.

Z — Areas exhibiting major, permanent, non-urban, man-made structures of recreational interest.

A typical map symbol has the format

$$
\begin{array}{ccc}
6 & 3 & 1 \\
5\,Q & 3\,N & 5\,V \\
J & Y & R
\end{array}
$$

This denotes a complex unit containing Class 5 upland with a diversity of natural landscape (Q) and possibilities for gathering and collecting (J); Class 3 shorelands with capability for lodging (N) and family boating (Y), and Class 5 upland with viewing possibilities (V) and interesting rock formations (R); in the proportions 6:3:1.

Carlisle and Calhoun (1979) and Leeson (1979) have discussed the evaluation of shorelands, floodplains, wetlands, coastal zones, and other wildland environments for a variety of land uses, including low-intensity recreational use, in the United States.

Rating land for visual qualities

If attractive landscape would be drastically altered by a proposed development a need may arise for grading 'attractiveness', and this was first attempted by Fines (1968). 'Beauty is in the eye of the beholder', so the procedure outlined by Robinson (1976) requires that at least four observers record their ratings without mutual discussion, a mean being taken subsequently. The assessment is usually made of squares of 0.5 to 5.0 km side, from viewpoints giving a comprehensive view of each square. The whole survey should be completed within one short period of good weather. A scale is recommended ranging from 100 as the best imaginable landscape to 0 as the worst.

Wildlife resource surveys

A specific analysis of the landscape using air-photographs is preferable to soil survey interpretation in evaluating conditions for most kinds of wildlife. In remote areas satellite imagery may be used, e.g. the study of caribou habitat in northern Canada by Thompson, Klassen, and Cihaler (1980).

The Canada Land Inventory Land Capability Classification for Wildlife (Perret 1969) has seven Classes which express the capacity of the land to produce and support ungulates or waterfowl. For all Classes except Class 1 the factors which limit the production of wildlife are shown as Subclasses and in the classification for ungulates, the major (indicator) species in the area is also given.Separate maps of land capability for ungulates and for waterfowl are published. A typical map symbol on an ungulate capability map is:

$$4 \, \underset{T}{\overset{7}{Q}} \, 3W \, \overset{3}{\underset{Q}{}}$$
$$D \quad EM$$

This represents an area of which 70 per cent (7) is class 4 for deer (D) with limitations due to snow depth (Q)and topography (T) and 30 per cent is Class 3 wintering area (W) for elk (E) and moose (M) with slight limitations due to snow depth.

The Capability Classification of Fresh Waters for Sport Fish (CLI 1965*a*) has only four numbered Classes (no, slight, moderate, and severe limitations to the production of sport fish) and seven Subclasses, denoting by letter suffix the nature of the main limitation.

10. Land evaluation and land-use planning and resource inventories

Land-use planning

The two principles which should dictate rational land use planning decisions are:

(i) Land should be used for the purposes for which it is well suited.

(ii) Land of high value for an existing land use should be protected against changes which are difficult to reverse.

These two principles are often in conflict. For example, land well suited to agriculture may also be well suited to urban development. Nevertheless, land evaluation is sometimes used solely for the negative purpose of preventing non-agricultural development on land of high agricultural quality, as in the Agricultural Land Classification of England and Wales (p. 76) or the recognition of Prime and Unique Farmland (p. 92) in the United States (e.g. Lex and Lex 1975; Reganold and Singer 1979). In some circumstances it may be necessary to zone urban expansion on to the better agricultural land, e.g. in the area round Townsville, Queensland (Murtha and Reid 1976), but it is often possible to identify areas of low agricultural value that are suited to urban expansion, e.g. around Christchurch, New Zealand (Raeside and Rennie 1974).

If the two basic principles are to be given practical expression, planning authorities need to have access to easily understood land evaluations, and sometimes a local planning authority will actually commission and pay for the soil survey on which the evaluation is to be based. Soil surveyors and land evaluators should ensure that their information is presented as simply as possible (e.g. Bidwell and Bohannon 1962; Smyth 1970a; Olsen 1977; Niemann and McCarthy 1979), and should avoid excessively large numbers of map separations. For example, Anderson, Kennedy, and Lewis (1978) have shown how the 128 soil mapping units of an area in Minnesota can be reduced to 18 'Landscape Planning Units' with little loss of important information.

The use of land evaluations by planners has become widespread in the United States, e.g. in Wisconsin (Bauer 1973; Zaporozec and

Hole 1976), New York State (USDA 1969), Minnesota (Anderson *et al.* 1978), California (Wohletz 1968), Illinois (Bartelli 1962), Connecticut (Hill and Thomas 1972), Maryland (Shields 1976), Virginia (Robinson, Porter, and Obenshain 1955; Pettry and Coleman 1973), Massachusetts (Zayach 1973), and Alabama (Culver and Clonts 1977). Bartelli *et al.* (1966), Soil Conservation Society of America (1977*b*), and Beatty, Petersen, and Swindale (1979) give further examples from the United States, of urban and other non-agricultural developments, such as roads, airports, utility corridors, and waste disposal areas, which were sited appropriately after a land evaluation exercise.

The various appraisals of the Canada Land Inventory (p. 196) were designed to be the basis for rational land-use planning (McCormack 1971; Coombs and Thie 1979). The Soil Capability Classification for Agriculture (p. 75) is particularly useful, since much of the land likely to be urbanized is now in agriculture, but it does not indicate the suitability of the land for building. Dumanski, Marshall, and Huffman (1979) described a procedure for deriving an urban suitability map for the Ottawa urban fringe which circumvented the agricultural bias of the CLI.

There is a similar conflict between urban and agricultural land uses in New Zealand (e.g. Raeside 1962; Smith and Forbes 1974), and in some particularly sensitive areas soil survey interpretations are made not only of the agricultural quality of the land but also its suitability for urban development (e.g. Cowie 1974).

In Britain soil survey information has been used, on an *ad hoc* basis, to assist land-use planning decisions of many kinds, e.g. the siting of quarries for glass-making sand near St. Helens, Lancashire (Hartnup and Jarvis 1979) or the integration of agriculture east of Doncaster, Yorkshire, with areas where future gravel working will create large water bodies (Casson, Hartnup, and Jarvis 1976). The Castleford area of West Yorkshire has been the location for a more comprehensive study of soil survey interpretation for planning purposes (Hartnup and Jarvis 1973; Casson *et al.* 1973), with interpretations not only of soil capability for agriculture but also for many of the recreational and urban uses discussed in Chapter 9.

The greatest use of soil survey information for land-use planning is in countries with high population densities, and in the Netherlands the staff of the Soil Survey Institute act not only as consultants but are directly involved in the planning process. Examples of the

Dutch approach to using soil survey information in this way are given by Edelman (1963), Haans and Westerveld (1970), Westerveld and Van den Hurk (1973), and Davidson (1980).

Even where urban pressures are not extreme, soil survey information can influence land-use decisions and the economic development. In Ireland, for example, Walsh and Gardiner (1976) have discussed how land appraisal has assisted in management decisions in commercial farming, regional planning for special purposes, the implementation of EEC directives, and national development planning. In developing countries land evaluation exercises are often related to areas assigned to particular projects, a subject discussed by Young (1968, 1973a, 1976), in many FAO publications, and reports of such bodies as the British Overseas Development Agency (Robertson 1970; Stobbs 1970; Baulkwill 1972; Murdoch *et al.* 1976)

Resource inventories

Introduction

Previous chapters have shown that many factors of the environment are important for development, including relief, surface drainage, climate, soil, geological resources (such as industrial minerals, construction materials and underground water) and biological resources (such as the natural or semi-natural flora and fauna, and the use of land for agriculture, grazing and forestry, and of waters for fishery). Liability to natural hazards, such as floods, volcanic eruptions and hurricanes is significant, as is the incidence of pests and diseases affecting man or plants or animals. There are considerable benefits from making an assessment of all these factors at the same time. Field-support staff, vehicles, and facilities can be shared, as can base maps, air-photographs and cartographic services. Furthermore, one type of specialist can often help another, and all can share in interpretative exercises, such as land capability assessment. In a technically advanced country much information about resources has already been obtained, but has not been brought together. Three examples of general resource inventories are described below.

The Malaysian Land Evaluation Programme

Among developing countries Malaysia has the advantages of moderate size, comparative prosperity, a network of good roads, and accurate 1:63 360 topographical maps. A schematic reconnaissance soil map of mainland Malaya was completed by 1968 (Law and Selvadurai 1968); one for Sabah was published in 1975 (Acres, Bower, Burrough, Folland, Kalsi, Thomas, and Wright 1975). Considerable information was availabale for the remaining area, Sarawak. A small-scale geological map was available for the whole of mainland Malaya, and key areas have been mapped at 1:63 360. So the Land Evaluation Programme initiated in 1964 did not require the production of topographical, geological and soil maps.

Panton (1970) has described the Land Evaluation Programme in mainland Malaya. A complete (black and white) air-photograph cover at 1:25 000 was produced. Using this where appropriate, seven maps were prepared:

(i) Present land use, in 32 categories, with a minimum separation of 1.2 ha. The legend is based on that recommended by the Commission on World Land Use Survey of the International Geographical Union.

(ii) Land alienation and gazettement. All land belonged originally to the States, and its passage into private ownership is called alienation. Alienated land was divided into agricultural, mining, and urban areas. Gazettement involves allocation to a use without passing out of state ownership, e.g. to forest reserves, and was shown on the map by six use categories. The extent of mineral prospection licences on state land was also shown.

(iii) Mineral potentiality. Land was assessed in six categories according to the likelihood that it contained workable minerals from prospection records, or, in default, by the interpretation of geological maps (see p. 187).

(iv) Soil suitability for agriculture. From soil survey records and pedological and agronomic experience the degree of limitation to agricultural development was assessed in five Classes.

(v) Forest productivity. Maps of forest type were compiled from air-photographs with limited ground checking. Productivity was grouped in five Classes. Class 1 included all productive plantations and actively managed forests. Classes 2 to 5 categorized unmanaged forests by the volume of standing timber present. Each Class was divided into two subclasses: Classes 1 and 5 into 'mangrove' and 'non-mangrove' and 2, 3, and 4 according to the proportion of 'commercial' species.

(vi) Water resources. This map shows catchment boundaries with the catchments labelled as utilized, proposed for utilization, or unused and also existing and proposed irrigation schemes and isohyets.

(vii) Land capability. This map is compiled from the mineral potentiality, soil suitability, and forest productivity maps. It is assumed that mineral working will take priority over agricultural development, and that agriculture will be preferred to forestry. Class 1 land possesses a high potential for possible mineral development. Class 2 land possesses a high potential for possible agricultural development with a wide range of crops. Class 3 land possesses a moderate potential for agricultural development because of a limitation in the range of crops. Class 4 land possesses a high potential for possible productive forest development. Class 5 land possesses little or no mineral, agricultural, or productive forest development potential, but may be suitable for possible alternative purposes, such as protective forest reserves, water catchment areas, game reserves, recreation areas, etc.

The Programme located 2 750 000 ha of unused land suitable for agriculture; it also showed that much of the land legally alienated for agricultural use was unsuitable or only marginally suitable; indeed no attempt was being made to use 850 000 hectares of it. Of 3 240 000 ha of forest reserve 1 130 000 ha was suitable for agriculture. However, 4 200 000 ha of productive forest are unsuited to agriculture, and much of this lacks formal protection, as does most of the 2 200 000 ha of unproductive forest, much of which ought to be protected to avoid soil erosion and silting of rivers and to conserve interesting flora and fauna. Fifteen regions, typically of about 200 000 ha, were located in mainland Malaya where potential agricultural land is unused, and there are others in Sabah and Sarawak. The planning of new roads, settlements, and processing facilities, e.g. for palm oil, has followed.

The Bahrain Surface Materials Resources Survey

The State of Bahrain relies on oil for 72 per cent of its present annual income, but oil reserves are almost exhausted. The land area is small (663 km²), so it is urgent to assess the resources and hazards relevant to the development of commerce, industry, tourism, and horticulture.

The Bahrain Surface Materials Resources Survey was a multi-disciplinary study resting on a strong base of geomorphological and soil survey (Brunsden, Doornkamp, and Jones 1979; Doornkamp, Brunsden, and Jones 1980). A team of 18 produced maps of:

(i) solid geology and structure;

(ii) geomorphology and surface materials, particularly those of use in civil engineering;

(iii) soils (Bridges and Burnham 1980);

(iv) land capability for irrigated agriculture;

(v) hazards to construction (especially saline groundwater).

The team worked simultaneously, not only sharing transport, equipment, maps, and air-photographs, but constantly interchanging information. One kind of survey was often used as input for another. For example, the soil map of the southern desert depended to a large extent on the geomorphological survey. Conversely, soil boundaries in the northern coastal plain provided geomorphological information. Data on the salinity of groundwater produced during the soil survey assisted the assessments of land capability for agriculture, and the hazards of construction (p. 165). Brunsden *et al.* (1979) present derived maps, e.g. groundwater depths, groundwater salinity, salt hazard for construction (on a 'points' system with 100 as the maximum), aggregate resources, archaeological features, and areas of landscape value. Finally a map and recommendations set out the regional planning implications.

The Canada Land Inventory

A multipurpose land capability survey of Canada was proposed by Hills (1961), and initiated in 1963 under the Agricultural Rehabilitation and Development Act (1961). As a result all the land which is conveniently accessible from the settled regions has been systematically assessed according to its physical capability. In general the data has been compiled and prepared for computer input on maps at a scale of 1:50 000, while published maps are at 1:250 000 (or 1:126 720) (Canada Land Inventory 1965/1970; Coombs and Thie 1979).

Most of the components of the Canada Land Inventory have been mentioned elsewhere in this volume. They comprise:

(i) Soil Capability for Agriculture (p. 75).

(ii) Land Capability for Forestry (p. 147).

(iii) Land Suitability for Recreation (p. 188).

(iv) Land Capability for Wildlife (specifically waterfowl and ungulates (p. 190).

(v) Capability of freshwater bodies for Sport Fish (p. 190).

(vi) Present land use. There are no published maps but the data is placed in computer storage.

(vii) Socio-economic Land Classification. (This is mainly based on census data, and again has been prepared for computer input).

(viii) Agroclimatic Classification. (This delineates climatic zones significant for crop production).

The Canada Land Inventory comprises a total of 20 000 map sheets, together with census data. Typical maps carry 50–250 m of category boundaries. Tomlinson (1970) rightly observes that this 'presents a formidable task of reading and analysis for even the most simple understanding of the material that is stored', so the Canada Geographic Information System (Tomlinson 1967), is based on a large computer. A simpler system uses tracing paper overlays (Sinclair et al. 1973).

The use of computers in resource data handling

Storing and presenting data

The simplest method of storing, manipulating, and presenting spatially organized data with a computer is to allocate all the data to the appropriate cells of a predetermined grid (e.g. Meyers, Kennedy, and Sampson 1979). All the cells need not contain entries (Wehda, Dalsted, and Worcester 1980). The SYMAP V package, developed by Harvard University (1968), has often been used to process the data (e.g. Tomlinson 1970). Alternatively GRID CAMAP may be used (Finch and Hotson 1974), as in preparing the Agricultural Atlas of England and Wales (Coppock 1976).

If the cells have suitable properties (not always square), maps can be produced by a standard line printer (US Bureau of Census 1969; Hotson 1976). Any one convenient symbol can be used for binary data, and can also be recorded on feature-punched cards which enable interpretations by simple combination without using a computer (Rudeforth and Webster 1973). A variable ordered into grades or bands can be shown by a series of tones of increasing density, of which the darker are achieved by overprinting more than one character. Six categories is probably the maximum consistent with clarity.

Computer processing of data for land evaluation

The entire operation of assigning land at a point or in some small area to a suitability or capability group or rating can be committed to a computer, if the procedure can be completely specified in an objective manner and suitable data supplied. Rudeforth (1975) for example, has presented a computer program to assign sites to categories of the Land Use Capability Classification (p. 76) and determine the suitability of sites for growing barley and early potatoes in Pembrokeshire, Wales. Nichols and Bartelli (1974) and Nichols (1975) have suggested a very simple system for generating a range of suitability maps from a soil map by superimposing a grid on the soil map, assigning each square to the dominant soil within it, and then using a computer to assign each square to the suitability class of the soil as printed in the county soil report. Jansen and Fenton (1978) have described a Map Information Processing System which can deduce the information needed by tax assessors in the United States from soil survey data, and can also provide interpretative maps for soil properties or crop productivity. Kloosterman and Lavkulich (1973) have developed a more unusual model, assigning monetary penalties to limiting factors, by which the computer can be used to rate soils for agricultural and engineering land uses.

Such procedures assume that a predetermined 'model' exists with a set of rules to relate soil classes or soil properties to land suitability or capability. The computer will use this to interpret any data set which may be offered, even when the answer seems unreasonable. The evaluator will generally wish to be free to adjust the rules to correct anomalies so that analogous cases yield a reasonable answer in future (cf. p. 115). The computer may help him apply multivariate methods to increase his understanding of the system and so improve his model (Chapters 2 and 8, and more fully in Webster 1977, 1978). There are computer procedures in which the model is constantly reviewed (e.g. Bie, Lieftinck, van Lynden, and Waenink 1976; Bie and Schelling 1978).

Advantages and disadvantages of computer data systems

A major advantage of computer systems is that much more data can be handled and can be stored compactly. Also, data can easily be transformed, even if the transformations are very complicated. Output is flexible, and may be statistical or in the form of maps of widely varying kind and scale. New material can be added, and new ideas tested very rapidly. There are some disadvantages, notably that computer data systems are costly, and subject to rapid technical change (Moore 1978).

Comprehensive land data banks

Pearcey and Chapman (1968) have set out the technical requirments of a computer-based national data store for information relevant to land evaluation. Examples are the Canada Geographic Information system which stores the Canada Land Inventory (p. 196), together with census data (Tomlinson 1968; Moore 1978), and the Working Community Information System for the Earth Sciences (WIA) which has been developed in the Netherlands (Bie and Schelling 1978), and incorporates not only SYMAP but WIACLAS, a learning system based on Bayesian statistics for generating and reviewing both land suitability classifications and site assessments.

Most information systems actually in use either cover a restricted area, e.g. New York State (Wiebe 1971, Moore 1978,), often one with changing land use (Lynch and Emery 1977), or a limited topic, e.g. the Ecomap of Britain sponsored by the Institute of Terrestrial Ecology, or the National Soil Fertility Data Bank for Australia (Moore and Bie 1977). Garbouchev and Sadovski (1978) give examples of soil information systems in European countries. Powerful systems have been developed in Canada and the United States for storing and processing information specifically concerning soils (e.g. McCormack, Moore, and Dumanski (1978). In Canada CanSIS has been designed to aid effective land evaluation and planning, but links with other relevant data banks (e.g. Canada Geographic Information System) are still incomplete. The United States Soil Conservation Service established the Resource and Management Information System (RAMIS) in 1976. Separate subsystems for storing and processing data concerning soil properties, soil classification, soil performance, and soil location are being developed, but are not yet fully interlinked. Soil performance subsystems, of which those for tree growth and range production are operational, are of greatest interest to land evaluators. For other uses only existing interpretations for the 50 000 actively used soil phases are on file, and the task of making revised interpretations from records of performance is far from complete.

The future of land evaluation lies in storing and processing data with computers, as ably foreshadowed by Meyers *et al.* (1979) who also warn of the magnitude of the task. France and Briggs (1980) note 'a serious lack of information in most developed countries on even the most fundamental environmental conditions', and that there was no consistent standard even in EEC countries. Moore (1978) points to technical drawbacks to existing information systems, and concludes: 'The usefulness of such systems is limited if producers and users of information and computer scientists do not work together throughout the development of the systems and in their subsequent operation.' Thus, although the computer will surely become the usual mechanism for applying land evaluation systems in the future, the land evaluator must continue to plan the collection of data, design new evaluation systems and consider how the output can be best suited to the user and his needs.

References

A list of abbreviations used is given on page 230.

Aandahl, A. R. (1953). Using soil survey information in land valuation for tax assessment. *Proc. Soil Sci. Soc. Am.* **17**, 293–4.

—— (1958). Soil survey interpretation — theory and purposes. *Proc. Soil Sci. Soc. Am.* **22**, 152–4.

AASHO (1961). *Standard specifications for highway materials and methods of sampling and testing*, 8th edn. American Association of State Highway Officials, Washington, DC.

Ableiter, J. K. (1937) Productivity ratings in the soil survey report. *Proc. Soil Sci. Soc. Am.* **2**, 415–22.

—— (1940). Productivity ratings of soil types. *Bull. Mo. agric. Exp. Stn* No. 421, 13–24.

—— and Barnes, C. P. (1950). Soil productivity ratings. *Trans. 4th Int. Cong. Soil Sci.* Vol. 1, pp. 360–4.

Acres, B. D., Bower, R. P., Burrough, P. A., Folland, C. J., Kalsi, M. S., Thomas, P., and Wright, P. S. (1975). The soils of Sabah, 5 Vols. *Land Resource Study* No. 20. Land Resources Division, ODM, London.

Adu, S. V. (1968). Studies of land capability for Scots pine in Strathdon. Ph.D. Thesis, University of Aberdeen.

Aitchison, G. D. (1973). Twenty-five years of application of soil survey principles in the practice of foundation engineering. *Geoderma* **10**, 99–112.

Alberta Institute of Pedology (1974). *A comparison of the Canada Land Inventory (CLI) for agricultural land evaluation and the Storie Rating System.* Alberta Institute of Pedology, University of Alberta, Edmonton.

Allan, J. A. (1980). Remote sensing in land and land use studies. *Geography* **65**, 35–43.

Allemeier, K. A. (1973). Application of pedological soil surveys to highway engineering in Michigan. *Geoderma* **10**, 87–98.

Allgood, F. P. and Gray, F. (1978). Utilization of soil characteristics in computing productivity ratings of Oklahoma soils. *Soil Sci.* **125**, 359–66.

Ama, J. T. (1970). Report on the detailed soil survey of the proposed oil palm research centre, Kusi. *Tech. Rep. Soil Res. Inst. Ghana Acad. Sci.* No. 82.

Anderson, J. L., Kennedy, P. N., and Lewis, R. A. (1978). Landscape planning units: incorporating soils data into regional and local land use planning. *J. Soil Wat. Conserv.* **33**, 193–5.

Anderson, M. L. (1961). *The selection of tree species. An ecological basis of site classification for conditions found in Britain and Ireland*, 2nd edn. Oliver and Boyd, Edinburgh.

Andrawis, A. S., Moore, D. G., and Doka, A. (1980). *Evaluation of Landsat data for disaster assessment and planning, Sudan Flood 1978.* Remote-sensing Inst., S. Dakota State University, Brookings, SD.

Andriesse, J. P. (1966). The classification and evaluation of land in Sarawak. *Proc. 2nd Malays. Soil Conf.*, Kuala Lumpur, pp. 135–51.

Anon (1975). Sun and salt — the scourge of concrete in the Gulf. *New civ. Engr* 19th June, 32–3.

Arens, P. L. (1978). Edaphic criteria in land evaluation. *Wld Soil Resour. Rep.* **49**, 24–31.

Argent, C. J. and Furness, R. R. (1979). Corrosion in soils. *Soil Surv. Tech. Monogr.* No. 13, 135–47.

Arlidge, E. Z. and Wong, Y. C. Y. (1975). Notes on the land resources and agricultural suitability map of Mauritius, 1 : 50,000. *Occ. Pap. Maurit. Sug. Ind. Res. Inst.* No. 29.

Austin, M. E. (1965). Land resource regions and major land resource areas of the United States (exclusive of Alaska and Hawaii). *USDA Agriculture Handbook* No. 296.

Avery, B. W. (1962). Soil type and crop performance. *Soils Fertil.* **25**, 341–4.

—— and Bascomb, C. L. (1974). Soil survey laboratory methods. *Soil Surv. Tech. Monogr.* No. 6.

—— Findlay, D. C., and Mackney, D. (1975). *Soil map of England and Wales, 1 : 1,000,000.* Ordnance Survey, Southampton.

Azevedo, A. L. and Cardoso, J. C. (1962). Soil classification in Portugal and its application in agricultural research. *Trans. Comm. IV and V, Int. Soc. Soil Sci.*, New Zealand, pp. 473–9.

Baeyens, L., Sweldens, V., and Deckers, J. (1964) [Preliminary investigations on the suitability of different soils for Cox's Orange Pippin/EM IX]. *Agricultura, Louvain* **12**, 263–339.

Bagenal, N. B. and Furneaux, B. S. (1949). Fruit growing areas on the Hastings Beds in Kent. *Bull. Minist. Agric. Fish. Fd, Lond.* No. 141.

Bane, W. A. and Jones, G. H. G. (1934). Fruit growing areas on the Lower Greensand in Kent. *Bull. Minist. Agric. Fish. Fd, Lond.* No. 80.

Barley, K. P. (1964). The utility of field experiments. *Soils Fertil.* **27**, 267–9.

Barnes, C. P. (1949). Interpretive soil classification: relation to purpose. *Soil Sci.* **67**, 127–9.

Barrera, A. (1961). *Handbook of soil surveys for the Philippines.* Republic of the Philippines Department of Agriculture and Natural Resources, Bureau of Soils, Manila.

Barrett, E. C. and Curtis, L. F. (1976). *Introduction to environmental remote sensing.* Chapman and Hall, London.

Bartelli, L. J. (1962). Use of soils information in urban-fringe areas. *J. Soil. Wat. Conserv.* **17**, 99–103.

—— (1978). Technical classification system for soil survey interpretation. *Adv. Agron.* **30**, 247–89.

—— (1979). Interpreting soil data. In *Planning the uses and management of land* (ed. M. T. Beatty *et al.*) pp. 91–116. ASA, CSSA, SSSA, Madison, Wisconsin.

—— Klingebiel, A. A., Baird, J. V., and Heddleson, M. R. (1966). *Soil surveys and land use planning.* SSSA, ASA, Madison, Wisconsin.

Bauer, K. W. (1973). The use of soils data in regional planning. *Geoderma* 10, 1–26.

Bauer, M. E. (1975). The role of remote sensing in determining the distribution and yield of crops. *Adv. Agron.* 27, 271–304.

Baulkwill, W. J. (1972). The Land Resources Division of the Overseas Development Administration. *Trop. Sci.* 14, 305–22.

Beard, J. B. (1973). *Turfgrass: science and culture.* Prentice-Hall, Englewood Cliffs, NJ.

Beatty, M. T. and Bouma, J. (1973). Application of soil surveys to the selection of sites for on-site disposal of liquid household wastes. *Geoderma* 10, 113–22.

——, Petersen, G. W. and Swindale, L. D. (1979). *Planning the uses and management of land.* ASA, CSSA, SSSA, Madison, Wisconsin.

Beckel, A. (1962). The application of soil classification, in agriculture, forestry, and other fields in the Federal Republic of Germany. *Trans. Comm. IV and V, Int. Soc. Soil Sci.*, New Zealand, pp. 388–98.

Beckett, P. H. T. and Burrough, P. A. (1971). The relation between cost and utility in soil survey. IV. comparison of the utilities of soil maps produced by different survey procedures and to different map scales and V. The cost effectiveness of different soil survey procedures. *J. Soil Sci.* 22, 466–89.

—— and Webster, R. (1971). Soil variability — a review. *Soils Fertil.* 34, 1–15.

Beek, K. J. (1974). The concept of land utilization types. *FAO Soils Bull.* 22, 103–20.

—— (1975a). Identification of land utilization types. *Wld Soil Resour. Rep.* 45, 89–102.

—— (1975b). Land utilization types in land evaluation. *FAO Soils Bull.* 29, 87–106.

—— (1977). The selection of soil properties and land qualities relevant to specific land uses in developing countries. In *Soil resource inventories.* Agronomy Mimeo 77–23, pp. 143–62. Cornell University, Ithaca, NY.

Bellamy, D. J. (1976). *Bellamy's Europe.* BBC, London.

Bendelow, V. C. and Hartnup, R. (1977). The assessment of climatic limitations in land use capability classification. *Proc. N. Engl. Soils Discuss. Grp* No. 13, 19–28.

Bender, W. H. (1971). Soils and septic tanks. *Agric. Inf. Bull.* No. 349.

Bennema, J. and van Goor, C. P. (1975). Physical land evaluation for forestry. *Wld Soil Resour. Rep.* 45, 103–17.

Berger, K. C., Hole, F. D., and Beardsley, J. M. (1952). A soil productivity score card. *Proc. Soil Sci. Soc. Am.* 16, 307–9.

Bergmann, H. and Boussard, J. M. (1976). *Guide to the economic evaluation of irrigation projects.* OECD, Paris.

Berryman, C. (1970). The problem of disposal of farm wastes, with particular reference to maintaining soil fertility. *Symp. on Farm Wastes*, pp. 19–23. University of Newcastle-upon-Tyne.

204 References

Bibby, J. S. and Mackney, D. (1969). Land Use Capability Classification. *Soil Surv. Gt Br. Tech. Monogr.* No. 1.

Bidwell, O. W. and Bohannon, R. A. (1962). Community meetings: a device for distributing soil survey reports and for training in their use. *Proc. Soil Sci. Soc. Am.* **26**, 503–6.

Bie, S. W. and Beckett, P. H. T. (1971). Quality control in soil survey. II. The costs of soil survey. *J. Soil Sci.* **22**, 453–65.

—— and Schelling, J. (1978). An integrated information system for soil survey. In *Factual data banks in agriculture*, pp. 45–53, Pudoc. Wageningen. Netherlands.

——, Lieftinck, J. R. E., van Lynden, K. R., and Waenink, A. W. (1976). Computer-aided interactive soil suitability classification — a simple Bayesian approach. *Neth. J. agric. Sci.* **24**, 179–86.

Birse, E. L. and Dry, F. T. (1970). *Assessment of climatic conditions in Scotland. 1. Based on accumulated temperature and potential water deficit.* Macaulay Institute for Soil Research, Aberdeen.

Blagovidov, N. L. (1960). Principles of soil and land evaluation. *Trans. 7th Int. Cong. Soil Sci.*, Vol. 4, pp. 357–64.

Blaney, H. F. and Criddle, W. D. (1950). Determining water requirements in irrigated areas from climatological and irrigation data. *Tech. Pap. Soil Conserv. Serv. USDA* No. 96.

Blaquière, C. and Meriaux, S. (1969). [Relationship between the'appellations d'origine' of white wine from the Côte de Beaune, and certain edaphic characteristics.] *C.r. hebd. Séanc. Acad. Agric. Fr.* **55**, 1065–77.

Bleeker, P. (1975). Explanatory notes to the land limitation and agricultural and use potential map of Papua New Guinea. *Land Res. Ser. CSIRO Aust.* No. 36.

Blyth, J. (1974). Land capability for forestry in North East Scotland. Ph.D Thesis, University of Aberdeen.

Boddington, M. A. B. (1978). *The classification of agricultural land in England and Wales: a critique.* Rural Planning Services, Ipsden, Oxfordshire.

Boersma, L. L. (1979). Application of thermal effluent. In *Planning the uses and management of land* (ed. M. T. Beatty *et al.*) pp. 705–32. ASA, CSSA, SSSA, Madison, Wisconsin.

Booher, L. J. (1974). Surface irrigation. *Agric. Dev. Pap. FAO* No. 95.

Borden, R. W. and Warkentin, B. P. (1974). An irrigation rating for some soils in Antigua W.I. *Trop. Agric.*, *Trin.* **51**, 501–14.

Bouma, J. (1971). Evaluation of the field percolation test and an alternative procedure to test soil potential for disposal of septic tank effluent. *Proc. Soil Sci. Soc. Am.* **35**, 871–5.

—— (1973). Use of physical methods to expand soil survey interpretations of soil drainage. *Proc. Soil Sci. Soc. Am.* **37**, 413–21.

—— (1974). New concepts in soil survey interpretations for on-site disposal of septic tank effluent. *Proc. Soil Sci. Soc. Am.* **38**, 941–6.

—— (1979). Subsurface applications of sewage effluent. In *Planning the uses and management of land* (ed. M. T. Beatty *et al.*) pp. 665–703. ASA, CSSA, SSSA, Madison, Wisconsin.

Bowser, W. E. (1940). Soil surveys in relation to land classification in Alberta. *Scient. Agric.* **20**, 285–90.

—— and Moss, H. C. (1950). A soil rating and classification for irrigation land in Western Canada. *Scient. Agric.* **30**, 165–71.

Box, T. W. and Dwyer, D. D. (1979). Planning the use of rangelands for public and private lands. In *Planning the uses and management of land* (ed. M. T. Beatty *et al.*) pp. 321–34. ASA, CSSA, SSSA, Madison, Wisconsin.

Brady, N. C. (1974). *The nature and properties of soils*, 8th edn. Macmillan, New York.

Bramao, L. and Riquier, J. (1967). Soil resources appraisal for development. *An. Edafol. Agrobiol.* **26**, 865–78.

Brammer, H. and Brinkman, R. (1967). A land capability classification for use in East Pakistan. *Pakist. J. Soil Sci.* **3**, 10–16.

Brenchley, G. H. (1974). Aerial photography for the study of soil conditions and crop diseases. *Soil Surv. Tech. Monogr.* No. 4, 99–106.

Bridges, E. M. (1974). Recent developments and applications of land use classification in Britain. In *Regional development and planning. British and Hungarian case studies*, pp. 197–207.Publishing House of the Hungarian Academy of Sciences, Budapest.

—— and Burnham, C. P. (1980). Soils of the State of Bahrain. *J. Soil Sci.* **31**, 689–707.

Brink, A. B. A., Partridge, T. C., and Williams, A. A. B. (1981). *Soil survey for engineering.* Clarendon Press, Oxford.

Brinkman, R. (1978). Land suitability evaluation for wetland rice: criteria and required standards. *Wld Soil Resour. Rep.* **49**, 32–8.

—— Smyth, A. J. (1973). Land evaluation for rural purposes. *Publs int. Inst. Ld Reclam. Improv.* No. 17.

Brunsden, D., Doornkamp, J. C., and Jones, D. K. C. (1979). The Bahrain surface materials resources survey and its application to regional planning. *Geogrl J.* **145**, 1–35.

Brzesovsky, W. J. (1963). Statistical studies in detailed soil mapping; an aid in predicting the suitability of soils for crops by means of air-photo analysis. *Neth. J. agric. Sci.* **11**, 341–50.

BSI (1976). *CP2001 Site Investigations.* British Standards Institution, London.

Building Research Establishment (1981). Concrete in sulphate-bearing soils and groundwaters. *Bldg Res. Establ. Dig.* No. 250.

Burger, D. (1972). Forest site classification in Canada. *Mitt. Ver. forstl. Standortskart.* **21**, 5–36.

Burnham, C. P. (1979). A new inventory of the land resources of England and Wales. *Area* **11**, 349–52.

—— and McRae, S. G. (1974). Land judging. *Area* **6**, 107–11.

Burrough, P. A. and Beckett, P. H. T. (1971). The relation between cost and utility in soil survey. *J. Soil Sci.* **22**, 359–94.

Butler, B. E. (1964). Assessing the soil factor in agricultural production. *J. Aust. Inst. agric. Sci.* **30**, 232–40.

Campbell, I. B. (1977). Soils of part Wanganui County, North Island, New Zealand. *Bull. Soil Bur. N.Z.* No. 40.

Canada Department of Agriculture (1964). *Handbook for the classification of irrigated land in the Prairie Provinces.* Prairie Farm Rehabilitation Administration, Regina, Saskatchewan, Canada.

Canada Land Inventory (1965*a*). Objectives, scope and organization. *The Canada Land Inventory Report* No. 1. Department of Forestry and Rural Development, Ottawa, Ontario, Canada.

—— (1965*b*). Soil capability classification for agriculture. *The Canada Land Inventory Report* No. 2, Department of Forestry and Rural Development, Ottawa, Ontario, Canada.

—— (1969). Land capability classification for outdoor recreation. *The Canada Land Inventory Report* No. 6, Department of Regional Economic Expansion, Ottawa, Ontario, Canada.

—— (1970). Soil capability analysis for agriculture in Nova Scotia. *The Canada Land Inventory Report* No. 8, Environment Canada, Ottawa, Ontario, Canada.

—— (1977). *Soil capability for agriculture in Alberta.* Alberta Environment, Edmonton, Alberta, Canada.

Cannell, R. Q., Davies, D. B., Mackney, D., and Pidgeon, J. D. (1979). The suitability of soils for sequential direct drilling of combine-harvested crops in Britain: a provisional classification. *Soil Surv. Tech. Monogr.* No. 13, 1–23.

Cardoso, J. C. (1968). Soil survey and land use planning in Portugal. *Trans. 9th Int. Cong. Soil Sci.*, Vol. 4, pp. 261–9.

Carlisle, V. W. and Calhoun, F. O. (1979). Land uses of shorelands, floodplains, wetlands and coastal zones. In *Planning the uses and management of land* (ed. M. T. Beatty *et al.*) pp. 813–28. ASA, CSSA, SSSA, Madison, Wisconsin.

Carmean, W. H. (1975). Forest site quality evaluation in the United States. *Adv. Agron.* **27**, 175–269.

Carroll, D. M. (1974). The soils of the Maiduguri–Bama area. *Soil Surv. Bull., Samaru* No. 40.

—— Evans, R., and Bendelow, V. C. (1977). Air photo-interpretation for soil mapping. *Soil Surv. Tech. Monogr.* No. 8.

Carruthers, I. D. (1968). *Irrigation development planning. Aspects of Pakistan experience.* Wye College, Ashford, Kent.

—— and Clark, C. (1981). *The economics of irrigation.* Liverpool University Press.

Carstea, S. (1964). Utilization of soil surveys in land capability classification for various agricultural uses. *Trans. 8th Int. Cong. Soil Sci.*, Vol. V, pp. 847–51.

CAS (1980). *Strategy for the U.K. forest industry.* Centre for Agricultural Strategy, Reading.

Casson, J., Hartnup, R., and Jarvis, R. (1973). Soil surveys for integrated land use planning. *J. R. Tn Plann. Inst., Lond.* **59**, 400–6.

Chapman, L. J. and Brown, D. M. (1966). The climates of Canada for agriculture. *The Canada Land Inventory Report* No. 3, Department of Forestry and Rural Development, Ottawa, Ontario, Canada.

Chen, F. H. (1975). *Foundations on expansive soils.* Elsevier, Amsterdam.

Chiang, S. L. (1971). A runoff potential rating table for soils. *J. Hydrol.* **13**, 54–62.

Chisholm, A. M. (1965). Towards the determination of optimum stocking rates in the high rainfall zone. *Rev. Mktg agric. Econ., Sydney* **33**, 5–31.

Chun, S. S. (1971). Land suitability classification in Korea. *Wld Soil Resour. Rep.* **41**, 215–25.

Chuchward, H. M. and Flint, S. F. (1956). Jernargo extension of the Berriquin Irrigation District, New South Wales. *Soils Ld Use Ser. CSIRO Aust.* No. 18.

Clark, C. (1970). *The economics of irrigation*, 2nd edn. Pergamon, Oxford.

Clarke, G. R. (1950). Productivity ratings. *Trans. 4th Int. Cong. Soil Sci.*, Vol. 1, pp. 345–8.

—— (1951). The evaluation of soils and the definition of quality classes from studies of the physical properties of the soil profile in the field. *J. Soil. Sci.* **2**, 50–60.

—— (1957). *The study of the soil in the field*, 4th edn. Clarendon Press, Oxford.

Clements, R. F. (1976). Criteria for assessing land for fruit production. *Tech. Rep. Minist. Agric. Fish. Fd* No. 31, 33–6.

Collis-George, N. and Davey, B. G. (1960). The doubtful utility of present-day field experimentation and other determinations involving soil–plant interactions. *Soils Fertil.* **23**, 307–10.

Comerma, J. and Arias, L. F. (1971). [*A system to evaluate the land use capability of land in Venezuela.*] Mimeo, Maracay, Venezuela. [quoted by K. J. Beek (1978). *Publs int. Inst. Ld Reclam. Improv.* No. 23.]

Condon, R. W. (1968). Estimation of grazing capacity on arid grazing lands. In *Land evaluation* (ed. G. A. Stewart) pp. 112–24. Macmillan, Australia.

Conklin, H. E. (1959). The Cornell system of land classification. *J. Fm Econ.* **41**, 548–57.

Cooke, R. U. and Doornkamp, J. C. (1974). *Geomorphology in environmental management.* Clarendon Press, Oxford.

Coombs, D. B. and Thie, J. (1979). The Canadian Land Inventory System. In *Planning the uses and management of land* (ed. M. T. Beatty *et al.*) pp. 909–33. ASA, CSSA, SSSA, Madison, Wisconsin.

Coppock, J. T. (1976). *An agricultural atlas of England and Wales*, revised edn. Faber, London.

—— (1980). The concept of land quality: an over-view. In *Land assessment in Scotland* (ed. M. F. Thomas and J. T. Coppock) pp. 1–7. Aberdeen University Press.

Corbett, J. L. (1978). Measuring animal performance. *Bull. Commonw. Bur. Past. Fld Crops* No. 52, 163–231.

Corcoran, P., Jarvis, M. G., Mackney, D., and Stevens, K. W. (1977). Soil corrosiveness in South Oxfordshire. *J. Soil Sci.* **28**, 473–84.

Coulter, J. K. (1964). Soil surveys and their application in tropical agriculture. *Trop. Agric., Trin.* **41**, 185–96.

Cowie, J. A. (1974). Soils of Palmerston North City and environs, New Zealand. *Rep. N.Z. Soil Surv.* No. 24.

208   References

Cowlishaw, S. J. (1969). The carrying capacity of pastures. *J. Br. Grassld Soc.* **24**, 207–14.

Cressman, D. R. and Hoffman, D. W. (1968). Classifying land for recreation. *J. Soil Wat. Conserv.* **23**, 91–3.

Crowe, S. (1978). The landscape of forests and woods. *Bookl. For. Commn* No. 44.

Culver, V. P. and Clonts, H. A. (1977). Alamaba's land resources: A review of the need for critical areas protection. *Bull. Ala. agric. Exp. Stn* No. 481.

Curtis, L. F., Doornkamp, J. C., and Gregory, J. K. (1965). The description of relief in field studies of soils. *J. Soil Sci.* **16**, 16–30.

Cutler, E. J. B. (1962). Soil capability classification based on the genetic soil map. *Trans. Comm. IV and V, Int. Soc. Soil Sci.*, New Zealand, pp. 743–8.

—— (1968). Soils of the Otago region. *Spec. Publs Soil Bur. N.Z.* No. 351.

Davidson, D. A. (1980). *Soils and land use planning.* Longman, London.

Davies, H. (1968). Influence of soil and management on the botanical composition and productivity of 20 years old reclaimed hill pastures in mid-Wales. *Occ. Symp. Brit. Grassld Soc.* **4**, 162–7.

Davis, A. G. (1976). Land use in the Mazoe Valley: Land Capability Classification. *Rhodesia agric. J.* **73**, 65–71.

Davis, K. P. (1966). *Forest management: regulation and valuation*, 2nd edn. McGraw-Hill, New York.

Dawkins, H. C. (1959). The volume increment of natural tropical high forest and limitations on its improvement. *Emp. For. Rev.* **38**, 175–80.

de Bakker, (1950). [Soil problems of some Zuid-Beveland polders and their adaption for fruit growing]. *Versl. Landbouwk. Onderzoek.* **56**, No. 14.

de Jager, J. M. (1971). Theory for the assessment of environmental potential. *Agro-chemo-physico* **3**, 67–70.

de Kievit, J. L. (1970). [A classification system for assessing the suitability of land for specific kinds of land uses.] *Ingenieur* **45**, 159–68.

de Leenheer, L. and Simon, M. (1950). The influence of soil type in the production of sugar beet and sugar. *Trans. 4th Int. Cong. Soil Sci.*, Vol. 2, pp. 222–8.

Desaunettes, J. R. (1960). [The binary classification of soils as a function of their value.] *Trans. 7th Int. Cong. Soil Sci.*, Vol. 4, pp. 379–87.

—— Somapala, H., Hettige, P. M. L., and Amarasinghe, L. (1974). Methodology proposed for land evaluation in the wet zone of Sri Lanka. *Trop. Agric.* **130**, 135–51.

de Vries, M. P. C. (1980). How reliable are results of pot experiments? *Communs Soil Sci. Pl. Anal.* **11**, 895–902.

Didic, V. (1964). [Classification of soils according to their suitability for irrigation.] *Trans. 8th Int. Cong. Soil Sci.*, Vol. V, pp. 891–6.

Digar, S. and Sen, A. K. (1960). Significance of slope and erosion in land capability classification in the Machkund catchment. *J. Indian Soc. Soil Sci.* **8**, 157–69.

Doornkamp, J. C., Brunsden, D., and Jones, D. K. C. (1980). *Geology, geomorphology and pedology of Bahrain*. Geobooks, Norwich, England.

Dumanski, J., Marshall, I. B., and Huffman, E. C. (1979). Soil capability analysis for regional land use planning — a study of the Ottawa urban fringe. *Can. J. Soil Sci.* **59**, 363–79.

—— Wright, J. C., and Lindsay, J. D. (1973). Evaluating the productivity of pine forests in the Hinton–Edson area, Alberta, from soil survey maps. *Can. J. Soil Sci.* **53**, 405–19.

Dyke, G. V. (1976). Criteria for assessing land for arable farming systems. *Tech. Rep. Minist. Agric. Fish. Fd* No. 31, 13–17.

Echelberger, H. E. and Wagar, J. A. (1979). Noncommodity values of forests and woodlands. In *Planning the uses and management of land* (ed. M. T. Beatty *et al.*) pp. 429–43. ASA, CSSA, SSSA, Madison, Wisconsin.

Edelman, C. H. (1953). Suitability of soils for horticultural crops and some related soil problems in the Netherlands. *Rep. 13th Int. hort. Cong.*, Vol. 1, pp. 80–95.

—— (1963). Application of soil survey in land development in Europe with special reference to experiences in the Netherlands. *Publs int. Inst. Ld Reclam. Improv.* No. 12.

Edwards, R. D., Rabey, D. F., and Kover, R. W. (1970). *Soil survey of the Ventura Area, California*. Soil Conservation Service, USDA, Washington, DC.

Elsner, G. H., MacGill, A. W., Schwarz, C. F., and Thor, E. C. (1979). Planning other uses for public rangelands. In *Planning the uses and management of land* (ed. M. T. Beatty *et al.*) pp. 335–62. ASA, CSSA, SSSA, Madison, Wisconsin.

Escritt, J. R. (1979). The location, construction and management of playing fields. *Soil Surv. Tech. Monogr.* No. 13, 148–51.

Fackler, E. (1924). [Soil classification for tax purposes.] *Wbl. landw. Ver. Bayern* **114**, No. 41.

FAO (1960). Soil erosion by wind and measures for its control on agricultural lands. *Agric. Dev. Pap. FAO* No. 71.

—— (1965). Soil erosion by water — some measures for its control on cultivated land. *Agric. Dev. Pap. FAO* No. 81.

—— (1972). *Background document for expert consultation on land evaluation for rural purposes.* (AGL/LERP 72/1.) [In Land Evaluation for rural purposes (R. Brinkman and A. J. Smyth (1973).) *Publs int Inst. Ld Reclam. Improv.* No. 17.]

—— (1973). *A framework for land evaluation*, draft ed. FAO, Rome. (AGL/MISC/73/14.)

—— (1974). Irrigation suitability classification. *FAO Soils Bull.* No. 22, 77–82.

—— (1975). Report on the Ad Hoc Expert Consultation on Land Evaluation. *Wld Soil Resour. Rep. 45.*

—— (1976). A framework for land evaluation. *FAO Soils Bull.* No. 32.

—— (1979). Land evaluation criteria for irrigation. Report of an expert consultation. *Wld Soil Resour. Rep.* 50.

FAO–World Bank (1976). *Estimation of water requirement of crops.* FAO, Rome.

Farquharson, F. A. K., Mackney, D., Newson, M. D., and Thomasson, A. J. (1978). Estimation of run-off potential of river catchments from soil surveys. *Soil Surv. Spec. Surv.* No. 11.

Fenton, T. E. (1975). Use of soil productivity ratings in evaluating Iowa agricultural land. *J. Soil Wat. Conserv.* **30**, 237–40.

—— Duncan, E. R., Shrader, W. D., and Dumenil, L. C. (1971). Productivity levels of some Iowa soils. *Spec. Rep. Iowa St. Univ. agric. Home Econ. Exp. Stn.* No. 66.

Ferrari, T. J. (1966). Principles of experimentation on the study of soil–crop relationships. *Trans. Comm. II and IV, Int. Soc. Soil Sci.*, Aberdeen, pp. 345–55.

Finch, A. and Hotson, J. (1974). CAMAPG and GRID CAMAP, *Inter-University Research Councils Research and Development Notes*, No. 13, University of Edinburgh.

Finck, A. and Ochtman, L. H. J. (1961). Problems of soil evaluation in the Sudan. *J. Soil Sci.* **12**, 87–95.

Fines, K. D. (1968). Landscape evaluation: research project in East Sussex. *Reg. Stud.* **2**, 41–55.

Finkenzeller, R. (1957). [Combine harvesting on slopes.] *Landtechnik, Wien* **12**, No. 1, 12–14.

Fookes, P. G. (1978). Middle East — inherent ground problems. *Q. Jl Engng Geol.* **11**, 33–49.

—— and Collis, L. (1975*a*). Problems in the Middle East. *Concrete* **9**, No. 7, 12–17.

——, —— (1975*b*). Aggregates and the Middle East. *Concrete* **9**, No. 11, 14–19.

Forbes, T. J. (1976). Criteria for assessing land for grass production. *Tech. Rep. Minist. Agric. Fish. Fd* No. 31, 5–12.

Fordham, S. J. and Green, R. D. (1980). Soils of Kent. *Bull. Soil Surv. Gt Br., England and Wales* No. 9.

Fourt, D. F., Donald, D. G. M., Jeffers, J. N. R., and Binns, W. O. (1971). Corsican pine (*Pinus nigra* var. *maritima* (Ait.) Melville) in Southern Britain. *Forestry* **44**, 189–207.

France, J. and Briggs, D. J. (1980). Environmental mapping of the European Community: a review of the proposed method. *J. Ops. Res. Soc.* **31**, 485–96.

Frankart, R. and Sys, C. (1974). Significance of soil characteristics used for soil appraisal in humid tropical regions. *Trans. 10th Int. Cong. Soil Sci.*, Vol. V, pp. 34–9.

——, —— and Verheye, W. (1972). *Contributions to the use of the parameter method for the evaluation of the classes in the different categories of the land evaluation proposed by the working group.* Mimeo Report, FAO Consultation on Land Evaluation, Wageningen, Netherlands. [Quoted by Vink (1975).]

Freeman, T. H. (1940). The Saskatchewan system of rural land assessment. *Scient. Agric.* **21**, 361–7.

Garbouchev, I. P. and Sadovski, A. N. (1978). Development and use of soil information systems in Europe. *Trans. 11th Int. Soc. Soil Sci.*, Vol. 3, pp. 132–42.

—— Trashliev, H., and Krastanov, S. (1974). Land productivity evaluation in Bulgaria. *FAO Soils Bull.* No. 22, 83–95.

Gardiner, M. J. (1972a). An evaluation of the influence of soil characteristics and climate on crop yields. *Ir. J. agric. Res.* **11**, 211–17.

—— (1972b). An evaluation of the influence of soil characteristics and climate on crop yields. 2. Influence of temperature. *Ir. J. agric. res.* **11**, 219–32.

—— (1974). Land evaluation studies in Ireland, *FAO Soils Bull.* No. 22, 96–102.

Gavrilyuk, F. Y. (1967). Criteria for evaluating soils. *Soviet Soil Sci.* 1–5.

—— (1977). History of land capability evaluation and soil rating methods in the USSR. *Soviet Soil Sci.* 144–51.

Geczy, G. (1964). [An index for the classification of Hungarian soils according their natural fertility.] *Agrokem. Talajt.* **13**, 325–44.

George, H. and Jarvis, M. G. (1979). Land for camping and caravan sites, picnic sites and footpaths. *Soil Surv. Tech. Monogr.* No. 13, 166–83.

Ghosh, R. K. (1980). Estimation of soil-moisture characteristics from mechanical properties of soils. *Soil Sci.* **130**, 60–3.

Gibbons, F. R. (1961). Some misconceptions about what soil surveys can do. *J. Soil Sci.* **12**, 96–100.

Gibbs, H. S. (1963). Soils of New Zealand and their limitations for pastoral use. *Proc. N.Z. Inst. agric. Sci.* **9**, 63–78.

—— (1966). The soil factor in the assessment of land resources. *N.Z. agric. Sci.* **1**, No. 6, 11–14.

Godin, V. J. and Spensley, P. C. (1971). *Oils and oilseeds*. Tropical Products Institute, London.

Gowaiker, A. S. and Barde, N. K. (1964). Soils series and land use classification of areas in Vidarbha, Maharashtra state. *J. Soil Wat. Conserv. India* **12**, 32–44.

Grange, L. I. (1944). A basic scheme for land classification. *N.Z. Jl Sci. Technol.* **26A**, 136–41.

Griffiths, E. (1975). Classification of land for irrigation in New Zealand. *Sci. Rep. N.Z. Soil Bur.* No. 22.

Haans, J. C. F. M. and Westerveld, G. J. W. (1970). The application of soil survey in the Netherlands. *Geoderma* **4**, 279–309.

Haantjens, H. A. (1963). Land capability classification in reconnaissance surveys in Papua and New Guinea. *J. Aust. Inst. agric. Sci.* **29**, 104–7.

—— (1965). Agricultural land classification for New Guinea land resources surveys. *Tech. Mem. Div. Ld Res. CSIRO Aust.* No. 65/8.

—— (1969). Agricultural land classification for New Guinea land resources surveys. *Tech. Mem. Div. Ld Res. CSIRO Aust.* No. 69/4.

Hagan, R. M., Haise, H. W., and Edminster, T. W. (eds.) (1967). *Irrigation of agricultural lands*. ASA, Madison, Wisconsin.

212   References

—— Houston, C. E., and Allison, S. V. (1968). *Successful irrigation: planning development management.* FAO, Rome.

Hall, D. G. M., Reeve, M. J., Thomasson, A. J., and Wright, V. F. (1977). Water retention, porosity and density of field soils. *Soil Surv. Tech. Monogr.* No. 9.

Hall, G. F., Wilding, L. P., and Erickson, A. E. (1976). Site selection considerations for sludge and wastewater applications on agricultural land. *Res. Bull. Ohio agric. Res. Dev. Center* No. 1090, 2.1–2.8.

Hall, W. A., Hargreaves, G. H., and Cannell, G. M. (1979). Planning large-scale agricultural systems with integrated water management. In *Planning the uses and management of land* (ed. M. T. Beatty *et al.*) pp. 273–89. ASA, CSSA, SSSA, Madison, Wisconsin.

Hamilton, G. J. and Christie, J. M. (1971). Forest management tables (metric). *Bookl. For. Commn.* No. 34.

Harris, K. (1949). Factors that give value to land or basic land values. *Bull. Ariz. agric. Exp. Stn* No. 223.

Harrod, T. R. (1979). Soil suitability for grassland. *Soil Surv. Tech. Monogr.* No. 13, 51–70.

—— and Thomasson, A. J. (1980). *Grassland suitability map of England and Wales, 1:1,000,000.* Ordnance Survey, Southampton.

Hartnup, R. and Jarvis, M. G. (1979). Soils in civil engineering and planning. *Soil Surv. Tech. Monogr.* No. 13, 110–34.

——, —— (1973). Soils of the Castleford area of Yorkshire. *Soil Surv. Spec. Surv.* No. 8.

Harvard University (1968). *Reference manual for synagraphic computer mapping SYMAP Version V.* Laboratory for Computer Graphics, Harvard University, Boston, Mass.

Hauser, G. F. (1970). A standard guide to soil fertility investigations on farmers' fields. *FAO Soils Bull.* No. 11.

Hedge, A. M. and Klingebiel, A. A. (1957). The use of soil maps. *Yb. Agric. US Dep. Agric.* 400–11.

Hernandez, S. C. (1955). A proposed score-card for rating land use capabilities. *J. Soil Sci. Soc. Philipp.* **7**, 98–105.

Hetherington, J. C. and Page, G. (1965). Forest site evaluation with particular reference to soil and physiographic factors. *Rep. Welsh Soils Discuss. Grp.* **6**, 58–70.

Higgins, G. M. (1975). A framework for land evaluation. *FAO Soils Bull.* No. 29, 79–85.

—— (1978). A framework for land evaluation and its application. *Wld Soil Resour. Rep.* **49**, 3–12.

Higginson, F. R. (1975). Determination of slope for topographic maps on aerial photographs. *J. Soil Conserv. Serv. N.S.W.* **31**, 123–8.

Hill, D. E. and Thomas, H.F. (1972). Use of natural resource data in land and water planning. *Bull. Conn. agric. Exp. Stn.* No. 733.

Hills, G. A. (1961). The ecological basis for land-use planning. *Res. Rep. Ont. Dep. Lds For. Res. Br.* No. 46.

Hockensmith, R. D. (1947). The scientific basis for conservation farming. *J. Soil Wat. Conserv.* **2**, No. 1, 9–16.

—— and Steele, J. G. (1943). Classifying land for conservation farming. *Frms Bull. US Dep. Agric.* No. 1853.

——, —— (1949). Recent trends in the use of the land-capability classification. *Proc. Soil Sci. Soc. Am.* **14**, 383—8.

Hodgson, J. M. (ed.) (1974). Soil survey field handbook. *Soil Surv. Tech. Monogr.* No. 5.

—— (1978). *Soil sampling and soil description*. Clarendon Press, Oxford.

Hoffman, D. W. (1975). Interpreting soil survey information. *Geoscience, Canada* **2**, 65–7.

Hogg, W. H. (1964). Climatic factors and choice of site with special reference to horticulture. *Symp. Inst. Biol.* No. 14, 141–55.

Holmes, W. (1968). The use of nitrogen in the management of pasture for cattle. *Herb. Abstr.* **38**, 265–77.

Holtz, W. G. (1969). Soil as an engineering material. *Wat. Resour. Tech. Publs Rep.* No. 17. United Stated Department of the Interior, Washington, DC.

Hooper, A. J. and Griffiths, D. J. (1971). Practical problems of the agricultural land classification system of the Agricultural Land Service and its relation to the Land Use Capability Classification system of the Soil Survey of Great Britain. *Proc. N. Engl. Soils Discuss. Grp* No. 8, 1–15.

Hooper, L. J. (1974*a*). Land use capability in farm planning. *Soil Surv. Tech. Monogr.* No. 4, 135–49.

—— (1974*b*). *Report of a visit to USSR. Soils, soil chemistry and land use.* Ministry of Agriculture, Fisheries and Food, London.

Hotson, J. M. (1976). Mapping by line printer. In *An agricultural atlas of England and Wales* (ed. J. T. Coppock) pp. 229–35. Faber, London.

Hudson, N. (1971). *Soil conservation*. Batsford, London.

—— (1975). *Field engineering for agricultural development*. Oxford University Press.

Hughes, R. (1970). Factors involved in animal production from temperate pastures. *Proc. 11th Int. Grassld Cong.*, Vol. A, pp. 31–8.

Hunter, R. F. and Grant, S. A. (1971). The effect of altitude on grass growth in East Scotland. *J. appl. Ecol.* **8**, 1–19.

Husch, B., Miller, C. I., and Beers, T. W. (1972). *Forest mensuration.* Ronald Press, New York.

Islam, A. (1966). Current status of soil and land capability classification in East Pakistan. *Cento. Conf. Ld Classif. non-irrig. Lds*, 81–4.

Israelsen, O. W. and Hansen, V. E. (1962). *Irrigation principles and practices*, 3rd edn. Wiley, New York.

Jacks, G. V. (1946). Land classification for land use planning. *Tech. Commun. Commonw. Bur. Soils* No. 43.

Jansen, I. J. and Fenton, T. E. (1978) Computer processing of soil survey information. *J. Soil Wat. Conserv.* **33**, 188–90.

Jarvis, M. G. and Mackney, D. (1973). Soil survey applications. *Soil Surv. Tech. Monogr.* No. 13.

—— Hazelden, J., and Mackney, D. (1979). Soils of Berkshire. *Bull. Soil Surv. Gt Br., England and Wales* No. 8.

Jefferson, J. R. (1976). *Route location with regard to environmental issues: report of a working party*. Department of the Environment London.

Johnston, D. R. (1975). Tree growth and wood production in Britain. *Phil. Trans. R. Soc.* **271B**, 101–14.

—— Grayson, A. J., and Bradley, R. T. (1967). *Forest planning*. Faber, London.

Jones, R. J. A. (1979). Soils of the Western Midlands grouped according to ease of cultivation. *Soil Surv. Tech. Monogr.* No. 13, 24–42.

Jumikis, A. R. (1967). *Introduction to soil mechanics*. Van Nostrand, Princeton, N.J.

Kay, D. E. (1973). *Root crops*. Tropical Products Institute, London.

Kellogg, C. E. (1951). Soil and land classification. *J. Fm Econ.* **33**, 499–513.

—— (1955). Soil surveys in modern farming. *J. Soil Wat. Conserv.* **10**, 271–7.

—— (1961). *Soil interpretation in the soil survey*. Soil Conservation Service, USDA, Washington, DC.

—— (1962). Soil surveys for use. *Trans. Comm. IV and V, Int. Soc. Soil Sci.*, New Zealand, pp. 529–35.

Kendall, M. G. (1975). *Multivariate analysis*. Griffin, London.

Kezdi, A. (1979). *Stabilized earth roads*. Elsevier, Amsterdam.

Kilkenny, J. B., Holmes, W., Baker, R. D., Walsh, A., and Shaw, P. G. (1977). *Grazing management for beef cattle*. Meat and livestock Commission, Bletchley, Bucks., England.

Kinney, R. R. (1966). Use of soil surveys in the equalization of tax assessments. In *Soil surveys and land use planning* (ed. L. G. Bartelli *et al.*) pp. 132–6. SSSA, ASA, Madison, Wisconsin.

Klingebiel, A. A. (1958). Soil survey interpretation—capability groupings. *Proc. Soil Sci. Soc. Am.* **22**, 160–3.

—— (1967). Know the soil you build on. *Agric. Inf. Bull.* No. 320.

—— and Montgomery, P. H. (1961). Land-capability classification. *USDA Agriculture Handbook* No. 210.

Kloosterman, B. and Lavkulich, L. M. (1973). A method of statistically interpreting soil data for agricultural and engineering land use. *Proc. Soil Sci. Soc. Am.* **37**, 285–91.

Knox, E. G. (1977). The role of soil surveys in the decision making process for development planning. In *Soil resource inventories*. Agronomy Mimeo 77–23, pp. 243–8. Cornell University, Ithaca, N.Y.

Kovda, V. A., van den Berg, C., and Hagan, R. M. (eds.) (1973). *Irrigation, drainage and salinity: an international source book (FAO/UNESCO)*. Hutchinson, London.

Krastanov, S. and Kabakchiev, I. (1975). Approaches to land evaluation in East European (Socialist) countries. *FAO Soils Bull.* No. 29, 71–7.

Lamb, A. F. A. (1972). Tropical pulp and timber plantations. *Proc. 7th Wld For. Cong.*, Buenos Aires. 7CFM/C:1/2G.

—— (1973). Pinus caribbaea L. *Fast growing timber trees of the lowland tropics No. 6*. Commonwealth Forestry Institute, Oxford.

Lang, D. M. (1973). Handbook of the land capability classification method for open-field (including mechanized) agriculture in northern Zambia. *Supplry Rep. No. 9, Ld Resour. Div*. ODM, London.

—— (1975). Land evaluation in Land Resources Division projects. *Wld Soil Resour. Rep.* **45**, 27–34.

Law, W. M. and Selvadurai, K. (1968). The 1968 reconnaissance soil map of Malaya, *Proc. 3rd Malays. Soil Conf.*, Sarawak, pp. 229–39.

Lea, J. W. (1979). Slurry acceptance. *Soil Surv. Tech. Monogr.* No. 13, 83–100.

Leamy, M. L. (1962). The correlation of soil classification and soil capability in the Upper Clutha Valley, Otago, New Zealand. *Trans. Comm. IV and V, Int. Soc. Soil Sci.*, New Zealand, pp. 749–54.

—— (1974). An improved method of assessing the soil factor in land valuation. *Sci. Rep. N.Z. Soil Bur.* No. 16.

Lee, J. and Diamond, S. (1972). The potential of Irish land for livestock production. *Bull. natn Soil Surv. Ireland* No. 17.

—— and Ryan, P. (1966). Soil survey interpretation for crop productivity determinations. 1. Relation between soil series and sugar-beet yields. *Ir. J. agric. Res.* **5**, 237–48.

—— and Spillane, P. (1970). Influence of soil series on the yield and quality of spring wheats. *Ir. J. agric. Res.* **9**, 239–50.

Lees, P. D. (1976). The mapping of potential vegetable producing areas in the north of England. *Tech. Rep. Minist. Agric. Fish. Fd* No. 31, 71–7.

Leeson, B. F. (1979). Low-intensity recreational uses for wildland environments. In *Planning the uses and management of land* (ed. M. T. Beatty *et al.*) pp. 445–64. ASA, CSSA, SSSA, Madison, Winsconsin.

Lemmon, P. E. (1958). Soil interpretation for woodland conservation. *Proc. 1st N. Am. For. Soils Conf.*, pp. 153–8.

—— (1970). Grouping soils on the basis of woodland suitability. In *Tree growth and forest soils* (ed. C. T. Youngberg and C. B. Devey) pp. 413–26. Oregon State University Press, Corvallis, Oregon.

LeVee, W. M. and Dregne, H. E. (1951). A method for rating land. *Bull. New Mex. agric. Exp. Stn* No. 364.

Lex, L. A. and Lex, L. (1975). Land use control: the Black Hawk County experience. *Soil Conserv.* **40**, 16–18.

Limstrom, G. A. (1963). Forest planting practice in the central states. *Agric. Handb. Forest Serv. U.S.* No. 247.

Lindsay, J. D., Scheelar, M. D., and Twardy, A. G. (1973). Soil survey for urban development. *Geoderma* **10**, 35–45.

Linell, K. A. and Tedrow, J. C. F. (1981). *Soil and permafrost studies in the Arctic.* Clarendon Press, Oxford.

Lines, R. and Howell, R. S. (1963). The use of flags to estimate the relative exposure of trial plantations. *Forest Rec., Lond.* No. 51.

Linnard, W., and Gane, M. (1968). *Martin Faustmann and the evolution of discounted cash flow.* Commonwealth Forestry Institute, Oxford.

Litton, R. B. Jr (1974). Visual vulnerability of forest landscapes. *J. For.* **72**, 392–7.

Lloyd, W. J. and Clark, W. M. (1979). Timber production on intensive holdings. In *Planning the uses and management of land* (ed. M. T. Beatty *et al.*) pp. 387–428. ASA, CSSA, SSSA, Madison, Wisconsin.

Loughry, F. G. (1973). The use of soil science in sanitary landfill selection and management. *Geoderma* **10**, 131–9.

—— and Lacour, W. D. (1979). Sanitary landfill site selection and management. In *Planning the uses and management of land* (ed. M. T. Beatty *et al.*) pp. 763–91. ASA, CSSA, SSSA, Madison, Wisconsin.

Loveday, J. (ed.) (1974). Methods for analysis of irrigated soils. *Tech. Commun. Commonw. Bur. Soils* No. 54

—— and McIntyre, D. S. (1966). Soil properties influencing growth of subterranean clover in the Coleambally irrigation area, New South Wales. *Aust. J. exp. Agric. Anim. Husb.* **6**, 283–95.

Loxton, R. F. (1962). Report on methods, criteria, terminology, and scales used for land-use planning and mapping in the Republic of South Africa. *Sols afr.* **7**, 81–100.

Lynch, L. G. and Emery, K. A. (1977). A regional information system for the Bathurst-Orange growth area. *J. Soil Conserv. Serv. N.S.W.* **33**, 43–6.

McArthur, W. N., Wheeler, J. L., and Goodall, D. W. (1966). The relative unimportance of soil properties as determinants of growth of forage oats. *Aust. J. exp. Agric. Anim. Husb.* **6**, 402–408.

McCormack, D. E., Moore, A. W., and Dumanski, J. (1978). A review of soil information systems in Canada, the United States and Australia. *Trans. 11th Int. Cong. Soil Sci.* Vol. 3, pp. 143–60.

McCormack, R. J. (1967). Land capability classification for forestry. *The Canada Land Inventory Report* No. 4. Department of Forestry and Rural Development, Ottawa, Ontario, Canada.

—— (1971). The Canada Land Inventory: a basis for land use planning. *J. Soil. Wat. Conserv.* **26**, 141–6.

McDonald, R. C. (1975). Soil survey in land evaluation. *Tech. Rep. agric. Chem. Brch Dept. Primary Indust. Aust.* No. 6.

McGown, A. and Iley, P. (1973). A comparison of data from agricultural soil surveys with engineering investigations for roadworks in Ayreshire. *J. Soil Sci.* **24**, 145–56.

Mackenzie, A. F. (1970). Agronomic groupings of southern Quebec soils: oat field trial results. *Soil Sci.* **109**, 53–9.

McVean, D. N. and Robertson, V. C. (1969). An ecological survey of land use and soil erosion in the West Pakistan and Azad Kashmir catchment of the River Jhelum. *J. appl. Ecol.* **6**, 77–109.

Mackney, D. (1974*a*). Soil survey in agriculture. *Soil Surv. Tech. Monogr.* No. 4, 13–26.

—— (1974*b*). Land Use Capability Classification in the United Kingdom. *Tech. Bull. Minist. Agric. Fish. Fd* **30**, 4–11.

—— (1979). *Land use capability map of England and Wales, 1:1 000 000*. Ordanance Survey, Southampton.

—— and Burnham, C. P. (1966). *The soils of the Church Stretton district of Shropshire*. Mem. Soil Surv. Gt Br. Harpenden, Herts.

MAFF (1966). Agricultural land classification. *Tech. Rep. agric. Ld Serv., Minist. Agric. Fish. Fd* No. 11.

—— (1968). *Agricultural Land Classification map of England and Wales. Explanatory note*. Ministry of Agriculture, Fisheries and Food, London.

—— (1974). *Agricultural Land Classification of England and Wales.* Ministry of Agriculture, Fisheries and Food, London

—— (1976). Agricultural Land Classification of England and Wales. The definition and identification of Sub-grades within Grade 3. *Tech. Rep. Minist. Agric. Fish. Fd* No. 11/1.

Mailloux, A., Dubé. A., and Tardif, L. (1964).[The classification of soils according to their suitability for agricultural utilization.] *Cah. Géogr. Québ.* **8**, 231–49.

Maker, H. J., Bailey, O. F., and Anderson, J. U. (1970). Soil associations and land classifications for irrigation, Luna County. *Res. Rep. New Mex. agric. Exp. Stn* No. 176.

Malcolm, D. C. (1971). Site factors and the growth of Sitka spruce. Ph. D. Thesis, University of Edinburgh.

Maletic, J. T. and Hutchings, T. B. (1967). Selection and classification of irrigable lands. In *Irrigation of agricultural lands* (ed. R. M. Hagan *et al.*) pp. 125–73. ASA, Madison, Wisconsin.

Malo, D. D. and Worcester, B. K. (1975). Soil fertility and crop responses at selected landscape positions. *Agron. J.* **67**, 397–401.

Mann, Q. V. (1963). A land capability classification system in relation to farm planning in the Natal Cane Belt. *Proc. 37th Cong. S. Afr. Sug. Technol. Ass.,* pp. 118–21.

Marin-Laflèche, A. (1972). [Land-use classification.] *Annls agron.* **23**, 5–30.

Mausel, P. W., Runge, E. C. A., and Carmer, S. G. (1975). Frequency distribution of tract productivity indexes and examples of their utilization in rural land assessment. *Proc. Soil Sci. Soc. Am.* **39**, 503–7.

Maxwell, T. J., Sibbald, A. R., and Eadie, J. (1979). The integration of forestry agriculture — a model. *Agric. Syst.* **4**, 161–88.

Mehta, K. M., Mathur, C. M., and Shankara-Narayan, H. S. (1958). A proposed method for rating lands for irrigation and its application to Chambal area. *J. Indian Soc. Soil Sci.* **6**, 125–39.

Meyers, C. R., Kennedy, M., and Sampson, R. N. (1979). Information systems for land use planning. In *Planning the uses and management of land* (ed. M. T. Beatty *et al.*) pp. 889–907. ASA, CSSA, SSSA, Madison, Wisconsin.

Miller, F. P. (1979). Defining, delineating, and designating uses for Prime and Unique agricultural lands. In *Planning the uses and management of land* (ed. M. T. Beatty *et al.*) pp. 291–318. ASA, CSSA, SSSA, Madison, Wisconsin.

Miller, F. T. and Nichols, J. D. (1979). Soils data. In *Planning the uses and management of land* (ed. M. T. Beatty *et al.*) pp. 67–89. ASA, CSSA, SSSA, Madison, Wisconsin.

Miller, M. F. (1924). *The soil and its management.* Ginn, New York.

Millette, G. J. F. and Searl, W. E. (1969). [Agricultural capability indices for the soils of pedological reports in eastern Canada.] *Agriculture, Montreal* XXVI, No. 3, 3–10.

Milne, J. D. C. and Northey, R. D. (1974). Microzoning for earthquake effects in Wellington. *Bull. N.Z. Dep. scient. ind. Res.* No. 213.

218   References

Mitchell, A. J. B. (1976). The irrigation potential of soils along the main rivers of eastern Botswana — a reconnaissance assessment. *Land Resource Study* No. 7. Land Resources Division, ODM, London.

Mitchell, J. (1940). A method for obtaining a comparative rating for Saskatchewan soils. *Scient. Agric.* **20**, 281–4.

—— (1950) Productivity ratings and their importance in the soil survey report. *Trans. 4th Int. Cong. Soil Sci.*, Vol. 1, pp. 356–60.

Montgomery, P. H. and Edminster, F. C. (1966). Use of soil surveys in planning for recreation. In *Soil surveys and land use planning* (ed. L. J. Bartelli *et al.*) pp. 104–12. SSSA, ASA, Madison, Wisconsin.

Moore, A. W. (1978). Some impressions of overseas developments in information systems for soil and related data. *Divl Rep. Div. Soils CSIRO Aust.* No. 28.

—— and Bie, S. W. (eds.) (1977). *Uses of soil information systems.* Pudoc, Wageningen, Netherlands.

Morrison, J. and Idle, A. A. (1972). A pilot survey of grassland in South east England. *Tech. Rep. Grassld Res. Inst.* No. 10.

Moss, H. C. (1962). *The relation between type of soil and yields of wheat in Saskatchewan.* Department of Soil Science, University of Saskatchewan, Regina, Saskatchewan.

—— (1972). A revised approach to rating Saskatchewan soils. *Ext. Publ. Sask. Inst. Pedol.* No. 218.

Mudd, C. H. (1976). Criteria for assessing land for stock enterprises. *Tech. Rep. Minist. Agric. Fish. Fd* No. 31, 1–4.

Mulcahy, M. J. and Humphries, A. W. (1967). Soil classification, soil surveys and land use. *Soils Fertil.* **30**, 1–8.

Muller, J. P. and Gavaud, M. (1976). [Agricultural land capability mapping in relation to soil mapping of the Benue Valley, Cameroon.] *Cah. ORSTOM, Pedol.* **14**, 131–59.

Murdoch, H. G., Lang, D. M., and Smyth, A. J. (1976). Land suitability assessment by Land Resources Division. *Misc. Rep.* No. 221. Land Resources Division, ODM, London.

Murray, W. G., Englehorn, A. J., and Griffin, R. A. (1939). Yield tests and land valuation. *Bull. Ia agric. Exp. Stn* **252**, 53–76.

Murtha, G. F. (1975). Soils and land use on the Northern Section of the Townsville Coastal Plain, North Queensland. *Soils Ld Use Ser. CSIRO Aust.* No. 55.

—— and Reid, R. (1976). Soils of the Townsville area in relation to urban development. *Divl Rep. Div. Soils CSIRO Aust.* No. 11.

Murthy, R. S., Jain, S. P., and Naga, B. S. R. (1968). Soil survey and land capability classification for sound watershed management in Kundah Project (Madras). *J. Indian Soc. Soil Sci.* **16**, 223–7.

Myklestad, E. and Wager, J. A. (1976). PREVIEW: computer assistance for visual management of forested landscapes. *USDA For. Serv. Res. Pap. NE-355.* Northeast For. Stn, Upper Darby, Pa.

Nelson, L. A. (1963). Detailed land classification — Island of Oahu. *Bull. Ld Study Bur. Univ. Hawaii* No. 3.

—— and McCracken, R. J. (1962). Properties of Norfolk and Portsmouth soils: statistical summarisation and influence on corn yields. *Proc. Soil Sci. Soc. Am.* **26**, 497–502.

Nichols, J. D. (1975) Characteristics of computerized soil maps. *Proc. Soil Sci. Soc. Am.* **39**, 927–32.

—— and Bartelli, L. J. (1974). Computer generated interpretive soil maps. *J. Soil Wat. Conserv.* **29**, 232–5.

Niemann, B. J. and McCarthy, M. M. (1979). Spatial data analysis and information communication. In *Planning the uses and management of land* (ed. M. T. Beatty *et al.*) pp. 187–222. ASA, CSSA, SSSA, Madison, Wisconsin.

Nieschlag, F. (1974). [The 1974 harvest shows the system of soil valuation is still valid.] *Mitt. dt. LandwGes.* No. 44, 1366–7.

Nix, H. A. (1968). The assessment of biological productivity. In *Land evaluation* (ed. G. A. Stewart) pp. 77–87. Macmillan, Australia.

Nix, J. S. (1979) *Farm management pocketbook.* Wye College, Ashford, Kent.

Norstadt, F. A. (1979). Locating animal feedlots and managing animal wastes applied to land. In *Planning the uses and management of land* (ed. M. T. Beatty *et al.*) pp. 733–61. ASA, CSSA, SSSA, Madison, Wisconsin.

Northcote, K. H. (1964). Some thoughts concerning agronomy and soil classification. *J. Aust. Inst. agric. Sci.* **30**, 241–6.

Northey, R. D. (1973). Insurance claims from earthquake damage in relation to soil pattern. *Geoderma* **10**, 151–60.

Norton, E. A. (1939). Soil conservation survey handbook. *Misc. Publs U.S. Dep. Agric.* No. 352.

—— (1940). Land classification as an aid in soil conservation operations. *Bull. Mo. agric. Exp. Stn* No. 421, 293–304.

Obeng, H. B. (1968) Land capability classification of the soils of Ghana under practices of merchandized and hand cultivation for crop and livestock production. *Trans. 9th Int. Cong. Soil Sci.*, Vol. 4, pp. 215–23.

O'Connor, J. (1962). Practical problems in classifying land for horticulture. *Tech. Rep. agric. Ld Serv. Minist. Agric. Fish. Fd* No. 8, 81–90.

Odell, R. T. (1950*a*). Measurement of the productivity of soils under various environmental conditions. *Agron. J.* **42**, 282–92.

—— (1950*b*). Study of sampling methods used in determining productivity of Illinois soils. *Agron. J.* **42**, 328–35.

—— (1958). Soil survey interpretation — yield prediction. *Proc. Soil Sci. Soc. Am.* **22**, 157–60.

—— and Oschwald, W. R. (1970). Productivity of Illinois soils. *Circ. Univ. Ill. Coll. Agric. co-op. Ext. Serv.* No. 1016.

—— and Smith, G. D. (1941). A study of crop yield records by soil types. *Proc. Soil Sci. Soc. Am.* **5**, 316–21.

Olivier, H. (1961). *Irrigation and climate.* Arnold, London.

—— (1972). *Irrigation and water resources engineering.* Arnold, London.

Olson, G. W. (1964). Applications of soil survey to problems of health, sanitation and engineering. *Mem. Cornell Univ. agric. Exp. Stn* No. 387.

—— (1973). Soil survey interpretation for engineering purposes. *FAO Soils Bull.* No. 19.

—— (1974). Land classifications. *Search Agric.* **4**, No. 7.

—— (1977). Principles of presentation of soil survey data for immediate use and application. In *Soil resource inventories*. Agronomy Mimeo 77–23, pp. 217–37. Cornell University, Ithaca, N.Y.

Omar, M. A. and El-Kalei, O. A. (1969). Optimum allocation of agricultural inputs to soils with variable productivities. *Beitr. trop. Landw. Vet. Med.* **7**, 19–25.

Osmond, D. A., Swarbrick, T. Thompson, C. R., and Wallace, T. (1949). A survey of the soils and fruit in the Vale of Evesham 1926–1934. *Bull. Minist. Agric. Fish. Fd, Lond.* No. 116.

Oyama, M. (1965). Land classification of Japan. *Wld Soil Resour. Rep.* **14**, 115–24.

Page, E. R. (1976). The assessment of land for vegetable production. *Tech. Rep. Agric. Fish. Fd.* No. 31, 19–31.

Page, G. (1968). Some effects of conifer crops on soil properties. *Commonw. For. Rev.* **47**, 52–62.

—— (1970). Quantatitive site assessment: some practical applications in British forestry. *Forestry* **43**, 45–56.

Pair, C. H., Hinz, W. W., Reid, C., and Frost, K. R. (eds.) (1975). *Sprinkler irrigation* 4th edn. Sprinkler Irrigation Association, Silver Spring, Maryland.

Palmer, R. C. and Jarvis, M. G. (1979). Land for winter playing fields, golf course fairways and parks. *Soil Surv. Tech. Monogr.* No. 13, 152–65.

Panton, W. P. (1970). The application of land use and natural resource surveys to natural planning. *Occ. Pap. Wld Ld Use Surv.* **9**, 129–38.

Parizek, R. R. (1973). Site selection criteria for wastewater disposal. In *Recycling treated municipal wastewater and sludge through forest and cropland* (ed. W. E. Sopper and L. T. Kardoz) pp. 95–147. Pennslyvania State University Press, University Park, Penn.

Paterson, S. S. (1956). *The forest area of the world and its potential productivity*. Department of Geography, Royal University of Göteborg, Sweden.

Patterson, G. T. and Macintosh, E. E. (1976). Relationship between soil capability class and economic returns from grain and corn production in south western Ontario. *Can. J. Soil Sci.* **56**, 167–74.

Patto, P. M., Clement, C. R., and Forbes, T. J. (1978). *Grassland poaching in England and Wales*. Grassland Research Institute, Hurley, Berkshire, England.

Pearce, S. C. (1976). Field experimentation with fruit trees and other perennial plants. *Tech. Commun. Commonw. Bur. Hort. Plantn Crops* No. 23.

Pearcey, T. and Chapman, T. G. (1968). Aspects of a computer based land evaluation system. In *Land evaluation* (ed. G. A. Stewart) pp. 221–230. Macmillan, Australia.

Perret, N. G. (1969). Land capability classification for wildlife. *The Canada Land Inventory Report* No. 7. Environment Canada, Ottawa.

Peters, T. W. (1977). Relationships of yield data to agroclimates, soil capability classification and soils of Alberta. *Can. J. Soil Sci.* 57, 341–8.

Pettry, D. E. and Coleman, C. S. (1973). Two decades of urban soil interpretations in Fairfax County, Virginia. *Geoderma* 10, 27–34.

Pijls, F. W. G. (1956). Applications of soil survey in the Netherlands. I. Horticulture. *Trans. 6th Int. Cong. Soil Sci.*, Vol. D, pp. 631–8.

Pollock, K. A. (1979). The effects of slurry application to soils. *Soil Surv. Tech. Monogr.* No. 13, 101–9.

Prickett, R. C. (1966). The Land Use Capability System. *N.Z. agric. Sci.* 1, No. 6, 17–21.

Protz, R. (1977). Soil properties important for various tropical crops: Pahang, Tenggara Master Planning Study. In *Soil resource inventories.* Agronomy Mimeo 7-23, pp. 177–88. Cornell Universit, Ithaca, N.Y.

PTB (1962). The planning procedures of the Federal Department of Conservation and Extension. *Sols afr.* 7, 7–17.

Purnell, M. F. (1978). Progress and problems in the application of land valuation in FAO projects in different countries. *Wld Soil Resour. Rep.* 49, 81–8.

—— (1979). The FAO approach to land evaluation and its application to land classification for irrigation. *Wld Soil Resour. Rep.* 50, 4–8.

Pyatt, D. G. (1977). Guide to site types in forests of north and south Wales, 2nd edn. *Forest Rec., Lond.* No. 69.

Raeside, J. D. (1962). Society, town planning and the soil map. *Trans., Comm. IV and V, Int. Soc. Soil Sci.*, New Zealand, pp. 854–8.

—— and Rennie, W. F. (1974). Soils of Christchurch region, New Zealand: the soil factor in regional planning. *Rep. N.Z. Soil Surv.* No. 16.

Reganold, J. P. and Singer, M. J. (1979). Defining prime farmland by three land classification systems. *J. Soil Wat. Conserv.* 34, 172–6.

Rennie, D. A. (1962). Methods of assessing forest site capacity. *Trans. Comm. IV and V, Int. Soc. Soil Sci.*, New Zealand, pp. 770–85.

—— and Clayton, J. S. (1966). An evaluation of techniques used to characterize the comparative productivity of soil profile types in Saskatchewan. *Trans. Comm. II and IV, Int. Soc. Soil Sci.*, Aberdeen, pp. 365–76.

Richards, L. A. (ed.) (1954). Diagnosis and improvement of saline and alkali soils. *USDA Agriculture Handbook* No. 60.

Richardson, S. J. (1976). Animal manures as potential pollutants. *Tech. Bull. Minist. Agric. Fish. Fd* 32, 405–17.

Richey, C. B., Griffith, D. R., and Parsons, S. D. (1977). Yields and cultural energy requirements for corn and soybeans with various tillage-planting systems. *Adv. Agron.* 29, 141–82.

Riecken, F. F. (1963). Some aspects of soil classification in farming. *Soil Sci.* 96, 49–61.

Rigg, T. and Chittenden, E. T. (1951). Classification of land in the Waimea County, Nelson for flue-cured tobacco. *N.Z. Jl Sci. Technol.* 33A, 30–6.

Rijkse, W. C. (1977). Soils of Pohangina County. *Bull. Soil Bur. N.Z.* No. 42

Riquier, J. (1972). *A mathematical model for calculation of agricultural productivity in terms of parameters of soil and climate.* (AGL/MISC/72/ 14.) FAO, Rome.

—— (1974). A summary of parametric methods of soil and land evaluation. *FAO Soils Bull.* No. 22, 47–53.

—— Bramao, D. L., and Cornet, J. P. (1970). *A new system of soil appraisal in terms of actual and potential productivity.* (AGL/TESR/70/6.) FAO, Rome.

Robertson, G. W. (1968). A biometerological time scale for a cereal crop involving day and night temperature and photoperiod. *Int. J. Biomet.* **12**, 191–223.

Robertson, V. C. (1970). Land and water resource planning in developing countries. *Outl. Agric.* **6**, 147–57.

—— and Mitchell, A. J. B. (1976). Land evaluation for irrigation development. *Misc. Rep.* No. 219. Land Resources Division, ODM, London.

Robinson, D. G. (ed.) (1976). *Landscape evaluation: report of the Landscape Evaluation Research Project to the Countryside Commission.* University of Manchester.

Robinson, G. H., Porter, H. C., and Obenshain, S. S. (1955). The use of soil survey information in an area of rapid urban development. *Proc. Soil Sci. Soc. Am.* **19**, 502–4.

Rodriguez, M. (1962). Soil classification and its application in Chile. *Trans. Comm. IV and V, Int. Soc. Soil Sci.,* New Zealand, pp. 332–7.

Rosell, D. Z. (1950a). The score card method of land classification and valuation. *J. Soil Sci. Soc. Philipp.* **2**, 173–80.

—— (1950b). Land classification, valuation and assessment for land taxation in the Phillipines. *J. Soil Sci. Soc. Phillip.* **2**, 238–48.

Rudeforth, C. C. (1975). Storing and processing data for soil and land use capability surveys. *J. Soil Sci.* **26**, 155–68.

—— and Bradley, R. I. (1972). Soils, land classification and land use of West and Central Pembrokeshire. *Soil Surv. Spec. Surv.* No. 6.

—— and Webster, R. (1973). Indexing and display of soil survey data by means of feature cards and Boolean maps. *Goederma* **9**, 229–48.

Ruhmann, H. (1957). Cultivation zones on gradients; practical limits of tractor work. *Landtechnik, Wien* **12**, 259.

Rust, R. M. and Odell, R. T. (1957). Methods used in evaluating the production of some Illinois soils. *Proc. Soil Sci. Soc. Am.* **21**, 171–5.

Ryan, P. (1962). Application of soil survey in related research fields. *Trans. Comm. IV and V, Int. Soc. Soil Sci.,* New Zealand, pp. 370–6.

Salter, P. J. and Williams, J. B. (1967). The influence of texture on the moisture characteristics of soils. IV. A method of estimating the available water capacities of profiles in the field. *J. Soil Sci.* **18**, 174–81.

Scotney, D. M. and de Jager, J. M. (1971). The assessment of environmental potential. *Agro-chemo-physica* **3**, 71–4.

Shelton, D. P., von Bargen, K., and Al-Jiburi, A. S. (1979). Nebraska on-farm fuel use survey. *Agric. Engrg, St. Joseph, Mich.* **60**, No. 10, 38–9.

Sheng, T. C. (1972). A treatment-orientated land capability classification scheme for hilly marginal lands in the humid tropics. *J. scient. Res. Coun. Jamaica* **3**, 93–112.

Shields, R. L. (1976). New generalized soil maps guide land use planning in Maryland. *J. Soil Wat. Conserv.* **31**, 276–80.

Shome, K. B. and Raychaudhuri, S. P. (1960). Rating of soils of India. *Proc. natn Inst. Sci. India* **26a** Suppl. I, 260–89.

Short, C. D. (1973). Land capability classification — an objective approach. *J. Soil Conserv. Serv. N.S.W.* **29**, 200–10.

Short, N. M., Lowman, P. D., and Freden, S. C. (1976). *Mission to Earth, Landsat views the World.* NASA, Washington, DC.

Schrader, W. D., Riecken, F. F., and Englehorn, A. J. (1957). Effect of soil type differences on crop yields on Clarion–Webster soil in Iowa. *Agron. J.* **49**, 254–7.

—— Schaller, F. W., Pesek, J. T., Slusher, D. F., and Riecken, F. F. (1960). Estimated crop yields on Iowa soils. *Spec. Rep. Iowa agric. Exp. Stn* No. 25.

Simonson, R. W. and Englehorn, A. J. (1938). Methods of estimating the productive capacities of soils. *Proc. Soil Sci. Soc. Am.* **3**, 247–52.

——, —— (1943). Interpretation and use of soil classification in the solution of soil management problems. *Proc. Soil Sci. Soc. Am.* **7**, 419–26.

Sinclair, G. A. A. Ambrose, J., Baker, R., McNeice, W., and van der Meer, J. (1973). A method of calculating carrying capacity, potential attractiveness and management input of a site for varied uses. *Forest Research Branch, Division of Forests, Research Report* No. 94. Ministry of Natural Resources, Ontario.

Singer, M. J. (1978). The USDA Land Capability Classification and Storie Index Rating: a comparison. *J. Soil Wat. Conserv.* **33**, 178–82.

—— Tanji, K. K., and Snyder, J. H. (1979). Planning uses of cultivated cropland and pastureland. In *Planning the uses and management of land.* (ed. M. T. Beatty *et al.*) pp. 225–71. ASA, CSSA, SSSA, Madison, Wisconsin.

Smith, A. W. and Forbes, I. G. M. (1974). The agricultural consequences of loss of productive land to urban use. *N.Z. agric. Sci.* **8**, 192–5.

Smith, G. D. and Smith, R. S. (1939). A study of crop yield records by soil types and soil ratings. *Proc. Soil Sci. Soc. Am.* **4**, 375–7.

Smith, L. P. (1953).Estimating the frost risk of an orchard site. *NAAS q. Rev.* **5**, 291–5.

Smith, W. H. (1968). Soil evaluation in relation to cast iron pipe. *J. Am. Wat. Wks Ass.* **60**, 221–7.

Smyth, A. J. (1966). The selection of soils for cocoa. *FAO Soils Bull.* No. 5.

—— (1970*a*). The preparation of soil survey reports. *FAO Soils Bull.* No. 9.

—— (1970*b*). Some concepts relating to the development of an internationally standardised system of soil survey interpretation. *Wld Soil Resour. Rep.* **40**, 121–8.

—— (1971). The aims and possibilities of standardising approach and presentation in the evaluation of land resources. (AGL/TLSR/71/21.) *FAO Latin American Land and Water Development Bulletin* No. 1 72-80. FAO Santiago, Chile.

—— (1974). The development of international standards of land classification. *Tech. Bull. Minist. Agric. Fish. Fd* **30**, 12–21.

—— Eavis, B. W., and Williams, J. W.(1979). Diagnostic criteria for evaluating land for irrigation. *Wld Soil Resour. Rep.* **50**, 14–20.

Snyder, J. H. and Weeks, D. (1956). Soil productivity ratings in economic analysis. *Soil Sci.* **82**, 101–16.

Soil Conservation Society of America, (1977*a*). Soil erosion: prediction and control. *Spec. Publs Soil Conserv. Soc. Am.* No. 21.

—— (1977*b*). *Land use: tough choices in today's world.* Soil Conservation Society of America, Ankeny, Iowa.

Soil Survey Staff (1951). Soil Survey Manual. *USDA Agriculture Handbook* No. 18, 365–95.

—— (1966). Aerial-photo interpretation in classifying and mapping soils. *USDA Agriculture Handbook* No. 294.

Sopper, W. E. (1979). Surface application of sewage effluent and sludge. In *Planning the uses and management of land* (ed. M. T. Beatty *et al.*) pp. 633–63. ASA, CSSA, SSSA, Madison, Wisconsin.

Speight, J. G. (1968). Parametric description of land form. In *Land evaluation* (ed. G. A. Stewart) pp. 239–50. Macmillan, Australia.

Spoor, G. and Muckle, T. B. (1974). Influence of soil type and slope on tractor and implement performance. *Soil Surv. Tech. Monogr.* No. 4, 125–34.

Spratt, E. D. and McIver, R. N. (1972). Effects of topographical positions, soil test values and fertiliser use on yields of wheat in a complex of black chernozemic and gleysolic soils. *Can. J. Soil Sci* **52**, 53–8.

Spurr, S. H. and Barnes, B. V. (1973). *Forest ecology*, 2nd edn. Ronald Press, New York.

Stallings, J. H. (1957). *Soil conservation.* Prentice Hall, Englewood Cliffs, N. J.

Stamp, L. D. (1962). *The land of Britain, its use and misuse*, 3rd edn. Longman, London.

Steele, J. G. (1967). Soil survey interpretation and its use. *FAO Soils Bull.* No. 8.

Stern, P. (1979). *Small scale irrigation.* Intermediate Technology Publications, London.

Stevens, M. E. and Wertz, W. A. (1971). Soil–timber species mix. *J. For.* **69**, 161–4.

Stobbs, A. R. (1970). Soil survey procedures for development procedures. *Occ. Pap. Wld Ld Use Surv.* **9**, 41–63.

Stoner, E. R. and Baumgardner, M. F. (1979). Data acqusition through remote sensing. In *Planning the uses and management of land* (ed. M. T. Beatty *et al.*) pp. 159–85. ASA, CSSA, SSSA, Madison, Wisconsin.

Storie, R. E. (1933). An index for rating the agricultural value of soils (revised 1937). *Bull. Calif. agric. Exp. Stn* No. 556.

—— (1944). Revision of the soil rating chart (re-revised 1948, 1953, 1955). *Leafl. Calif. agric. Exp. Stn* No. 122.

—— (1954) Land classification as used in California for the appraisal of land for taxation purposes. *Trans. 5th Int. Cong. Soil Sci.*, Vol. 3, pp. 407–12.

—— (1964a). *Handbook of soil evaluation*. Associated Students Bookstore, University of California, Berkeley, California.

—— (1964b). Soil and land classification for irrigation development. *Trans. 8th Int. Cong. Soil Sci.*, Vol. V, pp. 873–82.

—— (1976). Storie Index Soil Rating (revised 1978). *Spec. Publ. Div. agric. Sci., Univ. Calif.* No. 3203.

—— and Harradine, F. (1950). Soil survey data as a basis for the assessment of irrigation district lands. *Proc. Soil Sci. Soc. Am.* **14**, 327–9.

—— and Weir, W. W. (1942). The use of soil maps for assessment purposes in California. *Proc. Soil Sci. Soc. Am.* **7**, 416–18.

—— and Weislander, A. E. (1948). Rating soils for timber sites. *Proc. Soil Sci. Soc. Am.* **13**, 499–509.

Strzemski, M. (1972). [Awarding points in land classification.] *Pam. Pulawski* **55**, 199–210.

Sturdy, R. G. and Eldridge, D. J. (1976). Cereal yields in loamy and sandy soils in East Anglia. *Rep. Welsh Soils Discuss. Grp* **17**, 55–83.

Sweet, A. T. (1935). Soils of Orleans County, New York, in relation to orchard planting. *Bull. NY St. agric. Exp. Stn* No. 637.

Sys, C. (1975a). The pedology of rubber. *Wld Soil Resour. Rep.* **45**, 59–79.

—— (1975b). Guidelines for the interpretation of land properties for some general land utilization types. *FAO Soils Bull.* No. 29, 107–18.

—— (1978). The outlook for the practical application of land evaluation in developed countries. *Wld Soil Resour. Rep.* **49**, 97–111.

—— (1979). Evaluation of the physical environment for irrigation in terms of land characteristics and land qualities. *Wld Soil Resour. Rep.* **50**, 60–76.

—— and Frankart, R. (1972). Land capability in the humid tropics. *Sols afr.* **16**, 153–75.

—— and Verheye, W. (1974). Land evaluation for irrigation of arid regions by use of the parameter method. *Trans. 10th Int. Cong. Soil Sci.*, Vol. X, pp. 149–55.

Tabor, R. L., Bell, F. F., Buntley, G. J. Fribourg, H. A., and Springer, M. E. (1974). Agronomic productivity of the landscapes of three soil associations in Maury County, Tennessee: an analysis. *J. Soil Wat. Conserv.* **29**, 272–5.

Tahir, A. A. and Robinson, G. H. (1969). Interpretations of soil survey in the Sudan for the use and management of soils. *Tech. Bull. Minist. Agric. Sudan* No. 1.

Taichinov, S. N. (1971). A system for qualitative evaluation of soils. *Soviet Soil Sci.* 40–9.

Teaci, D. (1970). [*Evaluation of agricultural land.*] Editura Ceres, Bucharest, Romania.

—— and Burt, M. (1964). [Ecological criteria for qualitative classification of agricultural land.] *Trans. 8th Int. Cong. Soil Sci.*, Vol. V, pp. 853–64.

——, —— (1974). Land evaluation and classification in East-European countries. *FAO Soils Bull.* No. 22, 35–46.

—— Voiculescu, N., and Munteanu, M. (1974). Ecometry as a basis for farmland judging. *Trans. 10th. Int. Cong. Soil Sci.*, Vol. V, pp. 40–5.

—— Tutunea, C., Burt, M., Predel, F., and Munteanu, M. (1974). Aspects regarding the pedoclimatic zonation and rating of the agricultural land of Romania (Scale 1:200,000) by districts. *An. Inst. Cerc agron. Pedol.* **40A**, 389–408.

Thomas, R. G. (1962). Soil classification in Southern Rhodesia. *Trans. Comm. IV and V, Int. Soc. Soil Sci.*, New Zealand, pp. 507–14.

—— and Vincent, V. (1962). Classification of soils for land-use purposes in the Rhodesias. *Sols afr.* **7**, 25–34.

Thomasson, A. J. (1974). Soil type, water conditions and drainage. *Soil Surv. Tech. Monogr.* No. 4, 43–52.

—— (ed.) (1975). Soils and field drainage. *Soil Surv. Tech. Monogr.* No. 7.

—— (1977). Soil moisture assessments in land capability classification. *Proc. N. Engl. Soils Discuss. Grp* No. 13, 29–36.

—— (1979). Assessment of soil droughtness. *Soil Surv. Tech. Monogr.* No. 13, 43–50.

Thompson, D. C., Klassen, G. H., and Cihaler, J. (1980). Caribou habitat mapping in the southern district of Ikeewatin, N.W.T. and the application of digital Landsat data. *J. appl. Ecol.* **17**, 125–38.

Thompson, H.A. (1978). Land evaluation for sugar cane production. *Wld Soil Resour. Rep.* **49**, 73–80.

Thompson, T. R. E. (1979). Soil surveys and wildlife conservation in agricultural landscapes. *Soil Surv. Tech. Monogr.* No. 13, 184–92.

Thornburn, T. H. (1966). The use of agricultural soil surveys in the planning and construction of highways. In *Soil surveys and land use planning* (ed. L. J. Bartelli *et al.*) pp. 87–103. SSSA, ASA, Madison, Wisconsin.

Tice, J. A. (1979). Soil considerations in highway design and construction. In *Planning the uses and management of land* (ed. M. T. Beatty *et al.*) pp. 555–79. ASA, CSSA, SSSA, Madison, Wisconsin.

t'Mannetje, L. (ed.) (1978). Measurement of grassland vegetation and animal production. *Bull. Commonw. Bur. Past. Fld Crops* No. 52.

—— Jones, R. J., and Stobbs, T. H. (1976). Pasture evaluation by grazing animals. *Bull. Commonw. Bur. Past. Fld Crops* No. 51, 194–234.

Toleman, R. D. L. (1974). Land classification in the Forestry Commission. *Tech. Bull. Minist. Agric. Fish. Fd* **30**, 97–108.

—— and Pyatt, D. G., (1974). Site classification as an aid to silviculture in the Forestry Commission of Great Britain. *Proc. 10th Commonw. For. Conf.* 1–21.

Tomlinson, R. F. (1967). *An introduction to the Geographic Information System of the Canada Land Inventory.* Canada Department of Forestry and Rural Development, Ottawa, Ontario, Canada.

— (1968). A geographic information system for regional planning. In *Land evaluation* (ed. G. A. Stewart) pp. 200–10. Macmillan, Australia.

—— (1970). Computer based geographical data handling methods. *Occ. Pap. Wld Ld Use Surv.* **9**, 105–120.

US Bureau of Census (1969). Computer mapping. *Census Use Study Report* No. 2. US Department of Commerce, Washington, DC.

USBR (1953). *Bureau of reclamation manual.* Vol. V *Irrigated land use,* Part 2 *Land classification.* US Dept. Interior, Washington, DC.

—— (1967). *Instructions for the conduct of feasibility grade land classification surveys of the Lam Nam Oon Project Thailand.* Office of Chief Engineer, Bureau of Reclamation, US Dept. Interior, Denver, Colorado.

USDA (1967). Developing soil-woodland interpretations. *Soils Memorandum* No. 26 (Revision 2).

—— (1968). Soil interpretations for recreation. *Soils Memorandum* No. 69.

—— (1969). *Soils interpretation for regional planning.* US Department of Agriculture, Washington, DC.

—— (1970). Outline for preparing soil interpretations for range use in published soil surveys. *Soil Memorandum* No. 55.

—— (1971). *Guide for interpreting engineering uses of soils.* US Department of Agriculture, Washington, DC.

—— (1972). Soil interpretations for wildlife habitat. *Soils Memorandum* No. 74.

—— (1975). Prime and unique farmlands. *Land Inventory and Monitoring Memorandum* No. LIM 3.

—— (1978a). Application of soil survey information. *National Soils Handbook Notice* No. 24.

—— (1978b). Soil potential ratings. *National Soils Handbook Notice* No. 31.

US Dept of Defence. (1968). *Unified soil classification system for roads, airfields, embankments and foundations.* (MIL-STD-619B.) US Department of Defence, Washington, DC.

van de Geer, J. P. (1971). *Introduction to multivariate analysis for the social sciences.* Freeman, San Francisco.

van der Kevie, W. (ed.) (1976). Manual for land suitability classification for agriculture. *Tech. Bull. Soil Surv. Adm. Sudan* No. 21.

Van Heesen, H. C. (1970). Presentation of the seasonal fluctuation of the water table on soil maps. *Geoderma* **4**, 257–78.

van Liere, W. J. (1948). Soil conditions in the Westland. *Versl. landbouwk. Onderz. Ned.* **54**, No. 6.

van Volk, V. and Landa, E. R. (1979). Principles and processes involved in waste disposal and management. In *Planning the uses and management of land* (ed. M. T. Beatty *et al.*) pp. 611–31. ASA, CSSA, SSSA, Madison, Wisconsin.

Veatch, J. O. (1942). Agricultural land classification and land types of Michigan. *Bull. Mich. agric. Coll. Exp. Stn.* No. 231.

Vink, A. P. A. (1960). Quantitative aspects of land classification. *Trans. 7th Int. Cong. Soil Sci.* Vol. IV, pp. 371–8.

—— (1963a). Soil survey as related to agricultural productivity. *J. Soil Sci.* **14**, 88–101.

228   References

—— (1963*b*). The planning of soil surveys in land development. *Publs int. Inst. Ld Reclam. Improv.* No. 10.

—— (1975). *Land use in advancing agriculture.* Springer, Berlin.

—— and Van Zuilen, E. J. (1974). The suitability of the soils of the Netherlands for arable land and grassland. *Soil Survey Papers* No. 8. Netherlands Soil Survey Institute, Wageningen.

von Nostitz, A. (1929). *(Introduction to practical soil examination and valuation).* Parey, Berlin.

Wallace, T., Spinks, G. T., and Ball, E. (1931). The fruit growing areas on the Old Red Sandstone of the West Midlands. *Bull. Minist. Agric. Fish. Fd, Lond.* No. 5.

Walsh, T. and Clarke, E. J. (1943). Characteristics of some Irish orchard soil in relation to apple tree growth. *J. Dep. Agric. Repub. Ire.* **40**, 61–122.

—— and Gardiner, M. J. (1976). *Land resource appraisal for economic development.* An Foras Taluntais, Dublin.

Watt, G. R. (1972). The planning and evaluation of forestry projects. *Inst. Pap. Commonw. For. Inst.* No. 45.

Webster, R. (1977). *Quantitative and numeric methods in soil classification and survey.* Clarendon Press, Oxford.

—— (1978). Mathematical treatment of soil information. *Trans. 11th Int. Cong. Soil Sci.*, Vol. 3, pp. 161–90.

—— and Beckett, P. H. T. (1968). Quality and usefulness of soil maps. *Nature, Lond.* **219**, 680–2.

Wehde, M. E., Dalsted, K. J., and Worcester, B. K. (1980). Resource applications of computerized data processing: the AREAS example. *J. Soil Wat. Conserv.* **35**, 36–40.

Weiers, C. J. and Reid, I. G. (1974). *Soil classification, land valuation, and taxation. The German experience.* Centre for European Agricultural Studies, Wye College, Ashford, Kent.

Weir, W. W. and Storie, R. E. (1937). A rating of California soils. *Bull. Calif. agric. Exp. Stn* No. 599.

Wells, N. (1973). The properties of New Zealand soils in relation to effluent disposal. *Geoderma* **10**, 123–30.

Western, S. (1978). *Soil survey contracts and quality control.* Clarendon Press, Oxford.

Westerveld, G. J. W. and Van den Hurk, J. A. (1973). Application of soil and interpretive maps to non-agricultural land use in the Netherlands. *Geoderma* **10**, 47–65.

White, L. P. (1977). *Aerial photography and remote sensing for soil survey.* Clarendon Press, Oxford.

Wiebe, R. A. (1971). *LUNR classification manual: land use and natural resource inventory of New York State.* Office of Planning and Co-ordination, Albany, N.Y.

Wilkinson. B. (1968). Land capability: has it a place in agriculture? *Agriculture, Lond.* **75**, 343–7.

—— (1974). Quantitative basis for land capability interpretation. *Tech. Bull. Minist. Agric. Fish. Fd* **30**, 23–34.

—— (1977). The value of land capability in farm planning. *Proc. N. Engl. Soils Discuss. Grp* No. 13, 37–43.

Williams, G. D. V., Joynt, M. I., and McCormick, P. A. (1975). Regression analyses of Canadian Prairie crop district cereal yields 1961–72 in relation to weather, soil and trend. *Can. J. Soil Sci.* **55**, 43–53.

Withers, B. and Vipond, S. (1974). *Irrigation: design and practice.* Batsford, London.

Witwer, D. B. (1966). Soils and their role in planning a suburban county. In *Soil surveys and land use planning* (ed. L. J. Bartelli *et al.*) pp. 15–30. SSSA, ASA, Madison, Wisconsin.

Wohletz, L. R. (1963). Interpretive soil maps for land use planning. *Trans. 9th Int. Congr. Soil Sci.*, Vol. 4, pp. 225–33.

Wong, I. F. T. (1966). Soil suitability classification for dryland crops in Malaya. *Proc. 2nd Malays. Soil Conf.*, Kuala Lumpur, pp. 154–6.

Woodruff, N. P. and Siddoway, F. S. (1965). A wind erosion equation. *Proc. Soil Sci. Soc. Am.* **29**, 602–8.

Wright, J. W. (1982). *Land surveying for soil surveys.* Clarendon Press, Oxford.

Yates, R. A. (1978). The environment for sugar cane. *Wld Soil Resour. Rep.* **49**, 58–72.

Young, A. (1968). Natural resource surveys for land development in the tropics. *Geography* **53**, 229–48.

—— (1972). *Slopes.* Longman, London.

—— (1973*a*). Rural land evaluation. In *Evaluating the human environment* (ed. J. A. Dawson and J. C. Doornkamp) pp. 5–33. Arnold, London.

—— (1973*b*). Soil survey procedures in land development planning. *Geogrl J.* **139**, 53–64.

—— (1975). Land requirements for specific land uses. Crop/land relationships and the nature of decision making on land use. *Wld Soil Resour. Rep.* **45**, 85–7.

—— (1976). *Tropical soils and soil survey.* Cambridge University Press.

—— (1978). Recent advances in the survey and evaluation of land resources. *Prog. phys. Geogr.* **2**, 462–79.

—— and Goldsmith, P. F. (1977). Soil survey and land evaluation in developing countries: a case study in Malawi. *Geogrl J.* **143**, 407–31.

Zaporozec, A. and Hole, F. D. (1976). Resource suitability in regional planning with special reference to Wisconsin, U.S.A. *Geoforum* **7**, 13–22.

Zayach, S. J. (1973). Soil surveys — their value and use to communities in Massachusetts. *Geoderma* **10**, 67–74.

Zimmerman, J. D. (1966). *Irrigation.* Wiley, New York.

Zinke, P. J. (1959). Site quality for Douglas-fir and ponderosa pine in Northeastern California as related to climate, topography and soil. *Proc. Soc. Am. Foresters 1958*, 161–71.

230 References

Abbreviations

ASA   American Society of Agronomy.
BSI   British Standards Institution.
CSSA   Crop Science Society of America.
FAO   Food and Agriculture Organization.
MAFF   Ministry of Agriculture Fisheries and Food.
PTB   Planning and Training Branch, Federal Department of
      Conservation and Extension, Rhodesia and Nyasaland.
SSSA   Soil Science Society of America.
USBR   United States Bureau of Reclamation.
USDA   United States Department of Agriculture.

Index

The most important page references are given in **bold type**.